A PROPER DRINK

A PROPER DRINK

*The Untold Story of How a Band of Bartenders
Saved the Civilized Drinking World*

———

ROBERT SIMONSON

TEN SPEED PRESS
Berkeley

All rights reserved.
Published in the United States by Ten Speed Press, an imprint of the Crown
Publishing Group, a division of Penguin Random House LLC, New York.
www.crownpublishing.com
www.tenspeed.com

Ten Speed Press and the Ten Speed Press colophon are registered trademarks
of Penguin Random House LLC.

Portions of the chapter "Taking Back Tiki" were originally published in
different form on Eater.com.

Library of Congress Cataloging-in-Publication Data is on file with the publisher.

Hardcover ISBN: 978-1-60774-754-3
eBook ISBN: 978-1-60774-755-0

Printed in the United States

Design by Lizzie Allen

10 9 8 7 6 5 4 3 2 1

First Edition

To the memories of

DICK BRADSELL
(1959–2016)

and

SASHA PETRASKE
(1973–2015)

CONTENTS

PREFACE

I SAT AT THE CIRCULAR Carousel Bar of the Hotel Monteleone, one of those bars that slowly rotates—in this case counterclockwise, at the rate of four revolutions per hour. With its merry-go-round décor and absurd mobility, there was perhaps no better introduction to the circus atmosphere of New Orleans' French Quarter. It was 11 a.m., but that didn't seem to be stopping the barflies around me. So I ordered a Sazerac. I am compulsive about starting off new experiences correctly, and of all the drinks intrinsic to New Orleans culture, the Sazerac was the name I had heard most often since landing at the Louis Armstrong New Orleans International Airport. And I had never had one.

It was 2006. I wasn't much of a cocktail drinker at that point; more of a wine man. I'd order an occasional Gibson or Martini, and I had been known to play around with Gimlets and Tom & Jerrys at home. None of this prepared me for the Sazerac. The drink that was brought to me was startling: weirdly red (the Peychaud's bitters, I later learned) and oddly fragrant (the Herbsaint liqueur). It was ice cold and had no garnish. I took a tentative sip.

The edges of my vision suddenly blurred and my focus trained on the glass in front of me. I was simultaneously tasting three things I never had before: rye whiskey, spicy and bright; Herbsaint, as herbal as the name hinted; and Peychaud's bitters, which—well, what the hell were they anyway, and what did they do? But, more importantly, I was tasting them together, along with a bit of sugar and the effects of a lemon twist. It was a seamless, cultivated, elegant whole, and like nothing I'd ever experienced before. It was a drink with a story, a past, and more depth than most people I know. The world stopped.

Where had this cocktail been all my life?

The entire week at Tales of the Cocktail was like that. Tales was a cocktail convention. That phrase, "cocktail convention," sounded even more silly then than it does now. People had actually gathered from all over the nation to talk seriously about cocktails and mixology. Its founder was a scrappy blonde Southerner about the size of a whippet named Ann Rogers; I had met her by chance at an Illy Espresso pop-up in SoHo in New York, where she was working temporarily as a PR hired gun.

"I do this little cocktail thing down in New Orleans," she said. "You should come down."

New Orleans was something. I had been writing about wine for a few years. I loved wine and vineyards, but the wine world was a buttoned-up one. The cocktail world, while also dealing in intoxicants, was nothing like that. Hugs. High fives. Hawaiian shirts. Seersucker suits. Two-toned shoes. Hats on every head. Flasks full of wondrous potions, freely shared. Every time I stepped into the lobby of the Monteleone, I was handed a drink by someone. Thanks to tasting rooms, seminars, bars, and other events, I had many drinking opportunities at Tales. I made a list of all the cocktails I drank or sampled that first day. The total was sixteen. In addition to the Sazerac at the Carousel Bar, they included:

Pimm's Cup at Napoleon House
Hurricane at Pat O'Brien's
Milk Punch at Brennan's
Champagne Cocktail at Arnaud's
Ramos Gin Fizz at Carousel Bar

I sampled six vodkas at a seminar about that spirit and tasted absinthe, a spirit I thought was extinct and legally banned (it was), in a seminar led by absinthe authority Ted Breaux.

I learned to pace myself better the second day.

When I returned, newly converted to the cocktail, I scoured New York City for Sazeracs, my new favorite drink. Ten years earlier, I would have found no bars serving the exotic concoction. In 2006, however, it wasn't difficult. I could get one at a bar called Brooklyn Social, not far from where I lived in Brooklyn. I found a better one at The Good Fork, a restaurant in Red Hook, made by bartender St. John Frizell. I found other Sazeracs at bars in SoHo, Tribeca, and the Lower East Side.

Something was obviously afoot. When I had moved to New York in the late '80s, brew pubs and wine bars were hot. No one, bartender or patron, knew what a Sazerac was. When cocktails were drunk, Cape Codders and Cosmos and Dirty Martinis were the orders of the day. Now, unfamiliar libations like the Martinez, Aviation, and Corpse Reviver No. 2 were being called for. What was going on? A lot, I soon discovered, as, over the next year, I shifted my reportorial focus from wine to spirits and cocktails. It was nothing short of a revolution in the way people made mixed drinks and consumed them. And it wasn't just happening in New York and New Orleans. The world was revisiting the cocktail hour.

ABOUT THE "MODERN CLASSICS"

AT THE END OF MANY of the following chapters, you will find a cocktail recipe or two. A couple dozen of these are what I have determined to be "modern classics"—that is, drinks created during the cocktail renaissance that have been embraced by both bartenders and drinkers, and have shown some staying power. Most of them are served at bars worldwide.

I have tried to be unsentimental and impartial in compiling this list. There are many cocktails I admire that did not make the cut for various reasons: they remain popular, but only in one country or one city; they were ubiquitous for a time, then inexplicably faded from view; or they remained steadily ordered cult classics but never became full-fledged stars. Cocktails that made their mark but are not found herein are the Revolver (Jon Santer), Silver Lining (Joseph Schwartz), Wibble (Dick Bradsell), Russian Spring Punch (Bradsell), Greenpoint (Michael McIlroy), Waylon (Eben Freeman), Death Flip (Chris Hysted), Kentucky Buck (Erick Castro), Gordon's Cup (Toby Maloney), Porn Star Martini (Douglas Ankrah), and La Perla (Jacques Bezuidenhaut).

The drinks in the chapters "Bringing It All Home" and "Taking Back Tiki" are cocktails from the past that were once obscure or altogether unknown, but have been given new life and popularity through the efforts of cocktail bartenders and historians. Finally, the cocktails found at the back of the book are personal favorites that I feel deserve greater attention.

PROLOGUE

"There's this guy up in the Rainbow Room . . ."

IN 1988, DEL PEDRO, an affable Bermudan who had fallen in love with New York, was bartending at Sam's, a lavish restaurant inside the Equitable Center in midtown Manhattan. It had been built for $2 million and was owned by actress Mariel Hemingway, who christened it with her nickname. Though not as posh as its neighbors, Le Bernadin and Palio, it was opulent enough. There was a mural by James Rosenquist. Chandeliers hung from the twenty-eight-foot-high ceiling. And standing above Del atop the circular bar was a bronze bison. Sam's was certainly a change of environment from Pedro's previous bartending gig, a 125th Street dive under the West Side Highway called the 712 Club, where hardworking meatpackers and construction workers also drank hard, and a gun was kept in a drawer. It was there not to keep the patrons in line but to shoot the occasional intruding river rat.

The customers at the 712 Club wanted beer and shots. People at Sam's had different tastes. The headquarters of Time Inc. was nearby. Often, old-school publishing types, people who remembered the drinks of another era and hadn't lost their taste for them, wandered in. They called for Martinis, Manhattans, Negronis, and Gimlets. Occasionally, there'd be an order for a Sidecar or Stinger.

One night, a guy named Tommy came in. A well-lubricated Connecticut commuter straight out of a Cheever short story, he asked Del for a Negroni on the rocks. Pedro gave it to him in a highball. "Del, uh, what the fuck is that?" asked Tommy. "All right. Throw it out. I'll show you how to make a Negroni.'"

The women were no less exacting. One, coming in after brunch at Mortimer's, asked for a Sidecar. "Young man," she said to the blinking barman, "I can tell by looking at you, you have no idea how to make a Sidecar. For God's sake, don't put that lemon mix in it. Do you have fresh lemons?" And the lesson began.

Being dedicated and discerning drinkers, the customers at Sam's also knew *where* to drink. "One night this woman came in and asked for this crazy drink," remembered Pedro. "It was an old drink. I said, 'Well, I have the stuff to make it. I'll try.'" As Del went about his work, the woman added, "You know, there's this guy up in the Rainbow Room making these old drinks."

"This guy" was a former actor with a head of thick dark hair, an ever-present grin, and the marquee-ready name of Dale DeGroff.

I. THE ACTOR

THE MOST FAMOUS COCKTAIL BARTENDER in cinema history is, regrettably, the one played by Tom Cruise in *Cocktail*, the critically drubbed, commercially successful vehicle the toothy actor headlined in 1988, at the height of his newfound fame and popularity. His young audience recognized the type, no doubt. They'd seen bartenders of his stripe in the clubs and single bars and TGI Fridays, glad-handing and bottle-tossing and making time with the opposite sex. What they thought a cocktail was is another matter. Chances are it fell in line with the triumphal piece of doggerel Cruise delivers to a rapt crowd in the film:

> The Sex on the Beach, the schnapps made from peach
> The Golden Hammer, the Alabama Slammer
> I make things with juice and froth
> The Pink Squirrel, the Three-Toed Sloth
> I make drinks so sweet and snazzy
> The Iced Tea, the Kamikaze
> The Orgasm, the Death Spasm
> The Singapore Sling, the Ding-a-Ling.

The 1980s were dark days for drinking. Cocktails were simply uncool: establishment intoxicants of which your parents had drunk too many. They had been erased from youthful memory by the druggie haze of the 1960s, then relegated to the clubs of the 1970s and 1980s as just one of many stimulants on offer. By that point, any cocktails that were recognizable by name were made with vodka, the anodyne Harvey Wallbanger leading the pack. The Margarita and Daiquiri still had an audience, but in so whipped-up and tarted-out a form that their alcoholic base hardly mattered. Bourbon, America's native elixir, was in eclipse, undrunk. Rye, once bourbon's rival, was nearly extinct. Rum was a joke, something to do with those tacky tiki bars. Gin, a relic, contemptuously erased by the ascendant vodka.

An actor, not Tom Cruise, was about to change all that.

***

THROUGHOUT MUCH OF THE LATE twentieth century, the cliché went, bartending was a placeholder job taken by actors while they waited for their career to take off. It's perversely appropriate, then, that an actor should have spearheaded the bartending revolution.

Dale DeGroff, a Rhode Island boy and Navy brat, did do some acting, both in New York and Los Angeles. The stage dream died hard—in later years he put together a touring cabaret act—but he listened when, while working at the swanky Hotel Bel-Air in L.A., a colleague commented, "I know you want to do the acting thing, but you may want to consider sticking to bartending, because you're pretty good at it."

Compared to the other sidetracked actors behind L.A. bars, "Dale seemed to take bartending more seriously" than his colleagues, recalled his old childhood pal, Gerry Holland. "I noticed on his bookshelves some old bartending books."

DeGroff stayed at the Bel-Air for six years, beginning in 1978, teaching himself about spirits and cocktails simply out of a sense of self-preservation; he wanted to keep a good job he knew he wasn't qualified for. At a time when bartenders largely winged it, he chose to give a damn. His customers may have noticed, but the world did not. As longtime Los Angeles–based restaurant critic Jonathan Gold remembered it, "Dale

DeGroff was here for years and made no impact. Nobody heard of him or his cocktails."

A stint at Charley O's, a New York restaurant run by legendary impresario Joe Baum, had helped get DeGroff the Bel-Air gig. And it would be Baum who finally lent definition to DeGroff's pursuits. After his childhood pal Holland told him Baum was opening a fine-dining restaurant called Aurora, DeGroff convinced his wife to move back to New York in 1985.

Baum can, as much as anyone, be called the father of the modern cocktail era, though a rehabilitation of the bar was just one of the many ways he changed the way Americans dined out. He created some of the nation's first themed restaurants (Forum of the Twelve Caesars, La Fonda del Sol) and lent dining a sense of theatre. His exacting attention to detail extended far beyond the modern American twists on classic cuisines to service, décor, architecture, and menu execution. For Aurora, he wanted to have a classic cocktail bar, and he was auditioning Dale for the job of running it. He instructed the younger man to go out and purchase a certain book and study it.

"The son of a bitch said to me, 'You can find out a lot about this in a book called *How to Mix Drinks* by Jerry Thomas.' I went to bookstores looking for it. Finally one guy said, 'You know, this is familiar.' He looks it up and comes back. 'This book has been out of print since 1929. It was originally published in 1862.' Joe hadn't told me that."

Dale threw himself into creating the cocktail bar of Baum's dreams. It wasn't easy. Baum, whose instructions were often oblique, wasn't very specific. He mainly told DeGroff if he was veering right or wrong.

"Joe never told me anything," said DeGroff. "He tasted my Bloody Bull at Aurora and said, 'There's something wrong with it. Fix it.' I couldn't figure it out." One day DeGroff was at a Chinese restaurant and noticed the traditional dish Orange Beef on the menu. Suddenly he knew what was wrong with his the beef broth–based drink. "I gotta get my lemon and lime out of my Bloody Bull. As soon as I put in a twist of orange and a dash of orange juice, Joe tasted it and said, 'OK.'"

Baum insisted that the bar have no soda guns—a shortcut that had become pervasive in bars starting after World War II—and fresh juice instead of the widely used prefabricated sour mix that was squirted into any drink requiring citrus. DeGroff was hesitant. What if it got busy? Shouldn't they keep some sour mix on hand? Baum said that if DeGroff couldn't handle the work, he'd just find someone who could. The bartender decided to work it out.

DeGroff had known about Baum long before he worked for him. As young men in 1970, both DeGroff and his friend Gerry Holland got jobs in the mailroom at the famous Madison Avenue ad agency Lois Holland Callaway. (The Holland in the name was Ron Holland, Gerry's brother.) The firm handled Restaurant Associates Industries, the mammoth, industry-changing outfit at which Baum created and ran Four Seasons, the Brasserie, the Forum of the Twelve Caesars, and many others. Ron Holland had an expense account of $3,000 for Baum's restaurants. Dale and Joe would find out where Ron was going, and show up for a free meal. Everything was high design and high concept, each detail on the walls and on the plate seen to. It was a nice change from the slum apartment DeGroff and Gerry Holland occupied on West 74th Street, where people would lurk under stairwells, waiting to jump you.

DeGroff received an accidental culinary education. He often found himself at the same lunch table as Baum, so the restaurant industry lessons started early. DeGroff recalls walking into a restaurant when Baum stopped the maître d' short and asked, "'What's wrong with the consommé?' I say, 'Joe, c'mon. You can walk into this place and just by smelling find out there's something wrong with the consommé?' He said, 'There's always something wrong with the consommé.' That's Joe's style. Get them on their toes."

Dale's tour of duty with Baum began auspiciously. Aurora made a fortune. It was situated in a building full of bankers who came down to drink a lot. Then the 1987 crash hit. "The market went into an unprecedented spiral, at the time," recalled DeGroff. "And overnight, that place dried up. They fired two-thirds of the staff. Aurora never recovered from that."

As far as DeGroff's bartending career was concerned, however, it was just a bump. Baum had used Aurora's bar program as a laboratory for a larger project: the reopening of the 1930s-era Rainbow Room, on two floors at the top of Rockefeller Center. It was to be a nightlife showplace, and DeGroff wanted to be its chief barman.

"Joe worked on five-year plans," said DeGroff. "Aurora was the workshop. That's where he worked with Kevin Zraly, with Milton Glaser." Zraly, a former wine salesman, became a world-renowned wine educator, and Glaser was the legendary graphic designer who came up with the "I ♥ NY" logo. "I wanted to be a part of this. These were cool people." DeGroff presented a menu draft to Joe, drawing on bygone New York society meccas like the Colony and the Stork Club. Baum dismissed it. He'd already tried it all: he had done tiki at the Hawaiian Room; Pisco Sours at Fonda del Sol; fancy cocktails at Forum of the Twelve Caesars.

DeGroff regrouped. He put together a menu of classic cocktails from the glamorous era the Rainbow Room was meant to recapture, the just-post-Prohibition period when drinks like the Ramos Gin Fizz and Sazerac were not yet forgotten. Baum rejected the first attempt as too ambitious. "I tried to do twenty-six cocktails," said DeGroff. "It was a disaster. I had to go down to sixteen."

DeGroff wanted everything behind the bar to be premium; no junk brands. His principled stand took some fortitude. "The Rainbow Room became a magnet from the very beginning for anything cocktail related. I was fighting off liquor companies."

Despite the insistence on quality spirits and ingredients, Baum would not allow DeGroff and his fellow bartenders to use jiggers. Measurements had to be accurate, but free-poured, from bottle to mixing glass. "It was the times," explained DeGroff. "There was only one kind of bar that jiggered in the '50s, '60s, and '70s. Irish bars. An ounce and a quarter, if you're lucky. The perception was that if you jiggered, you were a cheap-ass little bar. He wanted people who came into the Rainbow Room to feel like they'd come into his house. He wanted that feeling of hospitality."

DeGroff's old mailroom buddy and lunch partner, Gerry Holland, witnessed DeGroff's hospitality skills quickly developing. "I think Dale used his theatre and acting skills to create what they now call the celebrity bartender," said Holland.

The reimagined Rainbow Room, as envisioned by Baum and executed over two years by architect Hugh Hardy, an expert in reclamations of classic New York properties, was—as it had been in the 1930s—about as swankily Manhattan an experience as possible; the kind of place that inspired proposals and lifelong memories; the only place, as Glaser put it, that matched the sweep and style of New York nightclubs as depicted in old black-and-white movies. There was a restaurant, grill, bar, and business dining rooms spread over two floors. The waiters wore tails. The dance floor revolved. "Finally, unabashedly, it's a theatrical experience, not just a functional one," Baum told the *New York Times*. "It's about the lift of being in New York."

DeGroff and his bar team—who had as a backdrop a five-foot-high model of a streamlined ocean liner designed by Norman Bel Geddes— were a big part of that lift. Jared Brown, who would become the author of many books about cocktails and spirits, was hired as a waiter at the Rainbow Room in 1990. One day, he heard a guy say, "Hey, you! Want to see a flaming twist?" (The flamed orange twist—in which the oils from a squeezed orange peel briefly feed a lit match, spritzing burnt citrus mist over the surface of a cocktail—was a trick that dated back decades. But few had seen it before DeGroff did it, and the bartender made it his calling card.)

"He was a very smooth, old-school bartender," remembered Brown. "Not a lot of flash. Not paying a huge amount of attention to the drink he was making. He was always busy engaging with the guest." DeGroff's bonhomie was effortless. He could talk about the horse races with the guy whose paper was open to the sports section and engage the visitor on tourist topics, deftly never letting the conversation circle around to him.

"He cut a good figure behind the bar," recalled William Grimes, who had written about drinks for *Esquire* in the 1980s and moved to the *New York Times* just after the Rainbow Room opened in 1987. "They had these spiffy uniforms. He squeezed the orange rind and ignited it. It was kind of like shooting your cuffs. There was a sense of a conductor at the head of a great orchestra."

Steve Olson had introduced classic cocktails and premium spirits at the various restaurants across the country where he had been sommelier and beverage director. But he had witnessed nothing like what he saw on his first visit to the Rainbow Room. He ordered a Manhattan and stared in wonder as DeGroff stirred—not shook, as was the common custom at the time—the drink. "I thought, *What the fuck is that?*" said Olson. "That was a moment that changed my life, watching Dale DeGroff stir a Manhattan."

Grimes started writing about DeGroff and followed him as his work behind the bar progressed. "He would forage for ingredients," said Grimes. "Got things in Jamaica. It was like adding keys to the piano keyboard. Everyone was working with twenty keys, and he had forty and sixty. He had the mighty Wurlitzer behind him."

"I was always hunting for lost ingredients," said DeGroff. "Proper maraschino liqueur—Luxardo wasn't available yet. Peychaud's bitters took some time to locate, and if I hadn't promised the distributor Spirit of Hartford to promote it, John D. Taylor's Velvet Falernum probably wouldn't be in the country." Quality bar tools, too, were difficult to find. The bowl-shaped, perforated Julep strainers needed to properly strain stirred drinks from a mixing glass, for example, were not widely used, and those available were cheaply made.

DeGroff and his team did not enjoy a trial period with the public. From day one, the bar was six deep. Patrons, thirsty for cocktails they hadn't seen in a generations—and done well—ordered them like there was no tomorrow.

Grimes observed how the cocktails were just one element of the spell DeGroff was trying to cast, an atmospheric tapestry that took in the décor, the views, the level of service, and myriad other details.

"The sun would set," explained Grimes, "it would shade into dark evening, the lights on the Manhattan skyscrapers would come out. It was like taking a romantic voyage up there. You felt removed from the rest of the world, kind of floating out from the skyline of Manhattan, and getting these absolutely tremendous drinks."

———

DEGROFF'S COCKTAILS SEEMED SO TREMENDOUS partly due to how starkly they contrasted to the dross then on offer at chain cocktail purveyors like TGI Fridays.

As the cocktail renaissance gathered steam in the early and mid-'00s, there was a predictable checklist of things all bartenders would repudiate out of hand as anathema to the movement. Sour mix, cheater ice, mixto tequila, vodka, and the Cosmopolitan were all poison. And it was an article of faith that TGI Fridays represented everything that was wrong about cocktails. The drinks were sweet and garishly colored, used bottom-shelf liquors, and were served in glasses the size of fishbowls.

But it hadn't always been that way. In its early days, TGI Fridays—and the other chains it inspired, like Hard Rock Café and Planet Hollywood—was an incubator of bartending skill and discipline during a period when bartending was considered a dead end.

"There would be no cocktail movement without them," said Philip Duff flatly. Duff, an itinerant cocktail consultant and speaker, knows this is an unpopular opinion, even an embarrassing one. "It's like saying Mussolini made the trains run on time or Hitler loved dogs. You just can't say it. It's absolutely true, but you can't say it."

Duff grew up in Scerries, a coastal town twenty miles north of Dublin. He started bartending at age fifteen. Scerries had twelve pubs for its five thousand people. One, Nealon's, was an oddity. The son of the owner had once gone to Dallas and seen one of the world's first TGI Fridays franchises. "He opened, to my knowledge, the first copy of a TGI Fridays anywhere," said Duff. (The first official UK TGIF wouldn't open until several years later, in Birmingham.) "This place was remarkable. Flair bartending, free pouring, cocktails, exotic things like tequila." That was where Duff got his start in the business.

Duff moved to London in the late '80s with a firm objective—to work at TGI Fridays. "It was the best training in the industry and the best money. If you got a job at one of the ones in London, you could potentially earn thirty-five thousand pounds a year. That was a fortune."

After a couple of bar jobs in Notting Hill and near Marble Arch, he was finally hired at the TGI Fridays in South Croydon. He went through six weeks of rigorous training and had to learn more than four hundred drinks. "You had to do food safety qualification, learn the food menu—before, I hasten to add, you spoke to a customer. And you were ranked every quarter according to your position in the bar program, as to how good you were. And the top three bartenders got to write their own schedules."

Many of the UK programs, including the first one in Birmingham, had been set up by "Magic" Mike Werner, one of TGI Fridays' globe-trotting master bar trainers. He and five other trainers lived in a six-bedroom London flat nine months out of the year. Finding UK bartenders to fit the TGI Fridays mold wasn't easy. The British barkeeps didn't tend to speak to customers until spoken to. "He had to Americanize them," said Werner.

Long before the mixology consultants and brand ambassadors of the twenty-first century began regularly dropping brand knowledge on bar staffs,

TGI Fridays trainees had to learn how spirits were made and the background of particular brands. They couldn't pour any bottle without an intimate knowledge of the contents. Hospitality was key, too. "You had to tell us fifteen jokes," said Werner. "They couldn't be racist or anything like that. The bartenders, while they made you a drink, they'd talk to you, tell you a joke, entertain you. You mingle with the people around you. That was the key function of the whole master bartender test. That master bartender had to know how to get customers involved."

TGI Fridays began as one corner joint on the Upper East Side. In 1965, Alan Stillman bought an old bar called the Good Tavern at the corner of First Avenue and 63rd Street. The neighborhood was home to a number of stewardesses and secretaries. His motivation for everything was: what would women like? He hired only jocks as bartenders, and dressed them in form-fitting soccer shirts. The handsome men—as well as the bright, cheery atmosphere, accentuated by red-and-white-striped awnings and Tiffany lamps—attracted women, who longed for a place where they could drink in comfort and peace. Soon, the women attracted young men. Lines formed outside and cordons were set up.

Stillman opened additional bars named after other days of the week—Tuesday's, Ice Cream Sunday's—but TGI Fridays was the one with legs. He began to franchise the restaurant in the early '70s. In 1972, Daniel R. Scoggin opened one in Dallas. The location performed phenomenally, and its raised square bar and multilevel seating became the industry standard. Werner was a teenage runaway from Milwaukee who had done a tour with the Navy. He used to go to the TGIF in Houston every night. In 1979, he began working there.

Though the chain now has a reputation as a family restaurant that also serves drinks, in its early years it was clearly a singles bar that happened to serve food. And the bartender was the top of the staff pyramid. "You were first a busser," said Werner, "then a waiter. When you were a top-ten waiter, you were eligible for barback. As barback, you were not allowed to look at or talk to the guests. You cut fruit, made mixes. Nine months later, you became a bartender. Typically, a bartender made more than anyone in the restaurant."

To become a bartender you had to learn four hundred drinks and pass a test. Twenty-five of those drinks you had to make blindfolded, in a certain amount of time, knowing through muscle memory where each bottle was. Werner climbed the ladder very quickly. Each quarter, his bartender rating rose, until he became head bartender.

The TGI Fridays of the '70s served very little beer. "It was a lot of Martinis, a lot of Scotch, and the rest were highballs," said Werner." The juices used in the drinks were freshly squeezed, and a house "sweet and sour" mix was made every day with citrus and fresh eggs. Everything was free poured, but with accuracy, and Martinis and Manhattans were properly stirred, not shaken as at most bars. At a time when few people outside of New Orleans knew what a Ramos Gin Fizz was, TGI Fridays in Texas made them every Sunday from scratch.

When TGI Fridays corporate found out Werner had been writing out a training manual in his spare time, they promoted him to trainer. Trainers were needed. The chain was purchased by Carlson Companies in 1975, and opened twenty-five to thirty new shops a year. Because of the increased workload, the vaunted training method was diluted. "To train like we used to at Fridays was almost impossible," said Werner. The instruction period for a bartender went from nine months to six weeks. Diminished, too, were the recipes.

Still, the TGI Fridays train chugged along and developed its acolytes, including David O'Malley, who would use what he learned from Werner when he opened his various bars in San Francisco, including Bix and Bacar. But it was in the London cocktail resurgence that the TGI Fridays effect had deeper roots.

"TGI Fridays is what this country needed," said Jason Crawley, a British bartender who became an influential cocktail consultant and trainer in Australia. "The drinks were shit, but we didn't know that at the time."

Angus Winchester, another bartender who became an important consultant, had a brother who bartended at Planet Hollywood in London. "TGI Fridays, Planet Hollywood, and Hard Rock for a long time had a proper bar program and a sense of pride and swagger," he said.

Having worked at a London TGI Fridays, Duff could thereafter write his own ticket. "It was like being in the first graduating glass of MBAs," he said. "Everyone wants you."

As the religion of craft cocktails began to rise in London in the late '90s, the influence of the big bar-restaurants began to wane until, by 2000, their name was mud. The veterans and insiders knew their training systems were solid. But brash young bartenders knew only that they served bad drinks.

Ironically, however, the cocktail movement's UK guru, Dick Bradsell, retained enough respect for the TGI Fridays model that he often hired their ex-bartenders for his own artisan watering holes. He knew that, underneath it all, they were "clean and efficient."

II. A BRITISH BARTENDER

BY THE TIME DALE DEGROFF was making headlines at the Rainbow Room, Dick Bradsell, who would become the London cocktail scene's own DeGroff figure, had been working his game for a decade or more, at Zanzibar and Soho Brasserie, serving Martinis and Pisco Sours, and even coming up with a few new drinks of his own.

In the world of British bartending, Dick Bradsell was an anomaly. Not because he was introverted, socially awkward, and sloppy (seeming drawbacks in his chosen profession)—though he was all those things. He was unusual because he was British.

The history of twentieth-century London bartending is the history of immigrants. Although there certainly were pubs owned by men and women of English blood, the posh hotel bars—those few places where cocktail culture was preserved—were for decades the domain of foreigners seeking a better life in England's capital.

In the late 1970s and early 1980s, the big names in British bartending were Italian: Peter Dorelli at the Savoy's American Bar, Salvatore Calabrese at Dukes Hotel, and Gilberto Preti, also at the Dukes. They were known for their old-school manners and habit. And they were union men.

"There were a lot of Italians," said Simon Ford. "They were making their cocktails in bars and doing it a certain way, and they were wearing white gloves."

Dorelli, a Roman, came to the UK in 1958 at age eighteen to escape both entering the family banking business and compulsory Italian army service. ("No one puts a gun in my hand," he said years later.) He did whatever he could to get by, working as a handyman and shoveling coal into boilers, outstaying his visa. A job at Stone's Chop House, part of the Savoy Hotel Group, led to a position at the adjoining Pebble Bar and then, finally, the famed American Bar. More than other London hotel watering holes, that bar kept the classic cocktail flame burning in London. Dorelli served Rickeys and sours to the over-forty crowd, many of them tourists.

Calabrese, considerably younger than Dorelli, came from the Amalfi Coast. He got his start behind the bar at eleven, when his father got him a job at a local hotel. He moved to London in 1980, where he found an English wife, who found him an English job, at the Dukes, a small, exclusive hotel off St. James Place. It was a tiny bar. Calabrese knew he couldn't work in quantity, so he focused on quality, collecting and selling rare spirits, and perfecting the house Martini, which was praised and made famous by Stanton Delaplane, a San Francisco-based travel and food writer. (Delaplane made the rounds of international bars. He is credited with introducing the Irish Coffee to America.) Over a dozen years ending in 1994, Calabrese forged a reputation as a silky, serious, and dignified bartender.

By the 1980s, Dorelli and Calabrese headed the United Kingdom Bartenders Guild, which was "an Italian mafia golf club," in the estimation of Simon Difford, who would found the drinks-world trade magazine *Class* in 1997. Difford recalled going to a UKBG meeting when he had just begun publishing *Class* and being told he wasn't properly dressed. "They were all standing there in their blazers and badges. That was not the cool scene that young bartenders wanted to be a part of."

Dick Bradsell admired the style of Dorelli. He'd hang out at the Savoy, studying the Italian, who had been trained by people whose training led back to famed Savoy barman Harry Craddock, author of the *Savoy Cocktail*

Book. Dorelli was thus one of the last few living links to the previous golden age of London cocktails. "It was very impressive," admitted Bradsell. But he found the place "shushy," and the union—the UK Bartender's Guild—stiff, with its uniforms and rule-bound cocktail competitions.

Even as his star rose in the '90s, he never joined the union. "I couldn't be bothered," he said, with characteristic contrariness. "They've asked me to join three or four times. I didn't see the reason."

Dorelli must have seen in Bradsell as unlikely a future for English bartending as Bradsell saw in Dorelli. "Dick is a great bartender, a mess as a human being," Dorelli quipped. "The British are all introverts: they are uncomfortable with people."

Dick Bradsell was a short, wiry man with a taut, sharp-featured face and a clipped, querulous way of speaking. He was raised on the Isle of Wight, the rebellious son of a man who worked for the ministry of defense. He left home in 1977 and took a hedonistic swan dive into London nightlife. According to Dick, the family was glad to see him go; a couple of home-destroying parties had attracted the attention of the local police and sent him packing. Still, it was the military that led him to what would become his career.

In London, Bradsell worked for his uncle, who ran the Naval and Military Club in Piccadilly, a proper gentlemen's club frequented by ex-army and navy people. Hired at nineteen, he worked through every single job in the place, including bartender, making Pink Gins for retired brass. By the time he left the club, he found he liked the bar business.

A friend got him a job in the late 1970s as a runner in the Zanzibar Club, a hip members' club in Covent Garden with a long bar and bartenders in waistcoats and ties. It was a place where "David Bowie was kept waiting at the door." The drinks were of a higher class as well. A bottle of exotic pisco was kept on the bar for a Chilean man who came in once a day and asked for a Pisco Sour. Ray Cook, the senior bartender, tossed the young barback a copy of his bible, *The Fine Art of Mixing Drinks*, a 1948 tome by David

A. Embury, an opinionated American attorney with a deep interest in the proper construction of a mixed drink.

Bradsell combed through Embury: the history of specific cocktails, theories on preparation and balance, and so on. It was all new to him, and he absorbed every word. Embury remained his driver's manual throughout his career.

"He was obsessed with Embury's book," said Nick Strangeway, who later worked under Dick Bradsell. "There was a copy behind every bar. He'd always start with the Embury version of something." (Because of Bradsell's ensuing and widespread influence, it can be argued that the subsequent London cocktail boom was largely rooted in Embury formulas. Bradsell sometimes cited the existence of the Embury book as the reason he didn't need to write one of his own.)

In those days, there were only three places to drink in London, according to Strangeway: "There were pubs, hotel bars, and illegal places." The pubs, by law, closed early. ("Our version of Prohibition was concentrated drinking periods," said Strangeway.) The hotel bars were stuffy. And the third option—well, that had its own drawbacks. Many of the latter were owned by Paul Raymond, the notorious, mustachioed, fur coat–wearing, porn-magazine kingpin who owned much of SoHo.

In answer to this vexing drinking dilemma came a new breed of private drinking den that catered to hip young night owls. These were membership clubs, but not like the stone mausoleums along Pall Mall and St. James Street. Those were for the old establishment. The new style of membership clubs would be like Fred's Club.

Fred Taylor worked alongside Bradsell as a bartender at the restaurants Zanzibar and Soho Brasserie, and wanted to create a bar of his own: a club for the "right" young people, the ones who couldn't (or didn't want to) get into the older, stodgier clubs and were tired of the proletariat pub scene. Taylor wanted to serve them cocktails as good as any that could be had in London.

When the two-floor Fred's Club swung its doors open in 1987, media people came in swarms, sitting on high stools along the long, gently curved wooden bar. Rockers went there for post-concert partying. "At the time, it was revolutionary," recalled Bradsell. "It was a big preclubbing bar. It was the drinking hole of the arty classes."

Fred's was the first place where Dick was given creative license, and he went on a tear, inventing a slew of modern classics, major and minor, that are still enjoyed today and at the time struck drinkers as thunderbolts of innovation. The Bramble was a gin sour when nobody was thinking much about gin, and made with crème de mure, a blackberry liqueur nobody thought of at all. The Vodka Espresso (today better known as the Espresso Martini) was a marriage of cold vodka, fresh hot espresso, and coffee liqueur that Bradsell may have invented at the Soho Brasserie, prior to working at Fred's—supposedly in response to a supermodel's request for a drink that would "wake her up, then fuck her up."

The drinks were good enough that they made an impression on patrons who were happy to get their hands on anything, liquid or powder, that helped their high. And everybody liked Dick. Strangeway, who graduated from the kitchen to the bar at Fred's while still a teenager, remembers the people he called FODs—Friends of Dick. "We literally just chucked out Sea Breezes, and he'd just be slowly stirring Martinis."

Bradsell would stay at Fred's as long as at any place he ever worked—five years. His next stage would also be in SoHo, but much more public in character. And it would make him the most famous bartender in Britain.

OLIVER PEYTON RAN IN THE same business circles as Bradsell—clubs and booze—and did very well by both. He had known the barman "forever" by the time he hired him for his new Atlantic Bar & Grill. To Bradsell, Peyton was "the golden boy who did stuff."

Peyton was Irish, born in County Mayo. Industrious and ambitious from a ridiculously young age, Peyton owned a nightclub called the Can in Brighton in 1982, when he was twenty, and another in London, Raw, soon after. Thin, awkward, bespectacled, he was hardly the club impresario type. Neither was he the liquor baron type. But that didn't stop him from becoming the largest retailer of Kirin beer in Europe, or convincing the Japanese to let him import Sapporo beer to the UK in 1986, or getting Absolut to let him do the same with their vodka. In the latter case, he beat out seventy other applicants.

In 1980s England, there was no brand consciousness where spirits were concerned. "My key job," said Peyton, "was to get people to stop saying 'vodka and tonic.' I wanted them to say, 'Absolut and tonic.'" He did that through an unorthodox array of stratagems, familiar today but unheard of at the time. He sold the brand bar to bar, ginned up a contest in which people were allowed to submit their own ad, and advertised in a gay magazine, buying the centerfold to showcase a "naked" bottle of Absolut. In the bars, he tried to create a cocktail culture where there was none, teaching bartenders how to make Bloody Marys and Vodka Martinis, and holding cocktail competitions, with trips to Sweden as the top prize.

"I don't remember brands until Absolut came along," recalled bartender Nick Strangeway.

Peyton, though openly "trying to make a living out of having fun," never had clubbing in his blood. It was a means to an end. By the time he opened the Atlantic Bar & Grill, he had tired of the culture altogether. "I was starting to get older," he said. "I got a bit bored of all that Ecstasy culture. I really wanted to sit down. Nightclubbing got younger. I wanted something more adult."

Something more adult was, to him, a restaurant. After some searching, he found a space on Glasshouse Street just off Piccadilly. A one-time "dodgy, rent-boy kind of nightclub," it turned out to be a secret portal to an underground lair full of surprises, an Escher puzzle made up of five or six different rooms on different levels. On his way out after inspecting it, he tore at a marble column he thought was a fake. Behind it, he saw a corniced ceiling. In the corridor, there was a historic license. It said the property was registered to stay open until 3 a.m. "Suddenly, it became very interesting."

The Atlantic arrived in 1994 with a cymbal crash. London had never seen anything like it: a fashionable night spot that wasn't private, wasn't sketchy, and didn't close early. The interior seemed to go on forever: a sweeping staircase leading down to a lobby that was likened to that of a 1930s ocean liner, a restaurant, and two bars. The more famous of the two was called Dick's Bar.

Peyton didn't actually promise Bradsell his own bar. But he did ask him to come up with a name. "I said, 'If we don't come up with a good name, I'm going to call it Dick's,'" said Bradsell. "He said, 'No, don't call it that.'" But Dick's Bar it was, and it changed the cocktail game in London, because it not only put craft cocktails in front of a thirsty public, but also placed the cocktail maker front and center.

"I think one of the seminal moments in the evolution of the London bar scene is when Ollie decided to name the members' bar at the Atlantic after Dick," said Ben Reed, who would soon become a celebrity bartender himself. It was, in Philip Duff's words, "the zero year of modern English bartending."

At Dick's, bartending involved a bit of social engineering. "You have to bear in mind that men didn't drink cocktails," said Nick Strangeway, who had followed Bradsell from Fred's Club to the Atlantic. "Or, rather, young men didn't drink cocktails. They didn't drink things in a martini-shaped glass. Places like Atlantic made it cool for men to hold a cocktail glass and drink something that wasn't a pint of beer."

Not everyone who went was enlightened when it came to spirits. According to Angus Winchester, an early bartender there, he sold a lot of

Champagne and wine, and the most popular drink in those early days was Pear Drop Shots—crushed-up pear candies mixed with shots of vodka. But the Atlantic answered a need, offering a middle ground between the stuffy, serious hotel bars and the vapid discos. Peyton was doing eight hundred to nine hundred covers a night and still booking dinners as late as 11:30.

The door was tough; being beautiful or famous helped you get past the bouncer. Kate Moss could get in; she was the first person served by bartender Winchester after he was hired. Artist Damien Hirst, who made it his business in the 1990s and '00s to be a fly at whatever bar was hot at the moment, was a regular. (Hirst himself would briefly own a restaurant and bar.) Alanis Morissette had a birthday bash there, and Def Leppard threw a launch party. Pierce Brosnan, then the reigning film Bond, ordered Martinis; Bill Murray stepped behind the bar and made his own drinks. Goldie Hawn, Robert DeNiro, Madonna—the list went on. Nevertheless, Peyton, chasing a certain nightlife democracy, ordered the doormen to keep the crowd eclectic, telling them to "go down and look at what the balance was of suits, trendies, women, men, blacks. It was a constant thing for me, the balance of people."

Once you got in, there was another cordon outside Dick's Bar, "a queue within the queue," as bartender Alex Turner put it. "It was smaller, we had better music, it was more intimate, we had a nicer-looking staff. We always had a hard-core crowd. They drank all the time."

With the mad popularity came a bit of actual madness.

"It was chaos," remembered Strangeway. Bradsell's work habits didn't help things. A genius at communicating matters of drink philosophy and creation, he was, in practice, a messy bartender. "Dick made brilliant drinks," observed Philip Duff. "But 'speed,' 'efficiency,' 'hygiene,' 'clean as you go' were strange words to him. He would make a drink, trash a station, move on to the next station, make a drink, and trash that."

Because he had put Dick's name on the bar, Peyton made Bradsell promise he'd stay a while. But Bradsell was gone in six months, putting into play a rolling-stone pattern he would follow for years to come.

"My doctor told me to leave," Bradsell said. "It was the most stressful place I ever worked. It was totally, impossibly disorganized."

Bradsell didn't suffer for his hasty retreat; he was already a legend in the industry and had no trouble finding work. Neither did Dick's Bar falter without Dick. The Atlantic marched on for years. The bar became a training ground for bartenders who would come to dominate the scene in the years to come, none more important than the men—Alex Turner, Dre Masso, Jamie Terrell, Doug Ankrah—who would eventually play a part in forming LAB, a cool abbreviation for London Academy of Bartenders. LAB began as a school and then morphed into the most influential bar to emerge in the wake of the Atlantic.

Vodka Espresso

DICK BRADSELL, 1980s, Soho Brasserie, London

2 ounces vodka

1 ounce espresso

½ ounce coffee liqueur

¼ ounce simple syrup

3 coffee beans, for garnish

No London bartender of the modern era invented more modern classics than Dick Bradsell, and the Vodka Espresso is neck and neck with the Bramble as his best known. Vodka Espresso is the original name of the drink, which has been served under many names, most frequently Espresso Martini. He famously created it for a supermodel who asked for something that would "wake her up, then fuck her up." (Dick never revealed the identity of the model. He was also vague about the drink's place of origin, sometimes naming Soho Brasserie, sometimes Fred's Club.) Fresh espresso is key to the success of this drink. The cocktail has become something of a religion in Australia, where good coffee is a national obsession.

Combine the vodka, espresso, liqueur, and syrup in a cocktail shaker three-quarters filled with ice. Shake until foamy. Strain into a chilled coupe. Garnish with three coffee beans.

Bramble

DICK BRADSELL, 1991–92, Fred's Club, London

2 ounces gin

¾ ounce fresh
lemon juice

½ ounce simple syrup

½ ounce crème
de mûre

Blackberry,
for garnish

Lemon wedge,
for garnish

Bradsell created this while working at Fred's Club, a private membership club favored by media and celebrities.

"This guy used to supply us with this really great cider," said Bradsell. "He brought us in these three great liqueurs—a cassis, a framboise, and a mûre. As soon as I tried the mûre, I was back in that blackberry patch on the Isle of Wight. It was spot-on, that flavor. I made a British drink with gin, lemon, and sugar. The scene was totally vodka then. It was like, modernity is vodka, fashion is vodka; seriousness is gin. I knew quite a lot about gin, the different gins; I knew that some brands were crap and some were really good." Bradsell thinks he first made the Bramble with Booth's Finest. "Gordon's would love me to say it was Gordon's, because that was our house gin. But it definitely wasn't Gordon's."

The Bramble was put on the menu at Fred's Club in 1991 or '92 (Bradsell was not sure) and became popular straight off. Its appeal widened after Bradsell put it on the menu of Jonathan Downey's Match. Soon the drink leaped the Atlantic. Its spread was helped along by the fact that it was easy to make. "You can do it at parties right away," said Bradsell. It's also very sessionable, being relatively light in alcohol. The fresh blackberry garnish gives the drink a striking presence.

Bramble, continued

Combine the gin, lemon juice, and syrup in a cocktail shaker three-quarters filled with ice. Shake until chilled. Strain into an old-fashioned glass filled with crushed ice. Drizzle crème de mûre on top of the drink. Garnish with the blackberry and the lemon wedge.

III. 'TINIS AND COSMOS

THE RAINBOW ROOM GARNERED CONSIDERABLE praise and press attention. But, for all the "cocktails are back" articles of the time, not much really changed behind New York area bars. As William Grimes observed, "I thought I was in the midst of a fad. I thought, *Five years from now, they're not going to be drinking these drinks.* I didn't see it having a longer life span than that."

Dale DeGroff worked largely in isolation. Nobody in New York—or anywhere else in the United States, really—was operating at his level and with his visibility. Still, some of his philosophy spread through a social circle called the Red Meat Club.

The group, which met monthly to devour steak and Martinis, was a collection of food and drink professionals, including Long Island winemakers David Page and Barbara Shinn; sommelier Fred Price; Michael Smith, the bar manager at Keens Steakhouse; Sam Barbieri, owner of the Brooklyn whiskey bar Pete's Waterfront Alehouse; Francis Schott, a New Brunswick restaurateur; and bartender Cory Hill. "We'd spend a lot of money and get roaring drunk on a Monday afternoon," recalled Hill. "But a lot of ideas got shared."

Few picked up on DeGroff's lead earlier than Schott. At one meeting, Schott got into a discussion with DeGroff about the seriousness of cocktails. Incredulous, Schott followed up with a visit the Rainbow Room.

"I walked in, and the first thing I realized was Dale was the best bartender I'd ever seen," recalled Schott. "I saw the people coming into the Rainbow Room—captains of industry, minor celebrities, people wearing suits that were half a year's salary to me. And by their body language, it was important to them that Dale knows them. Not that they know Dale; that Dale knows them. And he always did."

Then DeGroff started making cocktails. "He made me a Ritz cocktail. He made me a Whiskey Smash. He's using fresh juice. Unheard of. He's cutting garnishes to order. The glassware is beautiful, like something out of a movie. I walked out of that bar that night and thought, *I don't know anything about bartending.*"

Schott returned to New Brunswick and installed a new cocktail list, featuring a Caipirinha, Algonquin, Ritz, Stork Club, Flamingo, Bobby Burns, and Gin Sling. The bar squeezed fresh juice and remained the only New Jersey bar to do so for years. It shook drinks with egg whites. Schott also bought the first Kold-Draft ice machine—which produced stylish, chunky cubes rather than hollow, flimsy, standard bar ice—in the state.

When Cory Hill—who had worked at Keens Steakhouse—moved to Nosmo King, a restaurant with a healthy bent (as to the odd name, read: "No Smoking"), he made Watermelon Margaritas and Watermelon Martinis on the spot from fresh ingredients. "Dale was the inspiration for that," said Hill.

Those who couldn't gain DeGroff's wisdom for free through membership in the Red Meat Club could pay for it. In 1996, restaurateur Keith McNally opened his Soviet fantasy bar, Pravda, down some steps to the side of the Puck Building in SoHo. With vaulted ceilings and red-leather banquettes, it looked the way a dining car in a Moscow subway station might, if such a thing existed. There was an undulating zinc bar and sixty vodkas. McNally called DeGroff down from the Rainbow Room to train the bartenders. He also sent his Pravda staff uptown to see Dale work.

"It was a bottom-up sort of experience for these guys," said DeGroff. "They needed a complete training in the classics. I demo'd everything, then I set to work with these guys behind the bar one at a time, and they all learned from doing." Drink by drink, taste by taste, the young bartenders were schooled.

Head bartender was Eugene Masat, a Turk who was then in New York on an expired work visa bartending at the Copacabana nightclub. Masat was a veteran of Schumann's American Bar, a legendary Munich bar run by the even more legendary Charles Schumann. It was a bar the British McNally knew and respected.

Charles Schumann was a bartender as designed by Ian Fleming and Hollywood. He spoke four languages, was once a boxer, was the author of several books, and modeled clothing for Hugo Boss. And he owned what was then, and may still be, the most influential cocktail bar in Europe.

"If there is any legendary bartender anywhere on this planet Earth, it's that gentleman," said Stanislav Vadrna, of the bar Paparazzi in Bratislava. Bartender Philip Duff put it more succinctly: "If you say bartender to anyone in Germany, they'll say Charles Schumann."

Schumann's American Bar opened in Munich in 1982, serving classic cocktails and highballs. It was a success from the start. Most watering holes in Germany were in hotels; a free-standing bar was a novelty.

Schumann took the training of his staff seriously. Nothing was rushed, and nothing was left to chance. The bartenders free poured, but with great accuracy. In 1986, he gave Eugene Masat, who had grown up in Germany and was then just seventeen, a chance. Masat began by just washing glasses, standing next to the bartender, observing. He did that for six months. Then he was moved to the beer position, where he did nothing but draw beers for a year. He was then allowed onto the floor as a waiter. And so on. (Schumann, who shared a shoe size with Masat, sometimes had Eugene break in his bespoke footwear.)

When McNally was envisioning Pravda, "he wanted to have a dress code," recalled Masat. "Besides Rainbow Room, there were none." Masat showed McNally his crisp white Schumann's bar jacket, and McNally copied it exactly for Pravda. As for the female servers, little black dresses were the order. "It was like a Robert Palmer video," said Masat.

Like most McNally places, Pravda grabbed hold of New York's lapels almost immediately, serving vodka rocks and vodka Martinis to nightlife mavens and the wolves of Wall Street. The line waiting to get in extended down Lafayette around the corner to Prince Street. Celebrities flocked: JFK Jr., Sean Penn, Jim Carrey. But the bread-and-butter customers were the young, hotshot brokers.

"Mojito was our nemesis," recalled bartender Dushan Zaric, who got his start at Pravda before opening his own influential bar, Employees Only. "This is how it went down. Five o'clock. They would walk in, like six of them. From the door, he throws his credit card on the bar and says, 'Six Mojitos.' I start making six Mojitos. It required muddling. It would take a decent amount of time to make six of them. Five minutes. He would take them, bring them to the table and then say, 'Make another round.' They downed them right away. One by one they go to the bathroom to ski. They come back and then they start having three or four rounds like this. It's 5:45. Their tab is like $500. They leave me a $250 tip. They walk. Go somewhere else. We made really good money there."

DeGroff, still on McNally's payroll, continued to check in. "Pravda was going wild," recalled DeGroff. "They were selling caviar and fancy Champagne. I'm in there all the time, spending my money. I'm signing for my friends." When McNally's Balthazar was ready to go, the restaurateur had DeGroff train the staff there as well. "I send my invoice to Keith's office. I get this polite call. 'Actually Mr. DeGroff, you owe us $800.' They had never told me that my tradeoff was done at Pravda."

Whether due to DeGroff's influence or not, the cocktail ethos was spreading at other places at well. Martinis were the calling card, too, at Temple Bar, a Greenwich Village lounge that opened in 1989. Its fairly obscure entrance on Lafayette Street—an early harbinger of the speakeasy trend to come—opened up into a sophisticated, dimly lit drinking cave. At Global 33, a subterranean joint on Second Avenue with a 1950s, Pan Am airline vibe (it was named after a *Twilight Zone* episode), you could get Pimm's Cups and Dark & Stormys. Marion's Continental, another retro downtown place, served Gibsons and stirred Martinis.

At the Hudson River Club in downtown Manhattan, beverage director Nick Mautone managed to get chef Waldy Malouf interested in house-made cocktail garnishes when everyone else was content fishing them out of narrow bottles. "Waldy and I made cocktail onions. He literally brought cases of onions to brine." They also contracted for an entire cherry orchard so they could make brandied cherries for their Manhattans.

When Mautone moved to Gramercy Tavern in 1995, he brought his garnish mania with him, and he continued to collaborate with the kitchen, working with pastry chef Claudia Fleming and chef Tom Colicchio to accessorize the cocktails.

"Tom made roasted tomato chips that would float on top of a basil Martini," said Mautone. "Claudia made the cherries. If Claudia was using pineapple, I made drinks with pineapple. If Tom was using rosemary, I made drinks with rosemary."

"Mautone turned up the dial on cocktails way more than we had before," recalled Danny Meyer, owner of Gramercy. That was saying something, for Gramercy's initial general manager was Steve Olson, who insisted the wine and beer menus be joined by a list of classic cocktails with set specifications, including Manhattans made with then-exotic rye. Meyer wanted spirits behind the bar; he hadn't had any at the bar Union Square Café, which alienated drinkers, but he resisted the idea of a specific list.

"Danny thought it was pretentious to tell people what they should drink," said Olson, "that people who came in would know. I said, 'It's like a menu. Shouldn't we tell them what we're good at?'"

Meyer and McNally weren't the only New York restaurateurs to recognize the value of cocktails. In 1992, a group of five guys, refugees from other careers who had opened a string of thematic restaurants around the Village (Gulf Coast, Cowgirl Hall of Fame), opened Grange Hall on a bend in narrow Commerce Street. The space had formerly been the Blue Mill Tavern, a speakeasy, and the interior was little changed.

Co-owner Jay Suvulich decided to create a time capsule. He hired some Croatian woodworkers to transform the room into how it might have looked in the '30s. A period-appropriate mural was added. The original bartender, Danny Rosenberg, put together a menu by going through old cocktail books. The bar used fresh juices, house-made syrups, and infused vodkas and made *Glögg* at Christmas. Suvulich wasn't following anybody's lead. "It wasn't an attempt to be part of a trend," he said.

When Del Pedro joined the bar crew in 1995, he was impressed. Pedro committed himself to old-school bartending while at Grange Hall and developed a following. Pedro brought in Toby Maloney, who recalled Del as "the first person who ever said 'balanced' to me."

"That place was important," said David Wondrich, the cocktail historian. "It was the place you could go if you couldn't afford the Rainbow Room."

ALL THE BARS THAT TRIED on the cocktail thing in the 1990s, in both New York and London, relied heavily on two drinks. The first was the Martini, the one drink that everybody, however ignorant of American drinking history, recognized as the epitome of a cocktail.

Of course, during the 1980s and 1990s, Martini was a flexible term, basically covering anything a bartender cared to put in a cone-shaped, long-stemmed glass. Bars had "Martini menus," with many selections. This sort of thing made the Martini purists livid, but it kept the cocktail's name alive.

"Joe Blow had not experienced cocktails," argues Simon Difford, publisher of *Class* magazine. "But the Martini was a serious cocktail. The fact that they were drinking a Watermelon Martini turned a very simple drink into serious drink, simply because it came in a V-shaped glass and was called a Martini."

Bars and bartenders far and wide, endeavoring to promote their cocktail agenda, traded heavily on the one name people knew. In London, Salvatore Calabrese, one of the best-known bartenders in London throughout the '90s, achieved his most iconic creation with the Breakfast Martini, which mixed marmalade with gin. Dick Bradsell found similar success with the coffee-laced Espresso Martini (though first called the Vodka Espresso, it gained worldwide fame under its later name). LAB, a pivotal London bar in the late 1990s, offered a Porn Star Martini that came with a shot of chilled Champagne. The red-hot Met Bar, also in London, was all about fresh-fruit Martinis. The Appletini, which may have been born at a place called Lola's in Los Angeles, tore through U.S. bars in the last years of the '90s.

There were only a few cocktail books that came out in the '90s and early '00s, and most were solely about these "Martinis." Ben Reed, Gary Regan, the team of Jared Brown and Anistatia Miller, and Barnaby Conrad III all put out manuals dedicated to the drink.

The other drink order that New York cocktail bartenders of the 1990s could be assured of fielding on each shift was of more recent vintage.

The Cosmopolitan is a simple drink. It is basically a variation on the Kamikaze (a disco shot favorite with equal parts vodka, lime, and triple sec), made of Absolut Citron (which was released the same year the drink was created, 1988), fresh lime juice, Cointreau, and cranberry juice cocktail—the thing that gives the drink its famous pink color. It became internationally famous for a variety of reasons, not least of which was that it served as the primary form of sustenance for the four female characters on the HBO series *Sex and the City*.

But the real importance of the Cosmopolitan is not how it became famous and popular, but that it *did* become famous and popular. It is the only cocktail of its era that succeeded in becoming an international household word. The Martini was retro; however popular the drink was in the 1990s, the name was a throwback, a reminder that cocktail culture's heyday was in the past. The Cosmopolitan alone proved that the cocktail could be a thing of today.

The Cosmo also illustrates how, even in a time when media coverage blankets every moment of our lives, the origin of a popular drink can still be muddied by multiple and conflicting assertions of ownership. It's amusing, then, that the most convincing claim belongs to a contrarian who for many years refused credit.

Toby Cecchini is a querulous skeptic who likes to downplay his profession any chance he gets. He remained happily ignorant of the leaps mixology made during his first two decades as a bartender, from the mid-'80s to the mid-'00s. Rip Van Winkle–like, he woke up to the revolution he had helped set in motion only when his bar Passerby closed in 2008, and some of his younger colleagues dragged him out of the shadows and set him up as an idol and forefather.

Cecchini has worked in only four bars. The first was Odeon, the McNally brothers' 1980s Tribeca cradle of literary and celebrity life. Cecchini came from Wisconsin with dreams of becoming a writer, and he recognized the Odeon from the cover of Jay McInerney's *Bright Lights, Big City*. He quickly noticed that the bartenders were "ordained," whereas the waitstaff were chattel. Invited to train behind the bar, he happily agreed.

The Odeon, which opened in 1980, made classic cocktails and had its standards: no Long Island Iced Teas, and so on. After four years of serving the elite and becoming inured to celebrity, he was invited to run the bar at

Kin Khao in SoHo. The owner mandated that the bar needed some sort of Thai twists on drinks. "I tried infusing kaffir lime, every manner of ginger, lemongrass, pineapple, all in vodka," said Cecchini. "It would have never occurred to me to use gin or anything else. It was kind of groundbreaking at the time."

After six years there, his friend Gavin Brown, who had worked at Odeon, asked Cecchini if he'd be interested in opening a bar inside his Chelsea art gallery. Brown wanted a secret clubhouse for his art world friends, a place into which each art opening could spill over. Cecchini agreed, just as long as he could run the bar as he saw fit. But what most people remembered was the lighted disco floor, installed by artist Piotr Uklanski (a winningly ironic touch for a narrow space with no room to dance and no cabaret license).

Passerby was an odd place, a bar-world expression of the art concept of high and low; fabulously urbane arty folk were illuminated from below by Bay Ridge–style disco squares. The bar was on a gritty side street. The walls were plywood, and yet it appealed to a certain hipster eccentric searching for something original. Owing to its proximity to a lot of different New York communities, the crowd would change personality throughout the night, lurching from gay bar to wine bar to artist hangout to bridge-and-tunnel mess. It was, in short, a very New York bar.

Passerby opened in 1999, just as the cocktail scene in New York was about to blow up. It was popular and iconic in its way, but not trendy or a leader. Cecchini believed part of the reason for Passerby's lower profile was his connection to the *New York Times*, where he wrote a cocktail column. As long as he was working for the paper, the paper wouldn't write about him.

Some mixologists found Passerby, anyway. But it was only after it closed in 2008 that its true fame came about, and it passed into legend as one of New York's great lost bars. "Subsequently, everybody said, 'Oh my God, I loved your bar,'" said Cecchini. David Kaplan, co-owner of Death & Co, claimed to have visited several times. He lifted the disco floor motif wholesale when he opened Honeycut in Los Angeles years later. Adam Tsou, a former Passerby bartender, did the same thing when he opened Glass in Paris.

Cecchini's post-Passerby role in the brave new cocktail world was complicated. Young bartenders respected his veteran status and his writings (including the memoir *Cosmopolitan*, published in 2004). But they hated the drink he created—on principle. Struck by some Oedipal urge, they sought to kill the thing on which many of their careers had been built.

Cecchini remembered, "Years and years of bartenders saying: 'You! You invented the Cosmopolitan, you fuck!' And I'd be like, 'I'm sorry, man.'" (As to the details of the drink's creation, we'll get to that soon.)

Bartenders' rage toward the drink didn't stem entirely from a cool kid's knee-jerk urge to knock the trendy and popular, or from the natural hatred all bartenders feel toward any drink they're forced to make countless times. It was more that the drink required two artificial ingredients—flavored vodka and cranberry juice cocktail—that they, as artisans, had foresworn. *Fake* wasn't in the modern mixologist's vocabulary. Many cocktail bars didn't carry cranberry juice cocktail just so they wouldn't have to make Cosmopolitans.

It was a hard thing to own such a hated drink. So for many years Cecchini shirked his connection to it, developing the kind of cranky attitude toward his early work that Orson Welles had for *Citizen Kane* late in his career. That changed, though, as bartenders' feelings toward the cocktail began to relax, and as the number of credit hogs rose.

"Five years ago, I would have been, 'Look, I'm done with the Cosmo,'" Cecchini said in 2014. "'It's a drink I made up when I was twenty-five. Can I please be unshackled?'"

Cecchini still stands by the story of the drink's birth that he laid down in *Cosmopolitan* (which he had wanted to title *Behind Bars*). A fellow bartender at Odeon had friends from San Francisco who introduced her to a Bay

Area drink called the Cosmopolitan. She told Toby about the cocktail. "The Cosmopolitan was a kind of drink made of rail vodka, Rose's lime juice, and Rose's grenadine that was making the rounds of gay bars in San Francisco in the early '80s," he said. He didn't think much of it, and began tinkering. "I simply gave it the same treatment we were giving our Margaritas at the time, which was using fresh lime juice and Cointreau, and I swapped out the grenadine for a little Ocean Spray cranberry juice cocktail, which is what we were using in Cape Codders. And it became the staff drink. I remember being puzzled when the customers began to order one. *How do you know about our staff drink?* And I became really puzzled as I visited other bars and noticed this small diaspora around downtown New York and seeing people make it wrong and badly."

A Florida bartender named Cheryl Cook subsequently claimed to have invented the drink in the mid-1980s. (Improbable, as Absolut Citron wasn't introduced until 1988.) DeGroff began serving the drink at the Rainbow Room, which may have added to the drink's notoriety. In the end, the way Cecchini characterized the matter in *Cosmopolitan* best frames the nature of his achievement: "I did invent what you think of as the drink, the version everyone means when they order it."

The final irony of the Cosmopolitan is that it was invented in pre–cocktail revival days, when no one was looking for a new classic cocktail. And today's revivalists, who so desperately want to create new classics, have so far failed to put out anything even approaching the Cosmo in notoriety.

"I'm not sure we'll ever have a Cosmopolitan again," said Philip Duff, an international cocktail consultant and authority who has seen thirty years of cocktail trends come and go. "It was beautifully seeded by that television series, and we were all so hungry for it."

Cosmopolitan

TOBY CECCHINI, 1988, Odeon, New York

2 ounces Absolut Citron vodka

1 ounce Cointreau

1 ounce lime juice

1 ounce Ocean Spray cranberry juice cocktail

Lemon twist, for garnish

Arguably the only modern cocktail to become a household word. This phenomenally popular vodka cocktail illustrated that, even in the dark days of the 1980s, it was possible for a new, well-crafted drink to seize the public's imagination. Its origins have become quite murky over the years, with several bartenders and cities claiming a role in either creating or popularizing the drink. But the version that became recognized and enjoyed by millions as the Cosmopolitan—the one with Absolut Citron, which was introduced in 1988, and fresh lime juice, not Rose's lime juice—emerged from Odeon, the Tribeca hotspot where Toby Cecchini fashioned the cocktail as a staff drink.

Combine all the ingredients except the lemon twist in a cocktail shaker three-quarters filled with ice. Shake intensely. Strain into a chilled cocktail glass. Garnish with the lemon twist.

Breakfast Martini

SALVATORE CALABRESE, 1997, Library Bar,
Lanesborough Hotel, London

1 spoonful English orange marmalade

½ ounce fresh lemon juice

1⅔ ounces gin

½ ounce curaçao

Orange peel, for garnish

One of the earliest—and still the most famous—examples of jam as an ingredient in a cocktail revival era. Bartender Salvatore Calabrese created the drink at the Lanesborough, a posh hotel in Mayfair. "I'm a very typical Italian person," he said. "The first thing in the morning, all I can do is an espresso. I'm like a zombie." He said his wife made him eat marmalade. The bitter, tangy flavor intrigued him, leading him to create the cocktail. Some have noticed a similarity between this cocktail and the Marmalade Cocktail found in the 1930 *Savoy Cocktail Book*. Calabrese says he was not aware of the Savoy recipe when he created this drink.

Stir the marmalade with the lemon juice at the bottom of a cocktail shaker until it dissolves. Add the gin and curaçao. Shake with ice. Fine strain into a chilled cocktail coupe. Shred some orange peel on the top of the drink as a garnish.

IV. ANGELS IN THE EAST VILLAGE

NO COCKTAIL BAR THAT OPENED in New York in the 1990s was more important to the future of the cocktail revival than Angel's Share—even if it proved so sui generis and willfully isolated that it would largely be eclipsed and forgotten by the movement it helped to inspire.

It was located on the second floor of an angled street in the East Village, behind a door at the back of a Japanese restaurant. The owner wanted to create a Tokyo-style cocktail bar: small, intimate, and formal, with an emphasis on perfect drinks and service.

Japan's cocktail experience in the years following World War II was a world apart from America's. As U.S. dedication to mixology skill and credibility slackened and dwindled, Japan's intensified and became more rigorous. Formal and stylistic, Japanese-style bartending was devoted not to creating original drinks but to mastering and refining a few classics and presenting them with a highly detailed dignity. Japanese bartenders practiced their art in small, expensive drinking dens where nothing about the customer experience was left to chance.

"The process, it wasn't just about the final result, the cocktail," explained Stanislav Vadrna, a Czechoslovakia-born bartender who became an apostle of Japanese bartending. "It was about the whole process leading up to the cocktail. The Japanese customer is seeking beauty in every single movement. It's about these little details. The smell in the air. The setup on the bar. The way they were handling the equipment behind the bar."

Mixology has always been a trade characterized by little rituals. To some American bartenders, such rituals are given their due and even treasured. But to the Japanese, the myriad techniques leading up to the setting forth of the cocktail before the guest were as important as the drink itself and, they believed, directly influenced how the customer would enjoy the drink. "Westerners focus on results," wrote Kazuo Uyeda, a legendary Tokyo bartender, in his 2000 book *Cocktail Techniques*. "While the Japanese have been influenced by this focus to a certain extent in recent years, we, at heart, respect the process." Uyeda called this approach "the way of the cocktail," and it included the cleanliness and clothing of the bartender, the appearance of the cocktail (Midori and blue curaçao are not just ingredients to a Japanese bartender; they are paints on a palette), the beauty of the bar equipment and glassware, the look of the ice, the style of the shake, and things as intangible as sincerity of effort. The performances of Japanese cocktail bartenders are neat, elegant, and precise. It is Zen bartending, a perfectly put-together jigsaw puzzle that is a beauty to behold when whole, and, the thinking goes, utterly worthless when a single piece goes missing.

But Japanese bartending was also an isolated style, a hermetically sealed oddity not influenced by what was happening behind bars in London, New York, or San Francisco. Nor had those cities seen anything like Uyeda's renowed Tender Bar. Until Angel's Share came along.

It opened without notice in 1994. Shinichi Ikeda got behind the bar two years later. He had come from Japan, where he had worked as a bartender, to play music. "At the time, they didn't know how to run the bar," recalled Ikeda. "One day, the owner told me to run the bar. Somehow, he knew I used to work as a bartender in Japan." He retrained the bartenders to stir Manhattans and Martinis as he had learned in Japan, and he added classic cocktails to the menu as well as original cocktails with Japanese ingredients like shochu and shiso leaf. It was an exacting, decorum-centric bar entirely alien to Americans. There was no small talk (partly because many of the bartenders had limited English), no standing, no large parties. Martin Doudoroff, an amateur cocktail enthusiast who would come to play an important role in the movement, thought of it as not so much a bar as a Japanese-American cultural exchange program.

Hugh Garvey, who was writing a cocktail column for *The Village Voice*, was astonished. He ordered a Gin & Tonic. The bartender opened a fresh bottle of tonic, then pulled out a drawer and began chipping away at a large block of ice. Garvey recalls thinking, *Who are these guys with these shiny shakers and these bow ties tasting drinks on the back of their hands from barspoons and doing this balletic performance? I just don't understand this.*

Bartender Todd Thrasher remembers getting a lesson in Japanese-level service standards while on a visit from Virginia. "A barback was rude to a guest. He had rolled his eyes. The bartender told him to get something out of the bottom shelf. He was down on his hands and knees, and the bartender kicked him as hard as I've ever seen anyone get kicked."

The lasting impact of the Angel's Share was secured when a curious, dark-eyed local named Sasha Petraske came in the late 1990s. He marveled at the ice, the rules of etiquette, and the olives placed on the side of each Martini.

"He sat at the bar," recalled Ikeda. "He asked questions, about cocktails, skills. He told me, he wants to open a bar like Angel's Share."

He did. It was called Milk & Honey. And word of it quickly spread around the world. Word of Angel's Share, however, largely stayed put. In the years that followed, its owner didn't expand. None of its bartenders became stars. It put out no cocktail book. The bar remained insular and inward-looking, a "closed shop," as David Wondrich put it.

But the refusal to reach out went in both directions. Shingo Gokan, arguably the best-known bartender Angel's Share ever produced, joined the crew after he moved from Tokyo in 2006. The drinks movement was well along by then, but he never felt part of the cocktail community.

"I was there eight years. For the first six years, I didn't have any friends who were bartenders. I didn't know anybody at all. I was just working there. I didn't know who were the industry people. English is not my native language. We were always outside."

V. PRINCES IN EXILE

UNLIKE NEW YORK AND LONDON, San Francisco never had a distinct cocktail king. Instead, it had two princes in exile.

Tony Abou-Ganim and Paul Harrington were long gone by the time San Francisco's cocktail renaissance was in full swing. But their influence was felt in many bars, through the numerous young bartenders who, during the 1990s, passed under their tutelage at the Starlight Room in downtown San Francisco and Enrico's in historic North Beach. Harrington's time in town was the briefer, but his influence arguably more widespread, owing to his authoring one of the only historically minded cocktail books of the period. Well before DeGroff published his first cocktail book in 2002, Harrington's *Cocktails*, published by Viking in 1998, was read across the United States and overseas.

Unlike other American cities, San Francisco had never completely abandoned cocktail culture. Signs outside old-school restaurants advertised "cocktails" on nearly every block. In the 1950s, Martini culture was pervasive, remembers Barnaby Conrad III, whose father had owned Matador, a celebrity-studded nightclub during that decade. "My father said, 'Every time we ever had a fight in that bar, people were drinking gin.'" The Buena Vista Café has famously been serving Irish Coffees since 1952. Norman Hobday helped kicked off the fern bar movement—which fostered a culture in which young singles could mingle and meet—when he opened Henry Africa's in 1969 at the corner of Broadway and Polk, serving Daiquiris and Lemon Drops, a massively popular mix of vodka, triple sec, lemon juice, and simple syrup. The Zuni Café squeezed limes fresh for its famous Margaritas. At Stars, Jeremiah Tower's celebrated palace of fine gastronomy, the cocktail glasses were chilled, fine Carpano vermouth from Italy was used, and the bar served Negronis and pink gins. "We gave as much attention to the bar as we did to the food," said Tower. "It was a passion and the rules were strict."

Neither Harrington nor Abou-Ganim wanted to bartend. Abou-Ganim was an actor. Harrington pursued architecture. Abou-Ganim, at least, had bartending in his blood. He started working behind the stick in 1980 at the Brass Rail, his cousin's place in Port Huron, Michigan, on the Canadian border. (His parents had first met there, so you could say Tony owed his life to the tavern.) By 1985, he was in San Francisco, pulling pints and performing with a company made up of restaurant and bar employees called Pour Boy Productions.

Abou-Ganim landed a job at a brunch waiter at Balboa Café, a saloon then run by Hobday's brother Jack Slick and Doyle Moon. The Balboa was one of a trio of bars at the intersection of Greenwich and Fillmore dubbed the singles-scene "Bermuda Triangle" by columnist Herb Caen. (Hobday owned one of the others, the Dartmouth Social Club. The third was the Golden Gate Grill.)

"There was never a cocktail 'resurgence' with them. It never went away," Abou-Ganim said of Slick and Moon. They "understood fresh ingredients, they understood balance. There was no big buzz about it. It was just a great cocktail bar. Jack was doing Ramos Gin Fizzes in 1985. Outside of New Orleans, he was probably the only one." Abou-Ganim's rise at the Balboa was slow, but it was there he learned about how to build a cocktail and the importance of fresh juice.

From Balboa Café, Abou-Ganim moved on in 1991 to Harry Denton's, a bar run by its showman namesake. Denton, like Slick and Hobday, was a larger-than-life figure. Short and balding, he was a heavy drinker with a head as large and round as his belly, and a personality larger than that. "A wonderful guy who everybody loves, with a funny voice," as critic Michael Bauer put it.

Harry Denton's was run by another big personality, David O'Malley, who came out of Boston and was a prodigy of TGI Fridays' "Magic" Mike Werner. "He put together a classic cocktail menu there," Abou-Ganim said of O'Malley. "Sidecar, Old-Fashioned, Champagne Cocktail, Negroni. I'd never heard of the Negroni before." But Abou-Ganim quickly got the hang of bartending. "Tony was obviously our star," said O'Malley, "He rose above everyone." His acting background gave him presence, and his growing reverence for the history of bartending lent him gravity. Abou-Ganim called Denton's "where I really became a bartender."

But for Abou-Ganim, bartending was still a side job, and when he fell in love with his costar in the interactive stage production of *Tony 'n' Tina's Wedding*, he followed her to New York. In 1993, he got a job at a tiny Greenwich Village Italian restaurant called Po run by a nobody named Mario Batali. Batali told Abou-Ganim to check out the Rainbow Room. He went and ordered a Negroni from Dale DeGroff.

"That was one of the big aha! moments in my career," he remembered. "I sat at the bar with my Negroni watching him work for a couple hours."

In 1996, he returned to San Francisco to open up the Starlight Room, again working with Denton and O'Malley. The Starlight was a throwback, in its way the Rainbow Room of San Francisco. A rooftop lounge atop the Sir Francis Drake Hotel, it had been built in 1928, but had fallen from grace when Kimpton Hotels, O'Malley's employer, bought it in 1994. It was revamped and unveiled two years later as Harry Denton's Starlight Room. Like the Rainbow Room, the Starlight Room helped to put bartenders and their cocktail creations on an elegant pedestal, with the intended message being that both belonged there.

Abou-Ganim stayed only until 1998, while there creating the Cable Car, a sour made with spiced rum, curaçao, and a sugared rim, and his most famous drink. He left to take a command of twenty-nine bars and 250 bartenders at the Bellagio hotel and casino, becoming the first big craft cocktail force in Las Vegas—a gig for which DeGroff had recommended him. The Starlight Room, meanwhile, welcomed a stream of skilled bartenders who would go on to shape the San Francisco scene, including Marcovaldo Dionysus and Thomas Waugh.

PAUL HARRINGTON WAS BORN IN Yakima in central Washington. Relatives had opened casinos and bars, but his father, the son of jazz musicians, worked for the phone company. In college, Harrington made extra money selling marijuana to his fraternity brothers. But when someone he didn't know knocked on his door, he decided to leave his dealer days behind and take a year off school. In San Francisco, he got a job at a Houlihan's near Fisherman's Wharf. Disliking the Nielsen's Sweet Sour Mix he was forced to use, he began tweaking the corporate recipes.

When the Loma Prieta earthquake struck in 1989 and a section of the Bay Bridge collapsed, effectively closing the bridge, the commute to Houlihan's was suddenly a very long one, so he took a job at a place called Townhouse Bar & Grill in Emeryville, an industrial area in the East Bay near Oakland.

The Townhouse building dated back to the 1920s, when it was a speakeasy. Its owner when Harrington arrived, a Frenchman named Joseph LeBrun, had renovated the honky-tonk. LeBrun had a great selection of ports and Cognacs. Through him, Harrington became more interested in aperitifs. At Houlihan's, Harrington would play a trick on his fellow bartenders by serving them a Negroni as a shot. At Townhouse, he served the drink as is.

By a lucky coincidence, Dale DeGroff was friends with the owners of Bucci's, a restaurant near Townhouse. "He was the only bartender besides

Charles Schumann whose name I knew," said Harrington. Arriving at the bar at Townhouse, DeGroff ordered olive oil to start (to coat his stomach), then a Beefeater Martini. After a night of drinking around town, DeGroff returned at the end of the night. He recalled, "We drove [Harrington] crazy ordering difficult drinks."

Challenged, Harrington began collecting old cocktail books and introducing his own creations at the bar, including one, the Campari-laced Jasmine, that would go on to become a modern classic. In 1992, some friends recruited him to work at Enrico's in North Beach. Harrington stayed there only nine months, but it was Enrico's that turned him into an early cocktail authority.

Enrico's was an old beatnik holdout from the '50s with a boho vibe. (Its original owner, Enrico Banducci, had named himself after Enrico Caruso.) The space had stood vacant for years before it reopened in 1992 with new owners and Francis Ford Coppola as an investor. When Harrington started working there, his fellow bartender was the large, bearded Ward Dunham, a Vietnam vet, sometime bouncer, and famed calligrapher who had designed the logo for Bank of America. ("He was a scary individual," recalled Harrington.) Also on staff was a young waiter named Todd Smith, who was Harrington's roommate for a time and would eventually open a speakeasy called Bourbon & Branch.

Traffic was light until an article about the bar's Mojitos came out. (Though a future Enrico's bartender, Dave Nepove, would become known as Mr. Mojito, it was Harrington who got the drink going there.) Harrington served Billy Idol, Carrie Fisher, and members of the Oakland Raiders. He also served reporters, including Kate Corcoran of the *San Francisco Guardian* and Gary Wolf of the *San Francisco Weekly*. Wolf became editor of *Wired*, a new Bay Area magazine that touted itself as "the *Rolling Stone* of technology."

One of *Wired*'s editors, Laura Moorhead, wanted to create a cocktail channel on Hotwired.com, the magazine's website and the first commercial web magazine. Wolf sent her to Harrington, who by then was back at

Townhouse. Moorhead became editor of CocktailTime.com on Hotwired. com, while Harrington acted as a sort of in-house mixologist at *Wired*. Every two weeks, he'd go in and make a half-dozen drinks for the staff. Each drink was assigned to a writer or two.

"I'd make them drinks and tell them what I knew about the drink, and they'd go out and do the research," said Harrington.

Harrington never got a byline, but as the project built steam, Wolf asked him to write a column. It was called "The Alchemist," after a nickname Wolf had given Harrington in an article. Each column had a recipe and the history of that drink. The forum gave Harrington a chance to use the seemingly useless cocktail facts he had been accruing for years. "In my mind, I already ordered out families of drinks," he said. Harrington was thinking about cocktails in a way few bartenders in American were; more significantly, he was writing his thoughts down for public consumption.

Harrington left bartending in 1994, but he continued work on the column, which found an audience in pockets of curiosity throughout the world. "It was the first time I saw a recipe for a Daiquiri that didn't have sixteen kinds of fruit, and that treated the Cuba Libre as a classic cocktail and not just rum and Coke," said Jacob Briars, who was bartending in New Zealand.

Viking contacted Laura Moorhead and Harrington about turning the columns into a book. They worked on the book for five months, and *Wired* did all the production. In 1998, twenty-five thousand copies of *Cocktail: The Drinks Bible for the 21st Century* were printed. The book fell into the hands of a surprisingly wide variety of people.

"He started getting me into the history of these drinks," said Angus Winchester, then bartending and consulting around London. "It was a bit lyrical." At the Bellagio in Las Vegas, Tony Abou-Ganim used the book to train his staff.

There would never be a second printing of *Cocktail* (and, as *Wired*, now owned by a huge conglomerate, and Viking have no strong interest in the title, there may never be). But the book had a tremendous impact in a cocktail movement then just in its infancy. When Viking took the title out of print, Harrington bought the remaining stock. He sold them one by one through Amazon, mailing copies to every populated continent. (Today, new copies of the book are offered for $75 and up on Amazon.)

As Harrington's influence grew, however, his presence diminished. He began a degree in architecture after leaving the Townhouse. Today he lives in Spokane, Washington, where he manages, almost begrudgingly, a small bar called Clover. To many young mixologists who know his book and make the Jasmine cocktail, he is just a name.

"I've been called the D. B. Cooper of the cocktail world," said Harrington. "Nobody knows where I am."

Jasmine

PAUL HARRINGTON, 1990, Townhouse,
Emeryville, California

1½ ounces gin

¾ ounce fresh
lemon juice

¼ ounce Cointreau

¼ ounce Campari

Lemon twist, for
garnish

Paul Harrington named this drink after Matt Jasmin, a friend with whom he went to architectural school. He was working at Townhouse when Jasmin said, "Make me something you've never made before."

"The Pegu Club was really the drink I used to push on people," remembered Harrington. "I loved the Pegu. I literally thought about it for twenty seconds. I decided to use Campari instead of Angostura bitters, and use lemon juice instead of lime juice. I made it once, put a twist of lemon on it. It was a beautiful pink color. I handed it to him. He said, 'Wow, that's good. You just invented grapefruit juice.'"

The Jasmine gained wider fame when Harrington included it in his 1998 book *Cocktails*. Bartenders across the nation, and the world, who were looking for instruction, made it alongside the other, older drinks in the book.

Years after inventing the drink, Harrington realized he'd been spelling his friend's last name wrong all along; there is no "e" at the end. But by then, it was too late.

Combine all the ingredients except the lemon twist in a cocktail shaker three-quarters filled with ice. Shake until chilled. Strain into a chilled cocktail glass. Garnish with the lemon twist.

VI. INFORMATION, PLEASE

THERE IS NO GETTING AROUND the fact that there is an intensely geeky element running through the entire cocktail revival. Today's cocktail bartenders may look fiercely cool, with their tattoos, beards, and vests. But the modern mixology trade was built by people—some of them not bartenders at all, but full-blown computer nerds—who collected old books, knew their way around the Internet, and could talk for hours about ingredients and recipes and long-dead bartenders with a fervor to match the way science fiction nuts might discuss the backstory of Bobba Fett or the relative merits of the various incarnations of Dr. Who.

Beginning in 1933, in the wake of Prohibition, a flood of new cocktail books was released. As interest in that style of drinking declined over the decades, the flood narrowed to a trickle. Stan Jones's thick *Complete Barguide*, in 1977, was one of the last such major volumes. There were still annual manuals like the *Mr. Boston* guides, but those had no real authorial voice and were little more than compendiums of recipes, many poor and out of date.

The only recourse for those who thirsted after authentic cocktail know-how was to seek out of the old discontinued volumes, both those published before and after Prohibition. The people who amassed such collections in the 1990s and early '00s—independently and, as far as they could tell, alone in their mania—are surprisingly numerous. Cocktail nuts, as a group, proved to be the biggest bookworms in the culinary universe.

Brother Cleve, the godfather of the Boston cocktail movement (see chapter XXIII), collected books while touring with his band. One of his protégés, Jackson Cannon, found a family in Wisconsin selling a large library of cocktail books. Bartender Marcovaldo Dionysus found the answer to his questions in the "used" section of Powell's, the renowned independent bookstore in Portland, Oregon. His collection would eventually reach three hundred volumes. Amateur enthusiasts like Martin Doudoroff, who began with a waterlogged copy of the *Savoy Cocktail Book* his parents gave him, and Ted Haigh, who picked up Trader Vic's 1972 cocktail guide, went on to accrue hundreds of titles. British bartender Wayne Collins grabbed what he could find at book fairs. Much of this was done in the pre- and early Amazon days. It was hard work. It was a quest.

No one amassed more old cocktail books than a man named Greg Boehm. Boehm's grandfather founded Sterling Books. His father met suave Italian bartender Salvatore Calabrese at the Dukes Hotel in London and soon after bought the U.S. rights to the many cocktail books he had authored. Greg Boehm would go to the London Book Fair and spend his nights at Calabrese's latest perch, the Library Bar at the swank Lanesborough Hotel in Mayfair.

"I turned to my geeky book side and started collecting antique cocktail books," explained Boehm. "I was getting most of the things through antiquarian booksellers. Prices weren't as low as people think they were. Some were already pretty high." He had put together a collection of about six hundred titles before he got bored and packed them away. A couple years later, in 2005, he took them out of the boxes. "The world had changed in those two years," he said. "Suddenly, there were orange bitters on the market. The Internet had developed. If I didn't know what orgeat was, I could look it up and maybe buy it. These books that had been museum pieces were now working manuals." He started using the books every day, trying to make drinks. He also sold some on eBay. One of the first people to buy a book from him was a woman named Audrey Saunders, who would become one of the New York cocktail scene's first luminaries. "I said, 'I have all these other books if you want to come by and take a look.' She came by the next day," said Boehm.

By 2007, Boehm followed in his grandfather's and father's footsteps and began to publish. But his particular niche was reproductions of old cocktail books. Uncertain of the market for these, he began with six carefully chosen volumes—released under the Mud Puddle imprint, and initially sold only on the publication's website—including Jerry Thomas's *How to Mix Drinks* (1862), Harry Johnson's *Bartender's Manual* (1900), and *The Fine Art of Mixing Drinks* by David Embury (1948). (Most of the books were in the public domain. But for the last title, he tracked down Embury's surviving daughter and purchased the copyright.) Boehm followed up those original half-dozen volumes with many more. Suddenly, anybody interested in classic cocktails could acquire the books that Dionysus and Doudoroff had clawed and dug for.

Until Boehm republished these classics of the golden age, there was very little new content for cocktail book readers to enjoy. Apart from Harrington's 1998 *Cocktails*, there was *American Bar* by Charles Schumann, published in 1991 in German and then in English in 1995. It was found and bought by bartenders in England and the United States, including Sasha Petraske of Milk & Honey and Dushan Zaric of Employees Only.

In San Francisco, Barnaby Conrad III put out significant books about the Martini and absinthe. *Absinthe: History in a Bottle* came out in 1988, when the high-proof liqueur was still illegal in the United States but retained a romantic allure as the dangerous drink of Belle Époque Paris. It got a good review in the *New York Times* and remained in print for twenty-five years. Conrad published a book on the history of the Martini in 1995. He had a book launch party at the Rainbow Room, which Conrad had cold-called.

William Grimes's *Straight Up or On the Rocks* was one of the earliest cocktail histories of the modern age, published in 1993. Grimes joined the *New York Times* in 1989 after time at *Esquire*, where he wrote a column called The Drinking Man, waxing eloquent about Sidecars and Daiquiris. After he wrote a few columns, an agent asked him if he'd like to write a book. "The only thing that made sense was to construct a continuous narrative of the history of the cocktail," recalled Grimes.

He found the work difficult. No one had attempted anything similar, and, pre-Internet, basic facts were hard to come by. When he went to the Library of Congress to consult old cocktail manuals, he found a lot of them had been stolen. Nonetheless, he managed to put out a concise and elegant account of the cocktail, dating back to the early days of the republic. Not that many people cared at the time.

"It's not something that caught people's attention," he said. "It's the only time in my life I've been slightly ahead of the curve."

In 2002, as the cocktail movement was gathering steam, the book was reissued and had more of an impact. By then, however, Grimes had moved on. He was appointed the *Times*'s chief restaurant critic in 1999 and slowly but surely left cocktails behind.

One writer who didn't relinquish the drinks beat was Gary Regan. Regan was an expatriate British barman, the son of publicans from the Manchester area, trying to make a living in Manhattan. Regan was, and remains, a bon vivant eccentric, a devil-may-care libertine as blissfully unconcerned with his reputation as your average aging rockstar. Depending on the year, his well-worn face has been accented by shoulder-length hair, a full Smith Brothers beard, and eyeliner, and during his occasional bar shifts, he insists in stirring Negronis with his finger. He is an unlikely authority figure—more barfly than bar scholar. But an authority figure he nonetheless is, one of the accepted grand old men of the cocktail resurgence. He achieved this status primarily because he got there first.

Throughout the 1970s and '80s, Regan bounced around New York from bar to bar, even owning one for a time, until he got a job as assistant manager at the North Star Pub in the South Street Seaport. There he educated himself on the then-ascendant single-malt Scotches and met Dale DeGroff, who used to come in. Regan "was raucous, engaging, entertaining," said Jared Brown, a fellow bartender-turned-writer. "He was contagious."

Regan's whiskey work paid off. When *Time* magazine wrote an article on single malts in 1990, they interviewed him. And when Regan's wife, who worked at *Food Arts* magazine, showed her bosses the piece, the magazine hired him to write two articles: one on single malts, one on English pubs in America. As a writer, Regan was green, to say the least. "The editor said, 'How many words do you think you'll need?'" Regan recalled. "I said, 'I have no idea what you mean.'"

He won a regular column in *Food Arts*, and in 1991 published his first book, *The Bartender's Bible*. He went on to write *New Classic Cocktails* (1997), *The Bourbon Companion* (1998), and *The Martini Companion* (1999), all with his then-wife Mardee Haidin Regan. In the late 1990s, he did a radio show with spirits expert F. Paul Pacult called *The Happy Hour* on a New York station, inviting bartenders on the air. In 2001, he began writing a cocktail column for the *San Francisco Chronicle*. Regan had a clear motivation for his new career: "I wanted not to have to stand behind a bar."

All this time, he was waiting for the chance to pen his magnum opus, the book that would "prove to everyone I know what I'm talking about."

It would be called *The Joy of Mixology*. He'd had the proposal for years, but every publisher asked him to cut it down in size. "Finally, I went to [publisher] Clarkson Potter, to an editor who was an old friend of mine. He gets back to me and says, 'It's a good idea, but can you make it bigger?'"

The book was notable mainly for dividing cocktails into categories, illustrating how the drinks canon wasn't just a jumble of randomly mixed potions, but a family tree of workable liquid ratios that could be divided into sours, French-Italian cocktails (vermouth-based drinks), and other categories, many invented by Regan. It was a simple notion, but not a way that bartenders were thinking at the time.

"I realized I'd been stumbling around in the dark," said New York bartender Damon Dyer. The book was "not just what to do, but why you do it."

William Grimes, the only man at the *Times* who might have appreciated what Regan was going after, gave *The Joy of Mixology* a positive review. "Like Linnaeus," write Grimes, "he surveys the teeming, seemingly chaotic population of mixed drinks and imposes order."

The cocktail revival happened with greater speed than the food, beer, and wine revolutions that preceded it. And books, while they helped, didn't make that happen.

"We now have this avalanche of cocktail books. We didn't have that then," said Martin Doudoroff. "I don't think the market for these books would have developed without the Internet. The networking wouldn't have happened. The Rainbow Room would have come and gone, and that would have been that."

CocktailTime.com, Paul Harrington's collaboration with *Wired*, was just the beginning. It found an audience of cocktail geeks, but, given its limitations, didn't bring those readers together. In the late 1990s, a handful of techies with cocktail fetishes created a series of sites that connected the digital dots, making enthusiasts from New York to Seattle aware of one another.

In 1995, Ted Haigh figured out what the Internet was and was disappointed to see a lack of cocktail content there. He created an antique site and put pictures of old bottles on it, explaining what they were. It was just an IP address, and he doesn't know if he got any visitors. Then a friend showed him America Online, where there was a food and drink board. Under the handle agingwino@aol.com, he began "humbly answering people's questions," as he put it—questions from the likes of William Grimes, Gary Regan, and future rum expert Ed Hamilton. Soon, he was asked to host the board. Haigh, sensing his future as the first cocktail historian of the modern era, renamed himself "Dr. Cocktail."

Haigh had a head start on the other cocktail geeks. An itinerant, gregarious Hollywood graphic designer and former no-goodnik (there was a youthful folly of failed computer fraud in Canada), he'd been enamored with classic cocktails ever since, as a teenager, he'd found an old cocktail manual in his parents' collection. As he shifted from job to job, he collected old cocktail books and then, after examining the recipes, scavenged for the lost and obscure ingredients needed to make them.

When Haigh was working on location, he'd use his free time to hunt down old, neglected liquor stores, walk in, and ask for spirits and liqueurs that no one remembered. Sometimes he struck gold. The bottles he wanted would be gathering dust on a bottom shelf or top shelf. One weekend in L.A., he went to sixty-two liquor stores and found Cordial-Medoc and Forbidden Fruit, two once-popular liqueurs that only someone like Haigh would have remembered. Another time, he located a bottle of Swedish punch—a once-common elixir made from Batavia arrack, rum, sugar, and spices. "The clerk would look at me [and say] 'It's like you stepped out of a time machine,'" he recalled.

Haigh hit the Comstock lode while working on the John Hughes film *Baby's Day Out* in Chicago in the early 1990s. Driving by Division and Wells, he saw a sign: "Chicago's oldest wine and spirits merchant." The place, called the House of Glunz, had been founded in 1888. After a get-to-know-you chat, the old owner, David Donovan, poured him a glass of Zwetschgenwasser, a plum brandy.

"That began a long friendship," said Haigh. "I would come back every weekend with all of my per diem and spend it there." At first, the owner balked. But Haigh, who has a bit of the con man in him, is good at wheedling. A few stories, told with wide smiles, twinkling eyes, and overactive eyebrows, and he usually got what he wanted. A bottle of Nicholson gin from 1930s. A case of no-longer-made Abbott's bitters. Old crème de menthe. He boxed everything up and shipped it home to L.A.

Bitters were a particular mania. In the 1990s, Angostura was the only brand widely available. That would not do. Angostura is all well and good, an excellent product, but it was only one crayon in what had been a box that was full to bursting with color. When working on films in New Orleans, he bought the local Peychaud's bitters. He called the Angostura company in Trinidad and found out about Fee Brothers, a small Rochester company and the only place in the United States that made orange bitters. He spoke to Jack Fee himself. Curious about peach bitters, he mailed Fee a vintage minibottle of peach bitters, which led the company to produce a peach bitters.

Haigh also began fieldwork, visiting promising bars and asking for old drinks. "They'd say, 'Oh, we can't make that.' Out of my satchel, I'd bring a citrus squeezer, a bottle of bitters. They'd look at me, but they did it."

When Haigh found a kindred spirit, he invited them to his home.

"He greeted us at the door with Champagne cocktails made with vintage Abbott's bitters, and the night proceeded from there," recalled Chuck Taggart, whose website, Looka!, had a cocktail focus. Taggart and his partner, Wesley Moore, drank a Sazerac with Old Overholt rye distilled before Prohibition, as well as some Prohibition-era medicinal whiskey, and Crème Yvette. "We had to walk around the neighborhood for a while before we could drive home," said Taggart.

———

FARTHER NORTH, IN THE SEATTLE area, Robert Hess, an executive at Microsoft, used *Wired*'s CocktailTime.com to teach himself about drinks. In the Pacific Northwest, he was surrounded by good beer and wine. But the mixed drinks he ordered in local bars were abysmal.

On a trip to Paris, he encountered Colin Peter Field at the Ritz bar. "He knew what he was doing," said Hess. When Hess came back, he set to work on becoming a cocktail missionary. "I was an evangelist at Microsoft. I knew how to take technology and expose people to that technology. I wanted to try and find those bartenders who had the spark."

He launched the website Drinkboy in early 1998. Its chat room soon became an agora for the future leaders of the cocktail renaissance. Ted Haigh, Gary Regan, Dale DeGroff, Audrey Saunders, David Wondrich, and Martin Doudoroff all gathered to exchange intelligence and engage in friendly fights on the proper proportions for obscure cocktails, which old books to trust, and how to recreate drinks that called for discontinued ingredients.

Doudoroff rarely commented on Drinkboy. But, drawing on Harrington's book and Drinkboy, in 1998 he launched his own website, Bar Asterie, which included recipes and cross-referenced ingredients. In 2004, Haigh and Doudoroff launched the Internet Cocktail Database, a more comprehensive recipe databank, and the fruit of four years' work.

These IT guys' side passions for drinks made sense, in a way. "With cocktails, there's a very strong foundation of formulas," theorized John Deragon, himself a techie who would later grow from barfly to bartender. "Interpreting and building on them appeals to my ADD, OCD tendencies. Martin and Robert both have these similar, analytical tendencies."

As bartenders' cocktail skills progressed, a few sometimes found taking advice from committed and confident laymen a bitter pill to swallow. "For someone who's never been behind a bar," observed bartender Neyah White of Hess, "he has a lot of arrogance about how bartenders should do things." But overall, Hess's influence was positive.

"Don't underestimate the importance of Robert Hess in the cocktail world," said Angus Winchester. After visiting Drinkboy "you didn't feel so geeky about what you were doing, because there were other geeks out there."

Trident

ROBERT HESS, 2002, Seattle

1 ounce dry sherry

1 ounce Cynar

1 ounce aquavit

2 dashes peach bitters

Lemon twist, for garnish

No bar is mentioned as the birthplace of this drink. That's because Robert Hess has never been a bartender. The Trident is one of the few modern classics created by a layman. Hess's esoteric interests are betrayed in the ingredient list.

"I took the Negroni and twisted all the ingredients to the slightly obscure side," said Hess. "Rather than Campari, I used Cynar, which very few bars had. Rather than gin, I used aquavit. Rather than sweet vermouth, I used sherry. That's where my mindset was in those days. I was trying to bring those obscure ingredients back." Hess posted the recipe on his Drinkboy site a few times. Soon, it was showing up on cocktail lists.

Combine all the ingredients except the lemon twist in a mixing glass three-quarters filled with iced. Stir until chilled. Strain into a coupe glass. Garnish with the lemon twist.

VII. ALONG THE LEFT COAST

DURING THE 1990s, ROBERT HESS got in the passive-aggressive habit of testing bartenders by ordering an Old-Fashioned and seeing how they made the cocktail. Since he was looking for the fruit-free, pre-Prohibition rendering of the drink—the one without the muddled orange and cherry "garbage"—most of his unwilling contestants failed. When they did, he shifted to wine and beer.

Murray Stenson remembered Hess during this period. "Robert was known as the customer who would come in and bring his own bitters with him and have you make various drinks for him," he said.

Seattle didn't have many bartenders who were going to satisfy Hess's exacting standards. But it did have Stenson.

Bartending had been so decimated as a respectable profession in the final decades of the twentieth century that young mixologists of the new millennium didn't have many mentors to cling to. When they found a specimen they approved as an old-school standard bearer, they hurriedly hoisted him or her onto a throne, whether that barkeep liked it or not. This they did with Stenson, and, for the most part, Stenson—a shy man by nature—didn't like it. (When the annual Tales of the Cocktail convention named him Best Bartender in America in 2010, he declined to make the journey to New Orleans to claim the award.)

Stenson was an unlikely candidate for barroom bigwig. Born in rural eastern Washington state, he became a bartender in the early 1970s for the old reason—he couldn't figure out what else to do. He chose to work at the service end of the bar because he was an introvert. He lost that shyness over the years until, during a twelve-year stint at Il Bistro, he became something of a local legend. By the 1980s he had begun collecting old cocktail books, and he studied the art of old local bartenders.

"Everyone used to go there after work," recalled Karen Casey, then a rising chef in the area. "He was making all these cool drinks. He was so engaging and wanting you to try different things. You always wanted to sit at his bar and have cocktails."

A principled man who bridled at injustice, he quit Il Bistro one night in 2002 when management turned away a couple of faithful regulars. The couple went instead to the Zig Zag Café, an odd, hidden bar located midway on a outdoor staircase near Pike Place Market. They told the owners about Stenson's exit. The owners, spying an opportunity, called Stenson up. He began tending bar at the Zig Zag the next week. It was there his national fame as a cocktail beacon began.

By the time Paul Clarke, who would become an influential cocktail blogger, visited Zig Zag, Stenson's reputation preceded him. The Seattle style of cocktails at the time, said Clarke, "was Murray Stenson's style, which was basically classic. He's not making any of his own ingredients. There were no infusions."

Stenson's national name among the cocktail elite was secured when he discovered and began serving the Last Word, a pre-Prohibition-era cocktail of zero renown. He had discovered it in an old cocktail book, which credited it to a vaudevillian named Frank Farrell who had introduced it to the Detroit Athletic Club. It was made of equal parts of gin, lemon juice, Chartreuse, and maraschino liquor. In the early '00s, the last two ingredients were rarely seen in drinks; most bars didn't even carry them.

The drink—simple, yet arcane, and effortlessly delicious—soon reached the opposite coast. There are various accounts of how this happened. "Karen Casey hired a hotshot bartender, Ryan Magarian," said Stenson. "He came down to the Zig Zag and tried the Last Word, and I know he took that recipe back to New York around the same time as the eGullet thing."

The "eGullet thing" was the work of Sam Kinsey, who ran the drinks end of things on the foodie website. He noticed one poster chatting about "Murray Stenson giving her a Last Word. I thought to myself, *Interesting; I should try this.*" He made the drink, then went to the newly opened Pegu Club and talked it up to the bartenders there. "It's clear to me that it came through some combination of eGullet via me," said Kinsey. "The next thing you know, within six months every cocktail person in New York was making the drink."

However, Pegu owner Audrey Saunders remembers Robert Hess telling her about the drink after Stenson served him the cocktail.

However the cross-country pollination went down, the Last Word saga was an early example of a conscientious craft cocktail bartender resurrecting a lost liquid gem and delivering it to the people. It was a culinary drama that, with different bartenders and different drinks, would play itself out again and again in the following years.

———

WHILE MURRAY STENSON WAS SHAKING drinks in Seattle, a young hotshot was doing the same 170 miles to the south, in Portland, Oregon. He was younger and more extroverted, something signaled by his chosen name. Born Mark Johnson in Southern California, he moved to Seattle when he was twenty-one and changed his name to Marcovaldo Antonin Dionysus. Marcovaldo came from the short-story collection by Italo Calvino; Dionysus from Greek mythology; Antonin was slipped in there so his initials would read "MAD."

Marco worked his way up from busboy to bartender at an upscale Mexican place called Casa U-Betcha. He mainly made frozen Margaritas, and liked it. But one day a customer ordered a Singapore Sling. Dionysus asked two senior bartenders, but nobody knew how to make that drink. That didn't sit right. So Dionysus went to Powell's in Portland and bought his first cocktail book. He kept going back.

From Casa U-Betcha, he went to Saucebox and met Peggy Boston. Boston was another California native. When she was a teenager, her father drafted her to make drinks at his parties, and Dad, being a chemist, was serious about how the cocktails came out. She turned pro in the late '70s and by 1990 was in Portland, where she rang up friends Chris Israel and Bruce Carey (who has worked at Zuni Café in San Francisco, with its fresh Margaritas). They had just opened a restaurant called Zefiro. The trouble was they already had a bar manager. But not for long.

"The guy was saying, we're going to have Slippery Nipples, and I said, 'No, no, no,'" recalled Boston. In two weeks, Boston was bar manager. She refocused the drinks menu on classics.

"When I showed up in Portland in 1990, Zefiro was already pouring really good craft cocktails, using correct glassware, making sure the drinks were as good as the food," said Andy Ricker, who would go on to fame as the founder of Pok Pok, a Thai food trailblazer.

In 1995, Boston opened the bar program at Saucebox for Israel and Carey. The cocktails were a mix of classics and originals made with homemade syrups and infused liquors. The drinks were fruit-forward and rather simple, but daring nobody else in town was doing anything remotely as creative.

"I would give Peggy credit for really being the first kitchen-perspective person opening bars on the West Coast," said Ryan Magarian.

The Saucebox staff was rich with talent. Lucy Brennan came on after Ricker had left; she later opened Mint, Portland's first important cocktail bar. And then there was Marco.

Dionysus was charismatic and quick. He rapidly drew a following. "There're not many bartenders I would sit and watch with admiration," admitted Brennan. "He's one of those. His attentiveness. To do all that and execute a good craft cocktail is a rare breed."

"He used to drive everyone fucking nuts, because he ran around the place spinning cocktail trays," recalled Ricker. "He was this long-haired, cocky kid, and we just wanted to kill him."

He was also restless, and in 1996 he left for San Francisco. "I knew Portland was going to be really cool in ten years," he reflected years later, "but I didn't have the patience." *Portland Weekly* voted him Best Bartender Who Left Town.

His first San Francisco bartending job was at Enrico's. Paul Harrington was long gone, but the cocktails were still flowing. "It was the only place in San Francisco making Mojitos," said Dionysus. "Pretty simple drink, but nobody made them."

Otherwise, "there wasn't much going on," he recalled. "A cocktail menu at that point was, 'Here's a list of cocktails we know how to make.'"

In 1997, Dionysus was working at a club in the South of Market neighborhood when he got a call from Paul Hodges, a former manager at Enrico's, about a new project. Called Absinthe, it would be a French-style brasserie (dark walls, banquettes, murals) in the then-dead Hayes Street area. Dionysus certainly knew what absinthe was. The new place sounded cool.

Dionysus was given free license to do whatever he wanted. He aimed to create the best bar in San Francisco. Drawing on his library of cocktail books and years of research, he poured all he knew into a cocktail list as dense and annotated as a graduate school term paper. Every page was a history lesson, featuring not only classic cocktails such as the Sidecar and Sazerac but also each drink's place and date of origin.

The breakout drink was the Ginger Rogers, a simple mix of gin, lemon juice, ginger syrup, ginger ale, and mint. Dionysus had actually invented the drink in Portland in 1995, basing it on the Favorite Cocktail, a drink in the 1914 volume *Cocktails* by Jacques Straub. At Absinthe, they sold a thousand Ginger Rogers in a month. (In later years, San Franciscan bartenders would grumble about the similarities between the Ginger Rogers and the Gin-Gin Mule, a much more celebrated cocktail by New Yorker Audrey Saunders. They are, indeed, almost identical. Saunders claims she had never heard of the Ginger Rogers, or Marco, when she created her cocktail. "The Internet had just begun to get its sea legs," she said, "and back in those days, bars and bartenders were like islands unto themselves without any connection between them until a few years later. I also didn't know about Jacques Straub in those days.")

Dionysus had exceeded his own expectations. "I knew that Absinthe had made it when I stopped in the middle of a busy night and looked up and down the bar, and ever single person in the bar had a cocktail from our menu," he recalled. "No wine, no beer, no Cosmos, no Lemon Drops."

"Absinthe, Absinthe, Absinthe," stated bartender Neyah White. "Those are the first three influential bars in San Francisco."

The busiest part of the night was often midnight to 2 a.m. when industry people would drift in. Bartender Scott Beattie, who would later find fame with his ornate farm-to-table drinks, was served a cocktail at Absinthe so good that it made him reexamine his career.

"I looked at what I was doing," Beattie said, "which was Cosmopolitans and Lemon Drops with Chambord at the bottom. I saw what he was doing and thought, 'I want to be like that.' The fastest bartender I've met to this day. He's a machine. Really fast, really intense, really funny and witty, bordering on dickishness, but always just right. I think Marco was *the* influential figure."

Everyone who ever worked with Dionysus seems to have been slightly in awe of him. "We'd always have a competition on Friday or Saturday night, whose coat was the cleanest at the end of the night," said Thomas Waugh, who bartended with Dionysus at the Starlight Room. "Marco won, every single time. He never had to dry-clean his coat. And he would out-ring everyone." (Dionysus also studied classical violin and would occasionally whip out his fiddle. Waugh saw him play once. "We were drunk, and he was flawless.")

Dionysus stayed at Absinthe for three years and could easily have fashioned himself into the Dale DeGroff of the San Francisco cocktail scene. But it wasn't to be, mainly because Dionysus, like Harrington before him, didn't seize the mantle or seem to want it. He would put in time at Tres Agaves and Harry Denton's Starlight Room, and go on to launch important cocktail programs, like that at Michael Mina's Clock Bar in the late '00s.

"Absinthe was so early in the cocktail renaissance that he sort of went unnoticed, and people just learned about his presence later on," theorized journalist Camper English, a chronicler of the San Francisco cocktail world. "He's not really looking for glory, though he deserves it a lot."

But by the 2010s, he had found a place behind the bar at Smuggler's Cove, Martin Cate's ambitious tiki bar. He stayed there for years, long after the rest of the original bar staff had moved on. Dionysus became the rare startender who seemed most contented simply being a bartender.

"There's a moment on a Friday night when I am so buried and I have sixteen drinks going, and a lot of it is still muscle memory at this point," he explained. "And I'm keeping track of what I'm doing, keeping track of who's next and how many people there are in the bar, keeping an eye on whether people have to leave. That moment where: I got this. I realize I'm just watching myself work and more supervising than anything else. And it's the flow, the moment I'm in the flow—that's what I love about it."

Last Word

Classic

¾ ounce gin

¾ ounce Chartreuse

¾ ounce maraschino liqueur

¾ ounce fresh lime juice

This pre-Prohibition drink was uncovered and popularized by Seattle barman Murray Stenson. The drink was emblematic of the revolution in that every ingredient was symptomatic of the new work habits of the young breed of bartenders. Modern cocktail recipes that riff off the Last Word's equal-parts-sour template are legion.

Combine all the ingredients in cocktail shaker three-quarters filled with ice. Shake until chilled. Strain into a coupe glass.

Chartreuse Swizzle

MARCOVALDO DIONYSOS, 2002, San Francisco

1½ ounces green Chartreuse

1 ounce pineapple juice

¾ ounce fresh lime juice

½ ounce Velvet Falernum

Mint sprig, for garnish

Freshly ground nutmeg, for garnish

This was an early, and at the time radical, use of the herbal liqueur Chartreuse as a base spirits in a drink, as well as a modern example of the forgotten Caribbean cocktail category of Swizzles.

Chartreuse sponsored a cocktail competition every year. Dionysus entered for four years straight and usually did well. He was asked to compete again for a fifth year, but worried he had run out of ideas. "I thought, *Let me take it in a different direction*," he recalled. "*Let me do a tropical drink*. And it won." The creation of the drink didn't take long. "I had been using Falernum as my secret weapon. It was a brown-bag ingredient that I wouldn't even reveal until the competition." The drink was put on the menu at the Starlight Room right away. "It wasn't really successful. I put it on a couple other menus, too." When he went to Clock Bar, he put it on the list there as well. The drink was also served at other restaurants by chef Michael Mina. After Mina mentioned the cocktail in interviews, it finally took off. Though the cost of making the drink prohibits it from becoming widespread, it has appeared at bars in a wide variety of time zones.

Combine all the ingredients except the garnish in a cocktail shaker three-quarters filled with ice. Shake until chilled. Strain into a Collins glass filled with ice. Garnish with the mint sprig and nutmeg.

VIII. TWO CALIFORNIANS

TEQUILA DID NOT PLAY a big role on early menus of the cocktail revival. Bartenders were too busy rediscovering gin and whiskey and liqueurs. But the agave spirit formed the foundation of two restaurants—one in London and one in San Francisco—that served as unofficial and inspirational meeting houses for the young mixologiti. Both, interestingly, were run by native Californians: one, Julio Bermejo, trying to run away from his family's Mexican restaurant; the other, Tomas Estes, who saw a Mexican restaurant as his ticket to freedom.

Estes was a high school teacher in Los Angeles. After a 1970 trip to Amsterdam, he decided to move there. He filled a perceived hole in the Amsterdam food market by opening a Mexican restaurant, Cafe Pacifico, on the edge of the red light district. In 1982, he opened a second in London, where he had by that time moved.

Though Cafe Pacifico had a respectable selection of tequilas—unusual for London at the time—Tomas wasn't on a mission to spread the gospel on the spirit. "My main goal was to support myself," he said.

Because Londoners were unfamiliar with tequila, Pacifico's clientele skewed international and cosmopolitan. Much of the tequila went into Margaritas, which were made with Sauza Blanco and Giffard triple sec, to Estes' specifications, according to Danny Smith, the son of noted British poet Ken Smith, and the magnetic glad-hander who bartended there for ten years.

In time, ambitious young London bartenders, having few places to go for a proper cocktail, found Pacifico. Dick Bradsell came by early, praising Smith's drinks. "Dick said the first squeezed limes he saw were at Pacifico," said Tony Conigliaro, a Bradsell disciple who would become a science-based cocktail eminence in London. Conigliaro, like many others, ping-ponged between LAB and Pacifico in the late '90s. "You could literally walk from there to Pacifico and back and that was the Sunday routine," he said. "And everyone were there."

Following the success of the London restaurant, Estes opened Pacificos in Paris, Cologne, Milan, and Sydney, and a second tequila/Mexican place, La Perla, in SoHo. One night Danny Smith took fellow bartender Dre Masso to La Perla. "We stood at the bar and I took everything in—the Latin music, delicious aromas coming from the grill, and stunning Margaritas," recalled Masso. "I announced to Danny that I felt like I was at home."

In 2003, Masso attended a tequila workshop at Cafe Pacifico where several tequila owners and distillers were in attendance. Hosting alongside Estes was an American named Julio Bermejo.

At the end of the demonstration, Julio handed out his business card and said if anyone was interested in learning more they should come to San Francisco and visit him at Tommy's. Masso was indeed converted to the charms of agave. He flew out less than a year later and spent a six-month apprenticeship with Bermejo. Later, with Henry Bessant, he opened Green & Red, a London cantina that offered the largest collection of premium tequila in Europe. Both Bermejo and Estes officiated at Masso's wedding.

———

BERMEJO WAS THE YOUNGEST OF five children born into a family that lived off the proceeds of Tommy's Mexican Restaurant, a commonplace, unremarkable eatery in the Richmond district of northwest San Francisco. Longing to escape his parents' fate, he studied political science at UC

Berkeley, dreaming of becoming a diplomat. But he failed the foreign service oral interview and returned to the restaurant. He was miserable.

"It was embarrassing for me to come and serve people and wash dishes and take people chips, while my colleagues were going to law school and having jobs with suits and ties," he said.

He buried himself in the bar; it wasn't as mortifying as being on the floor. Eventually, he came to love tending bar. The drinks, however, were nothing special. "Our bar was like any other bar: Galliano, crème de cacao, sloe gin, crème de menthe, some bourbons, some Scotches. Tequila was not a focus or even a concern." Margaritas were made with fresh lime juice (just like El Sombrero, a competitor down the street), but also sour mix and cheap mixto tequila.

Bermejo had an epiphany one day in the mid-1980s when he sampled Herradura, a 100-percent-agave tequila brought into the United States by entertainers Bing Crosby and Phil Harris. "I made a decision, as a young person with no authority, to stop selling mixto tequila and only sell 100-percent agave and put Herradura silver in the well," said Bermejo. It was not a seasoned businessman's move; Herradura cost four times more, and drink prices were hiked only 75 cents, to $4.75.

People were slow to notice. Nobody was looking for, or expecting, a tequila oasis in the then-staid Richmond. But Bermejo persisted. He threw out the sour mix. When good new tequilas, like El Tesoro and Patron, entered the United States, he was among the first to carry them. He offered customers free sips of tequila. It all paid off in 1999 when a journalist for the *Wall Street Journal*, canvassing tequila distillers for an article, was told to go to Tommy's. The resultant article called Tommy's the epicenter of tequila in the United States. (Bermejo's father was not impressed. Far from being proud, he slapped his son's ears back, asking how many enchiladas he had sold that day.)

Bermejo, encouraged, charged ahead. When agave syrup came on the market, he adopted it, using it in Margaritas. To move the forty-plus tequilas that were gathering dust behind the bar, he began a tequila club, based on beer clubs he had seen. For every tequila you tried, your card was punched; try thirty-five and you got a diploma. Bermejo gave away the first five hundred cards for free, waiving the $10 membership cost. "We never thought people would give a shit," he said. The program slowly grew. He introduced a master's level, then a PhD. Participants took a written test with seventy questions. He started to put graduates on a waiting list to visit distilleries in Mexico. The group was winnowed through "Tequilapalooza," a party he threw in order to identify and weed out bad drunks.

Tony Abou-Ganim was one of the first bartenders to notice Bermejo's good work. When he moved on to the Bellagio, Abou-Ganim put Herradura in the casino's bar wells. (The night before the Bellagio opened, Bermejo drove down to Las Vegas with a load of lime juicers.) Abou-Ganim introduced Bermejo to David O'Malley, who followed Bermejo's lead and refused to carry Cuervo Gold at the Starlight Room, dumbfounding the distributor. (For a while, Tommy's was Herradura's largest independent customer in the United States.)

In 2000, at Abou-Ganim's urging, Bermejo visited London. There he met Masso, Wayne Collins, Jamie Terrell, Henry Bessant, Nick Strangeway, and other up-and-coming bartenders. A London connection was born, and many of the men made their way to Tommy's. Bessant, in particular, became a friend. Bermejo credits Bessant with popularizing the Tommy's Margarita—as the 100-percent-agave/agave syrup/fresh lime/no curaçao house drink was now known—in London. (When Bermejo met Dick Bradsell, he deferentially asked, "Dick, would you please make me a Bramble?" To which Bradsell replied, "Julio, would you make me a Tommy's Margarita?")

Bermejo continued to inspire. In 2004, Martin Cate, future owner of rum-and-tiki haven Smuggler's Cove, attended a tasting of tequilas at Tommy's. "I'd never seen anything like this in my life," he recalled.

"Passionate bartenders, a couple enthusiasts, tasting all this stuff." He called his girlfriend and said, "I think I know what I want to do with the rest of my life."

Eventually, both Estes and Bermejo would take their devotion to tequila to the source. Estes collaborated on Tequila Ocho, a collection of distinctive single-source tequilas, with the Mexican family that made El Tesoro and Tapatio. Bermejo married well; his wife, Lily, is a member of the same family. Together, they have developed their own tequila label.

Tommy's Margarita

JULIO BERMEJO, early 1990s, Tommy's Mexican
Restaurant, San Francisco

2 ounces reposado
tequila

1 ounce fresh lime
juice

½ ounce agave syrup

Lime wedge, for
garnish

Bermejo was an early voice in insisting on respect for
tequila. His version of a Margarita—which eschews
curaçao, uses agave syrup instead of sugar, and insists
on 100-percent-agave tequila—showcased, rather than
masked, the innate flavor of the spirit. The drink
came together slowly. First came the fresh lime juice.
Then Bermejo decided to replace the mixto tequila
in the well at his restaurant with Herradura. Agave
nectar didn't come onto the U.S. market until the late
1990s. Bermejo called it the house Margarita. Others
called it the Tommy's Margarita. Bermejo credits
the late London cocktail leader Henry Bessant with
"the internationalization" of the Tommy's Margarita,
spreading word of the drink far and wide. Because of
the simplicity of the drink, it is often found on menus
in the most prosaic of places. In 2014, a Denny's in
New York City offered it.

Combine the tequila, lime juice, and syrup in a cocktail
shaker three-quarters filled with ice. Shake until chilled.
Strain into a rocks glass filled with ice and partially
rimmed with salt, if desired. Garnish with the lime wedge.

IX. MILK & HONEY

"WHEN YOU THINK OF THE classical bartender, it's always a tall white guy with a funny mustache," said bartender Giuseppe Gonzalez. "You're not thinking a lesbian from Hawaii or a Long Island girl or a Puerto Rican from the Bronx. We don't fit the mold. We don't want to fit the mold. We do things differently. Out of the three best bartenders in New York City— Sasha, Julie, Audrey—two of them are women."

Dale DeGroff was central casting for the classic role of the bartender. He was a would-be actor, a charismatic yarn-spinner, and drawn from the male, European, immigrant stock that opened most of the bars in the United States during the twentieth century. His three most important protégés were Julie Reiner, the "lesbian from Hawaii," Audrey Saunders, the "Long Island girl," and Sasha Petraske, who went uncharacterized by Gonzalez (who was the "Puerto Rican from the Bronx" and has worked for all three). A native New Yorker, Petraske was part Communist upbringing, part Marine training, part Jazz Age wannabe, and all willful, reckless iconoclast.

Sasha Petraske was born in 1973 and raised in Greenwich Village on Jones Street near Bleecker. His father was a bureaucrat who worked in health care, and his mother was a proofreader and then a fact-checker for the *Village Voice*. His grandparents had been members of the U.S. Communist Party and knew the Rosenbergs well enough to have coffee with them. Young Sasha became disillusioned with the party by the time he was thirteen, but the system's basic tenets stayed with him, giving him an inbred distrust of capitalism and instinctual urge to deal fairly with employees.

When Petraske was growing up in the 1970s and 1980s, every weekend the middle Village would be flooded with bridge-and-tunnel party kids who would litter the streets around the Petraske home with spent six-packs and vomit. This, too, had its impact. "That informed my desire to sell alcohol in a way that wouldn't interfere with anyone's sleep," he recalled.

He attended Grace Church School, an Episcopalian grade school on 10th Street, a scholarship kid. There he was first forced to wear the ties that he would voluntarily don as a young bartender. He went on to Stuyvesant High School, but was an impatient and obstinate student.

"He wasn't going to graduate," recalled T. J. Siegal, one of the few friends he made at Stuyvesant. "He didn't care anymore. He was brilliant, wildly smart, too smart for his own good. It was a good high school, but still a public school. He takes tests very well. He was bored."

Siegal remembered when Petraske sat in the front row of class and taunted the Harvard-educated teacher. "He wouldn't let him get a sentence out without challenging him. That was typical of Sasha." He sometimes wore a T-shirt that said "Abstinence," which Siegal thought could have "meant a lot of things."

Petraske dropped out and took job at Caffe Vivaldi, an old-school coffee-house. "He was extremely critical of the owner and quite a few of the employees," said Siegal.

Petraske admitted he had contempt for his boss, but became enamored of the simple, repetitive tasks required to run a café. "My style of bartend-ing owes much to the barista as opposed to the state of the bartender," he explained. "Just the idea that innovation is not what this is about. Creativity is an afterthought."

Inspired or not, he was still lost, and soon he left New York to embark on a quixotic cross-country bicycle trip, following a girl he had dated in high school who had moved to Berkeley. But the expensive, antique Italian bike he bought for the purpose was stolen in New Mexico. Nearly broke, he took a bus the rest of the way to California. He stayed for four years.

Things didn't work out with the girl, and a job hunt in San Francisco proved fruitless. "Every day I would take two CDs from my record collection, sell them, and buy a *San Francisco Examiner* for the want ads, and get the two-slices-and-a-Coke deal at Escape From New York Pizza." After a month and no luck, he gave up and joined the army.

"He was an intense young man," said Siegal. "He thought that was a way of building character." It was grueling work. "They'd put you in a pair of slacks and T-shirt and drop you in subzero weather alone for three days," said Siegal. After three years, Petraske, looking for a way to be booted out, told the army he was gay. "They were not sad to see me go," he said.

Back in New York in the late '90s, he got a job at Von, a beer and wine bar on Bleecker Street with mismatched furniture and plenty of candlelight. Petraske poured glasses of wine. It was his first bartending job, and he did it for three years.

Barroom decorum obsessed him. If a customer was playing with the candle wax or peeling the label off their beer, it would drive him nuts. Mashing was equally frowned upon. Siegal detailed Petraske's technique: "If there are women at the bar, and some sleazy guy comes up and starts talking to them, trying to pick them up, he would start talking to that guy, leading him as far away from the girls as possible. And he was good at it. The next step was just writing up those rules."

He would write them up. And start a bar to go with them.

MILK & HONEY WOULD NOT have happened without Sasha Petraske's childhood pals. Chasing after an ad in the *Village Voice* that promised a commercial space on Eldridge Street on the Lower East Side at an unbelievable

$800 a month, Sasha was met by an old friend from the fifth grade whom he hadn't seen in years. The friend lived in the building. Petraske sealed the deal and began renovating the narrow 480-square-foot space, a former tailor shop and more recently a mah-jongg parlor. He was soon broke.

"He had been talking about it a few months before he finally said to me, 'The guy's coming in to do the plumbing, and I don't have any money,'" recalled Siegal. "It wasn't 'T. J., I want you to invest.' It was, 'I'm doing this thing, and I ran out of money.'"

For months, Siegal handed over all the cash he made at the restaurant he was working at. A couple more of Sasha's high school friends took on credit card debt for him. A beautiful wood floor was installed, only to be destroyed by a flood, after which another floor was laid.

Construction was never actually completed. When Petraske quietly opened on New Year's Eve 1999 (the Y2K scare was of no concern—Milk & Honey didn't have a POS system), some of the booths didn't have leather on them, just foam rubber; they stayed that way for years. There were pieces of blue painter's tape on the crown moldings. (In 2012, when Milk & Honey moved from Eldridge Street to 23rd Street, those bits of tape were still there.)

Siegal said dealing with Sasha was like talking to someone with multiple personalities. "On the one hand, you're trying to get more refined in the drinks and social aspect. And then there's blue tape and foam rubber and exposed plywood."

Some of the things Milk & Honey became notorious for were accidental. There was no outside indication of its being there, because Petraske had promised his noise-averse landlord that no one would know there was a bar inside. The controversial reservation policy was instituted to eliminate spillover crowds lingering on the sidewalk. And there was no menu, said Petraske years later, because he didn't know how to work a printer.

Other aspects, however, were intentional. "Rules of Etiquette" were posted in the bathrooms: "No standing; No name dropping, no star fucking;

Gentlemen will remove their hats; Gentlemen will not introduce themselves to ladies," and so on. They were largely borrowed, like much of M&H's aesthetic, from Angel's Share, and were Petraske's attempt to create the kind of civilized atmosphere he had not seen in any place he'd worked.

Milk & Honey was the first modern speakeasy, kicking off a genre of modern bar that persists today in cities and towns across the globe. Whether Petraske did it consciously is open to debate. Late in his career, Petraske insisted that Milk & Honey became a speakeasy by default, secret only because his landlord's demands forced it. Siegal isn't convinced.

"I differ with him in my memory of that," said Siegal. "The idea that it was like a speakeasy and you couldn't tell it was a bar from the outside, that was him. He wanted that. Absolutely."

(In 2000, Petraske told a reporter, "The service I'm offering is an idiot-free environment safe from celebrity sycophants and frat boys who read the listings in *Time Out*. Unfortunately, hiding my bar was the only way I could think of to do it these days.")

However the prissy, principled package of Milk & Honey came together, it struck the public and the media as elitist and pretentious. And they couldn't get enough of it. Eventually.

"It wasn't a smashing success" at first, recalled Siegal of the early, wintry days of 2000. "It's hard to get people to come to your bar when you don't tell them you have a bar."

For a while, to Petraske's few customers he seemed like a madman with a strange hobby. The sole owner and sole employee, he worked the bar six days a week; Sunday he closed. The bar might have died on the vine within a year had not a curious neighbor across the street, director of manufacturing for Harry Winston, wandered in one night. He told a friend, Dale DeGroff, about the place.

Petraske had never met DeGroff but had heard of him. His hands trembled as he made the older man a Martini, nearly knocking the glass over.

"It was kind of weird," remembered DeGroff. "The kid is just starting out. He's all alone. He had built his own bar. He was very proper: suspenders, the whole thing. He asked me a lot of questions. He was trying to figure it all out."

Petraske's education began then. DeGroff taught him how to make classic cocktails and lent him a copy of Trader Vic's cocktail manual. "He gave me the notion that the good stuff was in out-of-print books," Petraske recalled. Early on, he got his hands on a copy of *Here's How*, a 1941 recipe book by Ross Bolton. The book "laid the groundwork" for most of the drinks the bar made.

Other things Petraske figured out himself. There was no room for an ice maker behind Milk & Honey's tiny bar. So he made his own ice cubes, freezing water in large flat pans and then carving the ice into jumbo-size cubes for rocks drinks and spears for highballs. In a world of shoddy ice, he was adorning cocktails with crystalline jewels that sparkled in the glass and in the customer's eyes. It was a mother-of-invention solution, but one that would be copied by hundreds of bars.

"The thing about Sasha was, he was a solve-the-problem, common-sense kind of guy," said DeGroff, "because he had no money."

By Petraske's account, it took about a year for Milk & Honey to find its footing, with many mistakes along the way. He made Sazeracs incorrectly for a year, leaving out the sugar. And he regularly ran out of booze. "I would call and make a reservation," said bartender Eben Klemm, an early devotee. "Half an hour later, I would get a call from Sasha. 'Hey Eben, I see you're coming in tonight. Can you pick up a bottle of Campari on the way over?'"

But he did enough right to dazzle first-timers.

"Going into that bar, the whole ritual—the entrance, the setting—was very immersive," recalled Chad Solomon. "You're stepping into a netherworld. At that time, it was a big departure from any other nightlife experience." Solomon was then working at the Bryant Park Hotel. His coworker (and eventual romantic partner), Christy Pope, moonlighted as a server at Milk & Honey. In late 2001, Solomon finally visited Milk & Honey, ordering a rye fizz variation called Silver Lining from Joseph Schwartz, who invented it. "I remember watching him work. It was so foreign. And then when you tasted the drink: whoa. I walked out of there thinking, *I want to make drinks like that*."

Schwartz was a Brooklyn-born former teacher who began as a barback and graduated to bartending in late 2000. "To me, his concept made perfect sense," Schwartz said. "Why wouldn't you use nice ingredients and give people a place to sit and relax? We were all [sold] on the bill of goods that we should all be packed into an awful place with the cheapest possible spirits and largest margin."

People tend to remember their first drink at Milk & Honey, so heavily did the experience stamp them. For Jim Meehan, who would help found the bar PDT, it was the Gold Rush, a Whiskey Sour made richer by the addition of honey syrup. "Toby Maloney was bartending. Joseph Schwartz was on the floor," he remembered. "I remember both Joseph and Toby were wearing vintage shirt-tie-hat combinations. They had the silver tray with the candle on it. There was so much attention to detail—the clothes, the music, napkin, ice, glass, straw, liquor. That was the turning point for me; I went from pursuing wine first, to wine being my sideline and cocktails coming first."

Maloney was the first bartender Sasha hired. A dandy with a primitive upbringing, he was as unusual a case as Petraske. He had grown up in a log cabin on top of a mountain in Colorado with no running water or electricity, no television and no neighbors. His parents weren't back-to-nature hippies; Mom worked for the National Institute of Standards and Technology in Boulder, and Dad was a landlord, renting out other cabins. But they had priorities that superseded bourgeois domesticity.

"They decided early on that they wanted to spend money on education and travel and books," said Maloney. "So, by the time I was thirteen, they'd taken me around the world a few times. We had an old GMC truck with a camper on the back, and we'd do things like drive to Panama."

The day to day, however, was less glamorous. Toby walked three miles to the bus that took him to school. In summer, he ran or biked the distance; in winter, cross-country skis did the trick. Unsurprisingly, Maloney flew the coop by sixteen. After culling a few years of service experience at the only restaurant in Jamestown, the closest town, he relocated to Boulder.

He later moved to California, where he bailed after one semester of culinary school, instead getting a job at Monsoon, a four-star Bruce Cost restaurant in San Francisco. After a while, the wanderlust he'd inherited from his parents hit, and he pulled up stakes to tour the world for a year. He landed in Chicago in 1991 and got a job as a cook at a southwestern restaurant called Soul Kitchen. After a while, he asked if he could bartend. A single winter in Chicago convinced him he didn't want to go through that again, so the coming years followed a pattern of warm-weather work in the city, and world travel (mainly in Thailand) once the first cold breeze blew. Maloney kept that up until 1995, when he moved to New York, eventually getting a job at the cocktail bar Grange Hall alongside Del Pedro.

Maloney recalled, "One day, one of my friends who was a bartender came in and said, 'I'm going to take you to this bar. You're not going to believe it.'"

Milk & Honey blew him away. There was no vodka, no olives, on principle. Sasha made him a Daiquiri, not the frozen kind, but served elegantly and up. "I'd never had anything like it," said Maloney. "I'd never seen anyone use a jigger before."

Maloney began to visit four or five times a week. He was one of the few customers, and Sasha was the only bartender. Still, despite the empty seats, customers had to call for a reservation. Maloney didn't mind.

"The nightlife scene was so uncivilized at that point," said Maloney. "It was strawberry Cosmos and 'boom-boom.' Without him sticking to those rules, Milk & Honey would have been overwhelmed and turned into something horrible."

Sasha was exhausted. Toby offered to bartend every Thursday to give him a break. He didn't think Milk & Honey would amount to much at the time. Coming from the club world, where he banged out seven Cosmos in fifteen seconds, a bar that took fifteen minutes to make a single round of drinks seemed ludicrous, laughable. The place obviously made no money. But he might learn something here.

With his antiquated garb and slicked-back, 1930s labor-leader haircut, Petraske lent a bygone formality to the bar. The addition of the dandy Maloney doubled down on that aesthetic. "He'd come in with his three-piece suit and bartending equipment," recalled Petraske.

BY MAY 2000, THE DAYS of Maloney sitting alone at the bar were a thing of the past. The *New York Times* wrote a long article, ostensibly about "secret bars that spurn hype," but it focused almost solely on Milk & Honey. Petraske, as was his habit early on, gave the reporter only his first name, demanded the address not be revealed, and was otherwise at his cranky, contrarian best. "If Puffy showed up here in a limo," he said, in the piece's takeaway quote, "he could come in as long as he had a reservation and could obey my rules."

"At the time, Sasha hated the press, passionately," said Siegal. "He didn't want to be written about at all." The article made him "livid. He has always been extremely self-conscious. Anytime that a person says or writes something about him, his immediate reaction is, 'That makes me look bad.'" Siegal didn't agree. "I bought thirty copies."

Petraske's attitude regarding the press was perhaps more sophisticated than Siegal thought. He was, after all, the son of a *Village Voice* staffer, and he had seen how quickly bars got ruined by too much press. "The standard life cycle of a bar," he said years later, "was: open up; be cool for a year and not make much money; then they write about you and it gets real busy for a year; then those people drive away the original people who were coming; then you have a third year where you make real money; then those people realize there are no interesting people there and they move on. So my goal was to not get written up by the New York press."

Over its first two years, as crowds grew, a staff began to coalesce. From the beginning there were the barbacks—Kelvin Perez, who lived in the building, and José Gil, who laid the foundation for bartender support; Joseph Schwartz, the twin brother of Louis Schwartz, who took over for Sasha at Von, and worked at Von as well; Wilder Schwartz, who was no relation to Joseph, but had also worked at Von; Elizabeth Sun, an actress and musician raised in Glasgow, who later gained fame as a member of the gypsy punk band Gogol Bordello; and Christy Pope, an alabaster-skinned brunette who had come to New York from Louisiana to work in the music and art worlds. All drank the Petraske Kool-Aid, and loved it. A school of mixology, different from the DeGroff or Bradsell strains, was forming.

"Milk & Honey was the first bar I knew that ran itself as if it was a rock and roll band," said David Wondrich, the cocktail historian and *Esquire* columnist, "with the owner and bartenders having this strong camaraderie, like it's us against the world. It wasn't just a job, it was a cause."

DeGroff continued to come in, affable and encouraging, but nonetheless scaring the bejesus out of everyone. (A distraught Maloney forgot to put in the lime juice when the great man ordered a Mojito.) Eventually, he brought in an irascible Englishman named Jonathan Downey. Downey owned a few bars in London, including Match, and was also drinks editor for British *Esquire*. In spring 2001, DeGroff was doing one of his periodic "Cocktail Safaris," a business gig in which he and a few guests hit whatever cocktail hotspots there were to hit in Manhattan at the time. Downey asked to tag along, with the ulterior motive of getting DeGroff to England to train his bartenders.

"At the end of seven bars, we were the only two [tour members] still standing," remembered Downey. "We started down to Milk & Honey. It was 3 a.m. I met Sasha. Absolutely loved the place. There's nothing like it anywhere I'd ever been. I'd been offered a great site in London and didn't know what to do with it."

A plan was hatched almost instantaneously. The cash-strapped Petraske signed on more out of desperation than enthusiasm. "He said, 'Why don't we open one of these in London?'" recalled Petraske. "I said, 'Sure, let's do it.' I didn't have much of a choice. We were going to go out of business. Anything that helped."

So, with his fledgling bar only a year and a half old—already famous, yet struggling to survive—Petraske decamped to London for six months, leaving Milk & Honey in the hands of Siegal and Schwartz. He lived atop the Poland Street building in SoHo.

What opened in April 2002 was like Milk & Honey and not like Milk & Honey. The drinks, the ice, the candles, the attention to detail, the exacting service, the emphasis on civilized decorum and classic bartending skills—those were all there. A Gold Rush cocktail in London arrived with the same panache it did in New York, and tasted as good. But instead of one narrow room, there were four floors; instead of one bar, there were several. There was a party room. Like Fred's Club and other bars before it, it was a members joint. Patrons paid an annual fee. It was, in other words, Milk & Honey as reimagined by a businessman. And Jonathan Downey was nothing if not a businessman. Hard-nosed, hard-driving, a screamer, he was the toughest nut the nascent London cocktail scene had produced, building up a stable of high-performing, influential cocktail bars in the late 1990s and early '00s, and becoming the first defining force to emerge in London in the post-Bradsell/Peyton/Atlantic Bar & Grill era.

Gold Rush

T. J. SIEGAL, 2001, Milk & Honey, New York

2 ounces bourbon
(Elijah Craig single
batch recommended)

¾ ounce fresh lemon
juice

¾ ounce honey syrup
(recipe follows)

Siegal played an early, if largely unheralded, role in the establishment of Milk & Honey, lending founder Sasha Petraske seed money and managing the bar when Petraske went to London to establish a branch there.

Siegal is not a drink creator, and the Gold Rush is exceedingly simple. "He started making honey syrup," Siegal said of Petraske. "I said, 'Can you make one of those whiskey sours with the honey syrup instead of the sugar?' It was as simple as that." But in those early days, simple ideas could seem like revelations. The addition of the honey syrup lent the sour a rich, nearly decadent mouthfeel and flavor. It was an early hit at Milk & Honey and was soon being made at other bars.

Combine all the ingredients in a cocktail shaker three-quarters filled with ice and shake vigorously for 30 seconds. Strain into a rocks glass with one large cube.

To make honey syrup, combine three parts honey to one part water. Shake in a sealed container until integrated.

X. ROCK STARS

LAB STARTED AS A SCHOOL and became a bar. The school was a noble failure; the bar, a lurid success.

Doug Ankrah and Alex Turner had known each other for years. Before the Atlantic Bar & Grill, they had worked together, with Richard Hargroves, at the first Planet Hollywood in London in the mid-1990s. Alex and Doug formed the idea of starting a school that catered to people like themselves, the new breed of London bartender.

The Atlantic Bar & Grill and Dick's Bar had changed everything. Thanks to media attention and public adulation, it was now possible for bartenders, once blue-collar sloggers, to become idols—or rock stars, as the press began to label them—people's whose names were known in certain circles. Ben Reed had such a name.

"'Ben from the Met Bar' was a name that was massively bandied about," recalled Reed.

The Met Bar, more a club than a bar, was a tiny private box surrounded by velvet ropes inside the posh Metropolitan Hotel in Mayfair. Those few who gained access to it would often react "That's it?" Once Michael Jordan and his entourage walked straight across the floor to the bathroom, thinking the door led to a VIP room.

What was big were the names that got drunk there—the Gallagher Brothers from Oasis, members of their Brit Pop rival band Blur, and the ubiquitous Kate Moss and Damien Hirst (whom Reed banned from the bar several times)—and the drinks that got them drunk. These were mainly huge, fresh fruit "Martinis"—watermelon, pineapple, and other fruits. Their makeup wasn't much more complicated than vodka, muddled fresh fruit, and sugar, but they were greeted like a revelation.

People who couldn't get past the cordon rented a room in the hotel just to gain entry to the bar. Eventually, a second Ben, Ben Pundole, was drafted from the Groucho Club as general manager. He was all of twenty-two, but had the self-assurance of a man much older, and handled celebrities with ease.

Met Bar was so hot that it became the modern cocktail era's first-ever pop-up bar, chosen by Saks Fifth Avenue in Manhattan to be part of a fashion event called the British Invasion. (Pundole met New York nightlife impresario Amy Sacco on the trip. By the end of the year, he had moved to Manhattan to work at her Lot 61.)

Beyond an emphasis on fresh produce, Met Bar did little to advance the art of mixologist. What it did do was get drinks into the hands of the right people, the kind who got splashed across the papers.

Nick Strangeway went to the Met Bar a lot. His own place, Che, was right around the corner. Che, which opened in 1998, was one of the many London projects of ultrarich Hani Farsi, who was described by one newspaper as London's "supercool Saudi, the desert dandy." While attending university in America, Farsi had been spoiled by the selection of spirits. Now he wanted them in London. Che was stocked with bourbon and tequila and rum and cigars.

Strangeway wrote the cocktail list and hired Danny Smith away from Tomas Estes' Cafe Pacifico, where he had worked for a decade making Margaritas for bartenders just off their SoHo shifts. Smith was a big personality and was soon winning cocktail competitions all around town. "He's a wonderful front-of-house man," explained Strangeway.

Che made a splash, but it never made money. The bar and cigar lounge did well, but the restaurant was two flights up, reached by an ancient elevator that was constantly breaking down. Eventually, the restaurant dragged the bar down. Still, at the time, Smith knew he was in the right place. "The Met Bar was nearby, just opened," he recalled. "LAB about to open. I knew cocktails were coming on."

When LAB opened in 1996 with Hargroves as a partner, "There was only one other bartending school in the city," said Turner. "We wanted to do something contemporary, not flair," for the more cocktail-oriented bartenders. Advertisements ran in catering magazines, but enrollment was spurred mainly by word of mouth. Six hundred pounds bought a three-week course. LAB took on ten students at a time, teaching them about service, product knowledge, and sales—much more than cocktail-making skills. Classes were from 10 a.m. until 4 p.m. The last few days would involve shifts at bars run by people the LAB founders knew.

It was a different sort of business than Turner, Ankrah, and Hargroves were used to, and different money. "The only thing we did wrong was it was so badly underfunded," said Turner. "We were always one student away from not being able to run the following course. We all ended up having to work bar jobs. So we'd work at bars in the night and did training in the morning." Eventually, the school went bust. The name, however, did not, and soon symbolized something very different from classwork.

"The school didn't work out, so we opened a bar instead," said Turner.

The bar was intended as a living advertisement for the school. But today, not many know LAB began a school at all. It is easy to see why. LAB was a raucous, pulsating place that threw shade on everything in its radius. When, in the late '00s, New York bartenders were finally given charge of their own bars, they chose to set up serious temples to mixology like Death & Co and PDT. The bartender-owners of LAB had a different idea. They wanted a party bar, high volume and high energy.

"Other bars are very, very passively boring," said Ankrah. "LAB was a bar for people who rock every night. And everyone came there." It was a two-floor affair in a narrow building on Old Compton Street in the heart of what was SoHo's gay district. (The building had been a lap-dancing club.) Turner helped with the training and the drinks list, but left before the bar opened. "To be honest, our relationship became a bit fractious," he said. That left Ankrah and Hargroves. Ankrah called on Jamie Terrell, who had put in three years at Dick's Bar at the Atlantic. A few months in, Dre Masso joined the team, making LAB "a sort of halfway house for former Atlantic bartenders," as Angus Winchester put it.

"At the time, we wanted to make the best drinks in the world," recalled Terrell. "Doug and I wrote five different cocktail menus together, and each of those menus had two hundred drinks on it." The cocktails were flamboyant, as befit the personality of LAB and its bartenders. Ingredient-wise, they leaned heavily on the fruit-and-vodka foundation the Met Bar had built. "You'd walk into the LAB, and the backbar would be like a green-grocer," recalled Ben Reed. Glasses were filled with a forest of fruit flavors and a rainbow of colors, and—in an extreme overreaction to the iceless world of London pubs—mountains of ice.

"Everything was in a massive fourteen-ounce glass of crushed ice," said Turner. "People thought they were getting a lot. And it was lurid blue or green." The drinks had ribald names like Honey Rider, Cool Hand Luke, Absolutely Crushed, Nuclear Daiquiri, and—LAB's most famous drink—the Porn Star Martini.

The bartending approach was freewheeling. Though Terrell insisted he always used jiggers, patrons remember drinks being built on the fly, like a sculptor chipping away at a block until he found the desired shape.

"It was very much free pour and lots of ice and garnish, but it brought so much attention," recalled Simon Ford. "They brought a chef approach. They were putting straws in and sipping, then adding a bit more mint, a little more sugar, a dash of bitters, adjusting the drink. It was very unique at the time. I'd never seen anything like it."

Wayne Collins characterized the style as, "Muddled up, crushed ice, liquor, stir it up, bang!"

Getting a drink built in that fashion sometimes took time. "I always used to say about LAB, order two drinks," said Turner. "Order a drink and a beer, so you've got something to drink while they're making your cocktail."

At first, nobody paid much attention to LAB's pyrotechnics. The first few months of 1999 were slow. Then a good review came out in *Time Out London*. And Ken Livingstone, the mayor of London, and a regular, was quoted saying, "LAB is not a bar, it's a way of life." That did it.

Few LAB cocktails survived its heyday. And many of its most famous bartenders eventually left for the far corners of the earth. Its most lasting legacy was establishing once and for all the idea of bartenders as celebrities, not wage slaves, and for its role in knitting together the growing London bartending community.

Tony Conigliaro didn't go to LAB "necessarily for the drinks, but I loved what was going on," he said. "Everybody in the industry used to be at LAB. If you wanted to get hired, or hire, or meet a rep, that's where you went."

Giuseppe Gonzalez, a young American bartender then on a spree in London, couldn't believe his eyes. "It was a bartenders' bar. It was something I'd never seen," he said. He talked himself into barbacking at LAB for a while. "It was fucking amazing. If you just saw the drinks, you would have thought you hadn't seen anything like it. Apple fans, pineapple leaves, mint out the ass. Even the Martinis were great."

NOT EVERY LONDON BARTENDER WANTED to waltz the craft cocktail into the jungle room. Wayne Collins hated the fruit Martini, and he wrote an article in *Class* bashing it. He was a classicist. "I didn't like that it was called a Martini," he said.

Collins was from Camden Town, north of London; he began pulling pints at a relative's pub in Hoxton in the late 1980s. Collins's cocktail schooling came from Lee Chappell—who, according to Collins, was like the Bryan Brown character in *Cocktail* and knew five hundred drink recipes. (It's worth noting that Chappell ran the Long Island Iced Tea Shop in Covent Garden, which served bottled cocktails at a time when no one else did.)

Chappell beat the Martini into Collins's brain. "Why would anyone drink gin and vermouth? He'd say, 'You better start liking it. It's not about you, is it? It's about the guests.'"

As Collins moved from bar to bar in London in the mid-1990s, he retained his interest in the classics, reading old cocktail books and studying the talents of Peter Dorelli at the Savoy and Salvatore Calabrese at the Lanesborough. "There was something endearing about it that I wanted to know about. I knew there was something more than slinging whiskey in a bar that was five deep."

All that he learned was put into practice at High Holborn, where chef David Cavalier hired him as bar manager in 2000. His backbar was filled with rare bottles. Collins delivered a menu of classic cocktails to go along with the forty-seat bar's pre-Prohibition style. There were Manhattans, Daisies, and Punches. "I looked for drinks that I found in books that were not on lists around London," he said. "I wanted to do something different from LAB. LAB was a party bar. This was for serious drinkers." In a time when most London drinkers had never been served a cocktail without ice, Collins was stirring perfect Sazeracs and serving them in expensive glassware.

"An amazing bar to work in and a terrible restaurant," recalled Sebastian Reaburn, one of Collins's bartenders at High Holborn. "Its heart was so in the right place, and it influenced a lot of people," said Conigliaro. But it didn't last long. The restaurant was well-received and quickly won a

Michelin star, but didn't succeed the way the bar did. High Holborn closed within a year.

———

JONATHAN DOWNEY WASN'T A BIG FAN of LAB either. Or the Atlantic, for that matter. "LAB was bridge and tunnel," he said. "Atlantic was wealthy west London." But Downey liked few bars he didn't own; in his view, they didn't measure up. To be fair, though, most the bartenders who worked at LAB and the Atlantic weren't fans of Downey, either.

Divisive may be too mild a world to describe Jonathan Downey's position in the cocktail continuum. The mention of his name shuts most mouths in a wary silence. Any admiration of his achievements is begrudging. And bartenders who have never worked for him say so with an air that indicates that it is the best decision they ever made. Even Dick Bradsell, whose reputation Downey did much to burnish in the early '00s, chose his words carefully. "Jonathan has standards that he expects from people. Which is fair enough," Bradsell said. He then paused and smiled, before adding, "Is that diplomatic enough?"

But whatever one thinks of Downey, it's impossible to counter spirits educator Philip Duff's assessment that Atlantic Bar & Grill owner "Oliver Peyton, and Jonathan Downey, assisted by Dick Bradsell and later Dale DeGroff, changed drinking in London forever." That appraisal of Downey gains added heft when you consider that Downey hired both Bradsell and DeGroff.

Downey was never a bartender. He was a wealthy corporate lawyer who began opening bars because he was disgusted with what London was offering him in terms of drinking. His nightlife model was his native Manchester.

"I was living in London," he recalled. "There were no bars anyway. Just crap places full of old men. Just crap food. My hometown was Manchester. There was club culture in the 1980s. The scene there was great."

Following a year living and working in Hong Kong, he came back with two years of ex-pat cash saved up. He borrowed more from a bank and opened a bar and restaurant called Match.

"My idea was to open a bar in London that had the look and feel of a Manchester bar—music and an industrial atmosphere," he explained. But with New York drinks. He'd been to the Rainbow Room and been impressed. The name of his first bar and restaurant, Match, itself was a rebuke of the London bar scene. "I wanted a one-word name that was the antithesis of All Bar One, Pitcher and Piano, Dog and Duck."

In 1997, he met Dick Bradsell by chance. Bradsell had just left a bar called Detroit. Downey hired him as a consultant at Match. The opening cocktail list included something called "The Matchnificent Seven," classics that were renamed after actors from that film. (The Old-Fashioned was called the Steve McQueen, for instance, and the Cosmopolitan, the Robert Vaughn.)

The bar was open as a café during the day, and stayed alight until 1 a.m. Match's name had a practical application as well; all of the drinks were meant to go with food—an innovative idea at the time. "I was a bit of a drink fascist at the time," said Downey. "Mexican food and Mexican beer. Spanish food with Spanish drinks."

Match won the Evening Standard Bar of the Year award just three months after opening. A bit stunned, Downey moved fast. He opened a second, larger Match Bar in the West End, and renamed the first bar Match MC1 (after the postal code). Soon after, he took on a big space in the east London neighborhood of Shoreditch, adding a sound system and a state-of-the-art bar. Named Sosha, it acted like a Match club. In 2001, he took over Player, an existing bar in SoHo, and made it over in his fashion. In 2002 came the London version of Milk & Honey with Sasha Petraske. Within five years, Downey had built a cocktail dynasty.

"What Jonathan brought was the eye of the consumer and sex," argued Philip Duff. "He was relentless in making sure that his bars were fun and functioned brilliantly. He wrote once that his target market was the secretaries in the law office he used to work at. The secretaries were twenty-five to forty-five, single or married, they made OK money, they wanted to go out, they wanted good food, good drinks, and fun."

That success came at a cost, however. "He can be quite a difficult man, and he is famously difficult to work for," said Simon Difford, publisher of *Class*. "Everything has to be just so, and 'just so' is his way. He has a reputation for flying off the handle at the smallest thing. But Jonathan's personality strangely brings out the best in bartenders. It's almost like, a sergeant major who's a big soft will run a crap army. Having Jonathan at the helm, no one will answer back, everyone will do it his way, or they'll be fired. His influence is incredible. It was a culture of 'We're the A team, we're the best, we're the SAS [Special Air Service] of the army.' So many bartenders who are now running some of London's best bars went through his system."

"Without him," observed Duff, "the London scene might have conceivably fizzled out after the Atlantic Bar."

White Negroni

Wayne Collins, 2001, Bordeaux, France

1 ounce Plymouth gin

1 ounce Lillet Blanc

1 ounce suze

Grapefruit twist, for garnish

The Negroni was just beginning to make a reappearance on cocktail menus when British bartender Wayne Collins came up with this twist on the classic aperitivo drink. "It was done by default when I was in Bordeaux for the VinExpo [the famous wine exhibition]. I was in the cocktail competition for Plymouth gin, which I won. Nick Blacknell was global ambassador for Plymouth gin at the time. He wanted Negronis." Collins couldn't find any Campari, so he grabbed a bottle of suze, the French gentian liqueur. Then he decided to use Lillet, which was made nearby, instead of vermouth. Simon Ford took the recipe with him to New York, and its popularity spread from there.

Combine the gin, Lillet Blanc, and suze in a mixing glass three-quarters filled with ice. Stir until chilled. Strain into a cocktail glass. Garnish with the grapefruit twist.

XI. INVENTING THE AMBASSADOR

AS LONDON WAS THE FIRST city to foment a craft cocktail movement, British bartenders were naturally the first group to figure out how to make a buck off it in ways not limited to wages and tips (the latter were never a huge part of the British bartender's income anyway). Dick Bradsell, with the help of Jonathan Downey, had shown that a barkeep, once having established a reputation, could make a pile as a roving cocktail consultant, moving from bar to bar. Other younger barkeeps followed their lead. Almost every London mixologist of note formed a company in the late 1990s and early 2000s. If you had even touched Bradsell's sleeve, you were in. "'I worked with Dick.' That was your reason that you were a consultant," said Alex Turner, who, along with Angus Winchester and Ben Reed of the Met Bar, created in 1998 International Playboy Bartenders.

The International Playboy Bartenders (IPB) was a bartending consulting group, and the name gives an idea of how London mixologists saw themselves in those heady early days. (Winchester's "nom de bar" was Vince Champagne.)

"This was pre-brand-ambassador days," said Winchester. "We did work for Tanqueray, ended up working for Baileys, Smirnoff, Havana Club, Bacardi. We pretty much worked for everybody in those days, because the companies hadn't got into the ambassador status."

The IPB put together cool parties on the corporate dime. A "Financial Follies," held at the Hudson Theatre in New York and funded by Diageo, required flying eight bartenders over from London to man four bars. Everyone stayed at the swanky Paramount Hotel in Times Square. The money was very good.

"For me, because I don't come from a worldly place, it was insane," said Philip Duff, who began consulting in 2002. "As consultants, we made a fortune. We went everywhere business class. We were put up in $1,000-a-night hotels. You got to go to every corner of the world, and you were received as a god." Working for Bols, the Dutch genever company, he spoke to bartenders in Argentina. Other jobs sent him to Japan.

"We were pulling in a grand a day," recalled Reed, "each of us, from Bacardi, Pernod Ricard, Brown Forman, doing training for them. We were all over. Then Bacardi and Pernod Ricard and Bacardi woke up and thought, 'Wait. Rather than paying out thirty grand, forty grand a year for forty days' training from IPB, why don't we employ someone? We can pay twenty-five grand a year for 322 days of training a year.' That's when this whole element of consultancy dropped off. And then the brand ambassadors started happening. This was a kick in the teeth for us, but a massive development for the drinks industry."

———

"THE MOST IMPORTANT PERSON IN the industry of the last fifteen years isn't Dale DeGroff, it isn't Audrey Saunders; it's Simon Ford," declared Eben Klemm. "He's done more to create the international community than anyone else."

Ford—a name completely unknown to the drinking public but recognized by every career-minded mixologist across the globe—is the epitome of that modern profession known as the *liquor brand ambassador*. Brand ambassador is simply a fancy, twenty-first-century synonym for salesperson, but with a significant difference. A brand ambassador is a salesperson with an unlimited credit card, a salesperson with a license to throw parties, create events, foster general hedonistic mayhem, and treat bartenders like kings. They don't represent a brand; they embody it. More often than not, the ambassador is a former bartender who has fallen into a globe-trotting, luxury-living, meetings-in-the-morning-and-partying-at-night pot of jam. They are Good Time Charlies with a mission (spirits education), and an underlying motive (spirits sales), whose talent, more than anything else, is to make the people around them think something isn't being sold, when all the time, every waking moment, something is always being sold. The brand ambassador is a confidence man, but the kind that also gives other bartenders confidence in themselves.

Ford virtually invented the position, with the help of a large-boned, drawling marketing genius by the name of Nick Blacknell. In the late 1990s, Blacknell was called in to save a neglected gin called, and made in, Plymouth. It was a venerable gin; the British Navy had contracted with the company for decades. But the liquid inside had been dumbed down over the years and the brand forgotten. When Blacknell took it over, it was down to five thousand cases a year.

Blacknell had worked at Seagram's with Ford, a college dropout and former wine shop manager. When Seagram's laid Ford off in 2000, he used his severance package to open a cocktail bar called Koba in Brighton and gained some cocktail cred. In 2002, Blacknell sent Ford to New York to launch Plymouth. It was a suicide mission if ever there was one, but Blacknell had few options.

"We were caught between two things," he said. "As a small brand, we couldn't get in to the big distributors. They just weren't interested. And the smaller guys were not really effective at the time. There wasn't a culture of craft spirits, and no culture of gin at all. We thought the only way we stood a chance in hell was to get someone to hand-sell it."

"'All you have to do, Simon, is find the fifty best cocktail bars in America,'" Ford remembered Blacknell telling him. "He wasn't interested in the sales. He was interested in our being in the best cocktail bars."

Whether there *were* fifty good cocktails bars in 2002 that could be made to care about gin was an open question. But to Blacknell, Ford seemed the best man for such a desperate undertaking. Baby-faced, chatty, antic, and upbeat, with tousled dark hair, Ford laughed after every other sentence and was hard to dislike.

Colin Appiah, who had worked at LAB, remembers meeting Ford for the first time in Bath, where Appiah was opening a bar called Ring O Bells. "Guy walks in the door. 'Simon Ford, nice to meet you, sir. First day at work.' Welcoming, warm, lovely." Appiah was so charmed he told Ford which people he ought to look up in London. "Three months later," recalled Appiah, "I remember going back to London. Everybody said, 'Hey, you met this new kid, Simon Ford? He's great!' *Really?*"

"He had that irrepressible nature," said Blacknell, "which you needed. Because it was depressing, honestly, going to bars and trying to talk to people about gin." Blacknell sometimes joined Ford and remembers almost being reduced to tears by the work. "We didn't really know what we were doing."

Gradually, though, some people took heed. Ford sought out what few cocktail beacons New York had at the time: Audrey Saunders, Julie Reiner, Jerri Banks, writer F. Paul Pacult, and, of course, Dale DeGroff.

Ford's marching orders were decidedly different from those of any other booze salesman then working the New York pavement. "I never once walked into a bar and said, 'Hey, take ten cases and I'll buy you a television.' I never once sold a bottle. I said, 'Hey, can I teach you about my gin? Can I teach you about bartending?'" Soon he became known among bartenders as not a pest, but a helpmate.

"Here is what Simon intuited that most people didn't," said Eben Klemm. "The standard of all spirits back then was, 'Our product is better.'

To a group of bartenders who thought they were independent and free, he was selling their profession back to them. Obviously, Plymouth supports your free thinking."

Traditional American liquor salesmen, too, didn't initially know what to make of Ford. When the Jim Beam company took over distribution of Plymouth, they wanted nothing to do with whatever a brand ambassador might be. Blacknell was forced cut a deal: "Give him three months, and if you're not impressed with him, you can then tell me to get rid of him." Ford stayed.

Ford's reputation as someone who was truly interested in advancing bartenders' interests was solidified when he convinced Plymouth to invite a handful of American bartenders to visit the distillery in England. "This was a world without craft spirits," pointed out Blacknell. "To take people to a distillery with one still, two hundred years of history—I think it was quite mind-blowing for people."

It was the beginning of a form of jet-setting bartender education that only grew over the ensuing years. Humble drink-slingers who had never before been offered so much as car fare were being flown to Cognac, Kentucky, London, Peru, Brazil, Jerez, Poland, and beyond. It was also the start of profligate spending habits for the glad-handing Ford. "Knowing Simon, he probably didn't tell me how much it cost," said Blacknell of the Plymouth trips. "It was a bit chaotic, the invoicing. I didn't really mind; he was doing a good job."

Years later, when Ford was working for Pernod Ricard, promoting Absolut, he proposed a series of lavish press dinners in which celebrity Chicago chef Grant Achatz whipped up a tasting menu, each course accompanied by a different vodka drink. Ford had already spent $60,000 on the project when his bosses cut the entire budget. Rather than drop it, Ford forged ahead, holding five dinners at a cost of $330,000.

"I thought I might get fired," said Ford, "but the events were so well-received I got funding to do more."

The bartender trips back and forth between New York and the UK sparked a cross-pollination that helped spread one-on-one bartender encounters at an unprecedented rate. Ford would take Americans to LAB, Milk & Honey, and whatever London bars were cutting edge at the time. "They were blown away. Every single time," said Ford. The reverse trips didn't necessarily inspire the same shock and awe; London was much further along in cocktailing than New York at the time.

The New York scene "felt quite fragmentary," recalled Appiah. "[London] had a community that was really growing. I didn't get that same feeling in New York. Everyone was working in silos. I came from a background where, you take a classic and the world's your oyster. There are spices and syrups and fruits: Go! Use your imagination. Here, I found everyone was just classics, classics again, and classics again. They were playing the same Jerry Thomas cocktails."

But, however different their approaches, bartenders were meeting and talking. And their middleman was Simon Ford. "I think that Simon was making sure the conduits of conversation were happening through him," said Klemm. "What had largely been a local movement, he made it international."

Ford's efforts succeeded in making Plymouth stand for not only good gin, but also education, authenticity, and insider-y cachet. Soon there wasn't a single bar of merit in the United States that didn't pour Plymouth, which went from five thousand to a quarter of a million cases annually in five years. Eventually, both Blacknell and Ford went to work for Beefeater—which had been bought by the France-based Pernod Ricard—and worked the same magic, transforming a fusty, old man's brand into a respected, young maverick's spirit. Between Plymouth and Beefeater, Ford and Blacknell helped make gin the first poster spirit of the craft cocktail movement.

XII. LONDON ASSURANCE

WHILE PETRASKE WAS IN LONDON setting up the new branch of Milk
& Honey in early 2002, childhood pal and investor T. J. Siegal took over
operation of the New York Milk & Honey, and he made some changes.

"I like making money," said Siegal—no Communist he. "[Petraske's]
worry was always, 'There are too many people in here.' He wouldn't have
people standing. But I'd already run big dining rooms. The idea that that
you had to have reservations even when the place was empty—that's crazy.
I wouldn't take walk-ins because he didn't want it. But I would schedule the
place so that, as much as possible, it was full from the beginning to the end
of the night."

Siegal ran a tighter ship. He expedited the bar the way one would a
kitchen, getting the customers to order another round just as the bartender
was running out of tickets. "One of the rules is always keep the cooks
cooking," he said. "That probably didn't conform to Sasha's ideals. But it
increased numbers drastically."

Petraske returned from London with a lot of ideas, a passion for the
European style of service, and two Italians: Vincenzo Errico from Naples,
known to all as Enzo, and Laura Zanella from Rome.

Together they were known to the New York bartending crowd simply
as The Italians. It was the beginning of Petraske's habit of hiring foreigners, whose dedication, polish, and shine caused him to value them above

American bartenders. "They were great bartenders," he said. "That was the golden age of the bar, as far as I'm concerned."

Like many Italian bartenders before him, Errico went to London in 1999, at the age of eighteen, in search of opportunity. He fell into a job where Dick Bradsell did the training. By the time he met Sasha, he was working at Downey's Match Bar. Petraske was impressed and invited him to join the opening team at Milk & Honey London. When it came time to return to New York, Sasha asked Enzo to join him.

Errico's lasting contribution to Milk & Honey and the mixology world in general was the invention of the Red Hook cocktail, a riff on the all-but-forgotten Brooklyn cocktail, which itself wasn't too different from a Manhattan. (Amer Picon, a French amaro, was a key ingredient of the Brooklyn; when it ceased to be imported, the drink, never very popular to begin with, suffered a quick demise.) The Red Hook combined rye whiskey, the Italian vermouth Punt y Mes, and maraschino liqueur—three obscure ingredients then on the ascendant, thanks to curious bartenders.

The cocktail was quickly embraced by goggle-eyed bartenders as a eureka moment, proof that a simple riff on a classic could result in a unique and respectable libation. John Gertsen, a Boston bartender, said, "I took that drink to the bank. I brought that drink back to Boston and began serving it hand over fist."

For a few years, it was endlessly imitated, with a rye-vermouth-plus riff on it named after practically every neighborhood in Brooklyn. Julie Reiner's The Slope added apricot brandy to the mix; Michael McIlroy's Greenpoint Cocktail paired the rye with yellow Chartreuese; Chad Solomon's Bensonhurst called for dry vermouth and Cynar; Joaquín Simó reached for Nardini amaro for his Carroll Gardens; Maxwell Britten's Brooklyn Heights employed Luxardo Amaro Abano.

Unlike the flow of ideas between London and Australia, or New York and San Francisco, there has never been much of that between the London and New York cocktail scenes. The former views New York bartenders as hidebound in their devotion to the classics, while New York sometimes sees London's love of invention and flash as frivolous and shallow. Petraske's London trip was one of the few instances where English ideas were transplanted to a New York bar. Beyond the Italians, the London trip changed Petraske's mind about certain classic cocktails he thought he had known. Londoners made the Old-Fashioned sans the muddled fruit that Americans had become accustomed to since Repeal. Their drink was a simple construction of whiskey, bitters, muddled sugar, and a twist of citrus, often stirred over ice for minutes to secure what was thought to be the vital degree of dilution. (This peculiar practice can be traced to Bradsell, who claims he was only following the instructions of his mentor Ray Cook and author David Embury.) Even Dale DeGroff still made his Old-Fashioned with an orange slice and cherry. Petraske's stark version came as a shock. "That was total news," he recalled.

Schwartz and Maloney recall Petraske bringing back the 50-50 Martini—half gin, half dry vermouth—from London. Petraske doesn't remember it that way, but agrees he started making the drink that way around that time. Unlike the pared-down Old-Fashioned, the half-and-half Martini didn't look daring. It looked insane.

"There was this Martini contest sponsored by Tanqueray" and organized by *Esquire*, Petraske remembered. Several prominent bartenders were invited to make their version of the drink. "I made it one to two. Everyone was passing the vermouth over the bottle, using atomizers." (Petraske believed bartenders' and consumers' vermouth phobia was rooted in the problem of spoiled bottles. At Milk & Honey, he began buying vermouth in small sizes and storing it in the fridge.) The equal-parts Martini wasn't a new idea; recipes in the late 1800s called for those proportions. But it was so forgotten by 2002, it might as well have been new. And in a world where "wet," when placed before "Martini," was a dirty word, it amounted to an altogether new drink. (It wouldn't gain widespread acceptance until 2005, when Audrey Saunders put it on her opening menu at Pegu Club as the Fitty-Fitty.)

Despite its reputation as a trailblazer that was returning cocktails and bartenders back to respectability, Milk & Honey still wasn't for everyone.

"I felt like I was in a library drinking cocktails," Colin Appiah said of his first visit to the London bar. "I was told I couldn't do this, I couldn't do that."

"I don't know what to order, and the fucking bartender doesn't speak English," recalled Giuseppe Gonzalez of the New York bar. "Everything about it was intimidating. None of this was approachable."

Though Julie Reiner had been doing interesting things with cocktails well before Petraske set up shop on Eldridge Street, she didn't visit Milk & Honey until far into the run of her own groundbreaking bar, Flatiron Lounge. Passing through the metal door and heavy curtains, her first impulse was to laugh out loud. *"Wow, this is luxurious!"* she remembered thinking. *"This place is really tiny. How do they possibly make any money here?"*

Red Hook

VINCENZO ERRICO, 2003, Milk & Honey, New York

---

2 ounces rye

½ ounce maraschino liqueur

½ ounce Punt e Mes

For a bar that put slight importance on inventing new cocktails, Milk & Honey turned out more modern classics than almost any other bar of the twenty-first century. These include the Gold Rush (page 96), the Penicillin (page 170), and this creation. Vincenzo "Enzo" Errico, a Neapolitan whom Sasha Petraske brought back from London, worked at the bar for a couple of years. Errico wanted to created a new option for customers who didn't like drinks with citrus, fruit, cream, or eggs—a twist on a classic with just a few ingredients.

It began with an attempt to showcase a neglected product—in this case the strong Italian vermouth Punt e Mes. "It is different from the other vermouths, because while the others are dry, sweet or else, the Punt e Mes is a little bit on the bitter side," Errico said. "So, to me, that type of flavor matched in such a perfect way the sweetness and dryness of both rye whiskey and maraschino. The rye is dry but a little sweet from the corn. The maraschino gives you a dry mouth, but it is sweet with that flavor of marasca cherry. And the Punt e Mes, with its unique flavor, could balance and marry the other two ingredients. For the proportion, it was easy, since it was supposed to be a twist on a classic like a Manhattan." Joseph Schwartz suggested the name Red Hook, seeing the drink as a variation lying somewhere between the Manhattan and the Brooklyn. That Red Hook was traditionally an Italian neighborhood appealed to Errico.

The creation of the Red Hook made a big impression on Errico's fellow mixologists and led to a host of additional Brooklyn and Manhattan riffs (the "Neighborhood Drinks," as they're called), most of them named after sections of Brooklyn. The Yellow Chartreuse–laced Greenpoint, a near-classic by Michael McIlroy—another Milk & Honey bartender—is one of these.

––––––

Combine all the ingredients in a mixing glass three-quarters filled with ice. Stir until chilled. Strain into a coupe glass.

XIII. THE ANTI-SASHA

JULIE REINER WAS THE ANTI-SASHA. Of DeGroff's three greatest apostles, she became the best businessperson and the most successful. Quality cocktails were important, and conscientious bartenders were essential, but both were pointless if you couldn't meet the bottom line. Flatiron Lounge didn't serve perfect drinks to the appointed few. It served great drinks to the many. It was New York's first high-volume craft cocktail bar, a machine that, more than the Rainbow Room or any other cocktail bar before it, brought mixology to the masses, and became a breeding ground of expert bartenders that fed many of the subsequent New York cocktail bars.

No native New Yorker, Reiner came the farthest from home. She was born and raised in Hawaii and attended college in Florida after a family move to the mainland. Once independent, she split the cultural difference between the two by moving to San Francisco in 1994, "with the last boy I ever dated," she said, "and I made him drive the whole way." When stints in PR and the car rental industry bored her to tears, she returned to the bar work she had first learned in Hawaii. She began as a cocktail waitress at the Park 55 Hotel in San Francisco. She was taught how to bartend by Linda Fusco, manager of the Red Room Cocktail Lounge, whom she was then dating. "I would go to the Red Room and stand behind the bar, and she would yell six drinks at me, and I would have to make them really fast," Reiner recalled. "I learned classics and speed."

Eventually, she got a job at AsiaSF, an all-Asian drag queen restaurant where she was the only staff member who was born a woman.

San Francisco in the 1990s "was ahead of New York," said Reiner. "In New York, you couldn't get fresh juice anywhere except the Rainbow Room. In California, it was the norm."

As much as she loved San Francisco, New York beckoned. And so, with girlfriend Susan Fedroff, she packed up and moved in 1998. Fedroff, a former bar manager at Back Flip, Red Room's sister bar in San Francisco, got a call. C3, a place inside the Washington Square Hotel, needed a bar manager. Fedroff passed the tip on to Julie. It was Reiner's first gig managing a bar.

C3 had a strange setup. The parents of the owners owned the hotel and had handed over the space to their daughter. "She was, 'I always wanted to run a restaurant,'" explained Reiner. "And they were like 'Here you go, honey,' and turned what was a gallery into a restaurant. They dined there every day. It was odd." Moreover, the name reminded everyone of the droid C-3PO in *Star Wars*.

From the street, you could barely tell the C3 bar was there. Reiner, undeterred, went to work. "I'm a total overachiever girl," said Reiner. Like everyone, she had a twist on the Cosmopolitan; hers was made with blood orange. She threw tiki parties, serving Lava Flows. Reiner's creative energy wasn't rooted in the classics. She took a stab at anything that seemed fun and new and fresh. But it was her infusions that got her notice. She'd stick anything she could find in bottle of booze to see what came out.

What there was of a cocktail society back then found its way to Reiner. Ted Haigh, the movie graphic artist and cocktail nut, was in town working on *Riding Around in Cars with Girls*.

"He would come in every single night and sit at the bar and choose random stuff and say, 'Make me a drink with that!'" said Reiner. "Raspberry eau de vie or something. He'd choose the dustiest, weirdest bottle he could find. He challenged me to work with difficult spirits outside my comfort zone. And he would get absolutely hammered."

Haigh brought along DeGroff and another interested civilian, Martin Doudoroff. "She had loaded up the bar with demijohns," Doudoroff said. "Everything was called a Martini. Everything. The mixed drinks were terrible, but the enthusiasm was there. The one thing she did really well was infusions. That's what those demijohns were. Pineapple infusions. Apple vodka. Pineapple rum."

Reiner sold herself as much as the drinks. Gregarious, pretty, with a big smile and a bigger, borderline-wicked laugh, she was immediately likeable.

After a short while, the tail began to wag the dog at C3. The empty restaurant became a large, sepulchral walkway to the bar in the back. And then the press came. In fall 2000, Rick Marin of the *New York Times* wrote about her apple Martini, which she made not with vile Apple Pucker but with Granny Smith apple–infused vodka. Three months later, the *Times'* Amanda Hesser spotlighted her French 77, a French 75 with brandy and Chambord. Julia Duffy at *New York* magazine covered her, too. Suddenly, she was the most famous person working at C3. Bad development.

"The chef fired her because she was getting too much publicity!" laughed DeGroff. "It was the best thing that ever happened to her."

The C3 gig opened up a new world to her. She began by making interesting drinks to amuse herself, not thinking anyone else was interested. Then, some were. "Suddenly, it's like, 'Oh, there are six other people that care!' There's this tiny group of people," she recalled.

More importantly, the press cared. Journalists had few sources to turn to regarding cocktails. "I realized they wanted to write about cocktails and nobody else was doing anything of quality," said Reiner. "So, I was like, 'Holy shit! In a city where everything has been done and everything is saturated, this is a completely untapped market, and I need to open a bar focusing on cocktails tomorrow!'"

—————

DALE DEGROFF DIDN'T WAIT until tomorrow. He opened Blackbird in April 1999. For his first bar after leaving the Rainbow Room, he took one step forward in profile, two steps backward in affiliation. The space, which was the same one on E. 49th Street that had held the Baum group's Aurora, was Rainbow redux, but on the less-glamorous street level. This time, however, DeGroff was a star, and he was placed front and center at the marble-topped, horseshoe-shaped bar. He served Champagne cobblers, juleps, Caipirinhas, and Tom & Jerrys at the holidays. There was a standard drink list of ten cocktails, but, said Martin Doudoroff, "If you were someone who expressed an interest in more, he had a three-ring binder of drinks."

The space had been beautiful as Aurora. Since then, it had gone to seed, its banquettes and carpets in tatters. But DeGroff had a vision. "I wanted a downtown lounge, uptown," he said.

Like C3, the bar outclassed the restaurant, thus scuttling the whole enterprise. "When the bar got going, it was great," recalled Francis Schott. "But there was a real disconnect between the dining room and the bar. It never came together. When you got a critical mass at the bar, it was a fun place to hang out. But it started with one arm tied behind its back." The *New York Post* called it spooky, the "Bates Motel of doomed midtown restaurants," and criticized DeGroff for not being around enough.

The place closed by New Year's, lasting but a year. Aside from being the last bar DeGroff would regularly stand behind—what followed was a peripatetic existence of consulting, contest judging, classes, and speaking engagements—Blackbird was notable for introducing barflies and writers to Audrey Saunders, the only woman on the bar's all-male staff. A Long Island girl in search of a new life, she had been trailing DeGroff like a devoted puppy for years, happily working private events gratis whenever the great man called. Within six years, she would open a cocktail bar that would shift the paradigm as much as Milk & Honey had.

XIV. THE PROTÉGÉ

WHEN AUDREY SAUNDERS ASKED Sam Barbieri for a bartending job, she was in her early thirties, working in the corporate carpet and wall cleaning business with her soon-to-be-ex-husband. Sam owned Pete's Waterfront Ale House, an above-average bar with locations in Manhattan and Brooklyn.

"She wasn't happy with the business or the relationship either," recalled Barbieri. "She said, 'I love the bar business. Can I bartend?'" Barbieri had heard that plenty of times. He told her to go take a two-week bartending course, probably thinking that would get rid of her. She took the course. At her first shift, in 1995 at the Manhattan location, her hands shook. "I hadn't worked a soda gun," Saunders remembered.

She was fortunate in one coworker: Cory Hill, a fellow bartender, was a member of DeGroff's Red Meat Club. After a couple of weeks of trying to talk her out of bartending, Hill sent Saunders to a continuing ed class at NYU led by DeGroff. After four hours of hearing about pre-Prohibition cocktails, Saunders was sold. She walked to the front of the class and handed Dale her carpet cleaning business card. She'd work for free. She just wanted to learn.

"I couldn't hire her," recalled DeGroff. "But I did use her for pro bono work." The first was for Mayor Giuliani at Gracie Mansion. Dale put her in charge of making Mary Pickford cocktails. It would be four years of free work until DeGroff hired her for Blackbird. In the meantime, she kept her job at Pete's, taking her training where she could find it. One memorable shift, she entertained a regular named Sterling Youngman with endless Margarita modulations. "We did proportions, we did different types of orange liqueurs, trying all sorts of tequilas." It was a preview of what would become her career R&D process in creating cocktails.

At Blackbird, as short as its lifespan was, her eyes were opened. "It was really that year with Dale that I learned about cocktails," she said. "I found out about the Negroni, the Old-Fashioned. Every day was like Christmas with him. He was always coming in with a rare book or some ritual."

Following Blackbird's implosion, Saunders was lured over to another nearby Restaurant Associates project, Beacon, on 58th Street, where chef Waldy Malouf was in charge. The first years of twenty-first-century New York featured many jealous chefs who came to resent the increasing attention lavished on their bar directors. But Malouf was free of spite. He had been seasoned through years of working with Nick Mautone at the Hudson River Club and then DeGroff at Rainbow Room, where he was executive chef and director of operations. A flow of ideas between the kitchen and the bar was normal for him.

"Because we took so much care in the food, it became a natural extension," said Malouf. "If you had a great meal and you ordered a cocktail and it wasn't a great cocktail—it just didn't make sense."

Malouf and Saunders put together the food menu and the cocktail menu at the same time. If Malouf was cooking with pumpkins and gooseberries, Saunders was welcome to them. The wood-burning oven was used to roast tomatoes for Bloody Marys. Given such freedom, Saunders created modern classics that would become her calling cards. The Gin-Gin Mule—a Moscow Mule crossed with a Mojito, but made with gin—was introduced at Beacon, using a homemade ginger beer recipe cadged from a Jamaican kitchen staffer. The ginger beer also went into the Jamaican Firefly, a Dark and Stormy with lime juice and simple syrup. It was simple, but complex enough in 2001 for Julie Reiner to think, *"This is the best thing I've ever had!"* And Saunders began work there on the Old Cuban, another Mojito riff topped with Champagne.

As with C3 and Blackbird, the city's small coterie of cocktail geeks sniffed out Beacon, trying whatever Audrey was working on.

"I remember drinking a lot of Manhattans," recalled Doudoroff. "I do remember Audrey was making Grasshoppers with chocolate magic shell. This is where we were." Orders were all over the place. People asked for easy classics like Martinis and Sidecars, obscure forgotten drinks like the Monkey Gland and Satan's Whiskers, more modern creations like Lemon Drops and Cosmos. It was hit or miss, trial and error, for both barflies and bartenders. And there were a lot of failures.

"We pretty much screwed up anything from the nineteenth-century books," remembered Doudoroff. "Just about everything from Jerry Thomas. We'd look at that stuff and our eyes would glaze over. The terminology is just bizarre in that book."

But for the time being, the enthusiasts were happy. "I could go there and sit at the bar and there was no competition," said Doudoroff. "I could irritate Audrey for two hours."

Saunders stayed about a year at Beacon, when an offer of triple the salary lured her to Tonic, a Chelsea restaurant with a beautiful old mahogany Anheuser-Busch bar that had been in the building, in its various iterations (most famously Harvey's Chelsea House), since the late 1800s. The cocktail crowd followed here, and all was well until 9/11.

THE AFTERMATH OF THE ATTACKS on September 11, 2001, affected business in restaurants everywhere in New York City—including Tonic. Everywhere but Bemelmans Bar, nestled inside the ritzy residential fortress known as the Carlyle. Economic downturns didn't much affect Bemelmans:

it was dead whether times were good or bad. A plush Upper East Side land-mark, Bemelmans had been quietly keeping the hotel-bar torch burning for nearly three-quarters of a century. The interior was elegant and unique. The light from the tiny lamps on the tiny tables bathed everyone and every-thing in a cinematic amber glow, including the namesake murals executed by illustrator Ludwig Bemelmans.

The artworks' enveloping embrace had always ensured that wit, art, and New York café society history would never quit the room. But everyone else had. When the Rosewood Hotels chain took over the Carlyle in 2000, they determined to give the bar a jumpstart.

Dale DeGroff was brought in. They wanted him to redo the work man-ual for the bar, do training sessions, and write a new cocktail menu that at least brought the bar into the late twentieth century. DeGroff had his work cut out for him. The Carlyle was a union hotel, with stubborn, immov-able bartenders. "The least senior guy was seventeen years on the job," he recalled. "Those guys looked at me like a side dish they didn't order." The longest-serving veteran was Tommy Rowles. Manning the bar since 1958, he was a local legend, but one almost perversely proud of doing no more than absolutely necessary. In his charmingly Irish way, he refused to serve an ornate oyster shooter drink devised by DeGroff, because it contained food.

"'You know it's such a pleasure to be working for you; you're such a famous young man,'" said DeGroff, doing a spot-on Rowles impression. "'But I won't be able to serve the oyster shooter. It's such a lovely drink, but I can't handle food. I can't go against the union, after all these years; what would happen?'" The oyster shooter was struck.

When DeGroff's contract was up, he was asked who Rosewood should hire to manage the new program. DeGroff said, "I know the man for the job, and she's a woman."

It was an almost impossible assignment. Not belonging to the union, Saunders couldn't step behind the bar or make a single drink. And the men who could were not inclined to put in the effort needed to make a Gin-Gin Mule when a Martini took one-quarter the time and made them the same money. But Saunders wore them down bit by bit.

"She charmed the pants off these guys," said DeGroff. "But that didn't change the fact that she had to make all the special stuff in the kitchen. She'd call me up crying, 'Oh, Dale, I can't stand it. These guys are driving me crazy!'"

Despite these trials, within a short time Saunders succeeded in turning Bemelmans into a drinking destination. The room and the staff would always be, to a certain extent, ineffably themselves. But the cocktails were better, and the place seemed relevant again. And she benefitted professionally.

"There were years there that any time any journalist wanted to talk about cocktails, they'd called Audrey," said Doudoroff. "That was the time that Audrey became *the* Audrey Saunders."

Gin-Gin Mule

AUDREY SAUNDERS, 2000, Beacon, New York

¾ ounce fresh lime juice

1 ounce simple syrup

6 sprigs of mint, some leaves reserved for garnish

1½ ounces Tanqueray gin

1 ounce ginger beer

The crowning achievement, in gin terms, of early gin advocate Audrey Saunders. This is essentially a Mojito (a rum drink) crossed with a Moscow Mule (a vodka drink), but made with gin. It also illustrates the wide influence the omnipresent Mojito had on bartenders at the turn of the twentieth century. "Dale [DeGroff] showed me his recipe for a classic Mojito with a dash or two of Angostura. Having a cocktail that had a fresh herb in it—who knew? Wow, that's amazing. For me, the Mojito base, mint and lime, was really, really enjoyable. At that point, I dove head first into gin. So sub out the rum and try the gin and see how that tastes." Saunders found a recipe for homemade ginger beer from a Beacon kitchen staffer. "It had a lot more sugar in it, so I tightened it up," said Saunders. "I'm adding simple syrup in cocktails anyway, so let's make it drier. Then I can control how much sugar I can put in it. So that was it: Gin Mojito. My quest was helping people get over their phobia about gin. And I thought, *Wow, this drink is really good and accomplishes just that.*" She used Bombay gin at the beginning, but finally settled on Tanqueray, which had the heft she wanted.

Combine the lime juice, syrup, and mint in a mixing glass and muddle. Add the gin and ginger beer and ice and shake well. Strain into a highball glass filled with ice. Garnish with mint leaves.

Old Cuban

AUDREY SAUNDERS, 2001, Beacon/Tonic, New York

¾ ounce fresh
lime juice

1 ounce simple syrup

6 whole mint leaves

1½ ounces
Bacardi 8 rum

2 dashes
Angostura bitters

2 ounces Champagne

Saunders was a master of taking old classics and giving them inventive new life. She began work on the drink while working at Beacon and completed it when at Tonic. "The working title was El Cubano." As with the Gin-Gin Mule, she was tinkering with the Mojito model. Instead of white rum, she put in aged rum. "So, OK, Old Cuban. There. Then, let's make it festive and top it with Champagne." Call it a Mojito Royale. The drink is probably seen on more menus worldwide than any other Audrey Saunders creation, particularly in London.

Muddle the lime juice, syrup, and mint in a mixing glass. Add the rum, bitters, and ice, and shake well. Strain into a cocktail glass, and top with the Champagne.

XV. FOAM AND FLAMES

FAR FROM THE QUIET HALLS and tinkling piano jazz of the Carlyle, within the tangled, postindustrial streets of Tribeca, things were being attempted that would have made a Bemelmans bartender's lip curl. For all their innovation, DeGroff, Saunders, and Reiner were working within classical cocktail boundaries. (Petraske strayed even less from the straight and narrow.) Their drinks were sometimes surprising. But they were not weird.

Eben Klemm and Albert Trummer were weird. And contentedly so. They topped drinks with foam and set them on fire. The roots of what became the more ornate branches of the cocktail revival, including the phenomenon known—almost always derisively—as "molecular mixology," began with them, at least in New York. (Around the same time, in the late '90s, Todd Thrasher was trying similar tricks in the DC area.)

Of the handful of mixologists who kick-started New York's cocktail movement, Trummer was one of the few not from the United States, and he brought a particularly European sensibility to his cocktail making. His family ran a restaurant in Graz, Austria (the same town that gave the world Arnold Schwarzenegger). After harvest, cherries and pine shoots, among other things, would be harvested and fermented in bottles that sat on the roof for three months. Albert was formally trained at a restaurant school in Austria for three years. Possessed of a flamboyant streak, he gravitated toward the bar. He cut his teeth in hotel bars in Hong Kong, Italy, and the Philippines, all the time dreaming of New York.

After a chance meeting in 1998 with chef David Bouley, that dream came true. Bouley, impressed with a drink Trummer concocted for a private party the chef threw, hired him to manage the bar at Danube, his Austrian-themed Tribeca restaurant. For a signature drink, Trummer reached back to the flavors of his homeland, mixing exotic Austrian elderflower syrup with Champagne. The Danube cocktail was perhaps New York's first elder-flower-flavored cocktail, created long before the elderflower liqueur St. Germain became "bartender's ketchup" in the mid-'00s. Priced at $14 a pop, Danube handily sold one hundred a night.

Bouley let Trummer use whatever he could find in the kitchen, though Bouley was sometimes frustrated when needed cooking ingredients went missing. If Trummer needed a special herb, Danube got it for him. Fruity cocktails reigned, but so did the classic American drinks that Trummer had learned to make while at school.

He won a bigger stage at Town, in the Chambers Hotel, where chef Jeffrey Zakarian hired him a few weeks after the midtown restaurant opened in 2001. He cleared the backbar of its regiment of flavored Bacardis, streamlined the liquor stock, and began to make dozens of tinctures. The bar staff was dressed in suits and ties, like "Savile Row salesmen," quipped *New York* magazine. Trummer decided what he was doing had gone beyond mere bartending. He christened himself a "bar chef"—the first person to use that momentarily trendy title.

"I started as a bartender," he explained, in his soft, Austrian-tinged English. "I learned the skills to make a good cocktail. I also have kitchen expertise. I'm combining the two titles. That's why I'm a bar chef."

As at Danube, Trummer did not shy from showmanship or a high sticker price. For the Truffle Martini, a Sidecar-like mixture was topped with shav-ings from a truffle that has been soaked in Cognac for six weeks. It went for $25. (Regular drinks began at $15, an unheard-of price for cocktails at the time.)

But his pièce de résistance was the absinthe show. Absinthe, the high-proof, wormwood-infused liqueur that had famously addled so many brains in fin de siècle France, was still illegal in the United States. But Trummer found a way around the ban.

Trummer still worked occasional events for Bouley. During one catering job in southern France, he met an old man who still made and fermented absinthe, growing all the necessary plants for his potion. Once back in New York, Trummer ordered six or seven herbs and infused them in alcohol in old absinthe bottles he had found in New Orleans. He finished the recipe through pyrotechnics.

"I needed to turn it back in time and make it the David Copperfield style," he explained. To do that, he "finished the fermentation" of the liquor by lighting it on fire. He'd set up wine glasses and go from glass to glass, pouring in the fiery liquid. Rivulets of fire ran down glass stems and onto the bar. These were eventually doused by Trummer with a little mineral water. "It's almost like a Blue Blazer," he said, citing the once-famous nineteenth-century flaming drink. "It creates an amazing show."

The potion that ended up in the glass was nothing like absinthe, aside from a vague herbal flavor. And certainly the method with which he served it resembled not at all the absinthe drips of the late 1800s. But his audience had never tasted absinthe and knew little about its history; and the show alone—Trummer dimmed the lights and played music each time, creating a frenetic atmosphere, like a birthday party on the East Village's Indian Row—seemed worth the $25 they were paying.

The press ate it up. At a moment when the bar world seemed to be crying out for celebrities, Trummer was happy to oblige. Cocktail purists, however, weren't as convinced that Town was headed in the right direction.

"He had some pretty dopey drinks, but they were creative," recalled the cocktail historian David Wondrich, then a relatively unknown *Esquire* writer. "I was very doctrinaire at that point. It was classic, classic, classic. Let's bring back classic cocktails. Why are you fucking around? Can't you just make me an Aviation or something?"

If Trummer's cocktails were a mixed bag, in Martin Doudoroff's judgment, they also "brought this kind of European sensibility that we didn't have a lot of. He had the ornamental bitters bottles on the bar before anybody else."

One night, Stanislav Vadrna, on his first trip to New York, walked into Town. He knew about Trummer from the Internet, and he was fishing for ideas to improve Paparazzi, the cocktail bar he ran in Bratislava. "It changed my life," he said of the visit. "It was beautiful, decadent, sexy, stylish."

Eben Klemm was one American mixologist who felt Town played a significant role. "That bar was important in making cocktails mainstream," he said. "It was his misfortune to not have been well-liked by other people of that generation. So I don't think we talk about him as much as we should. He was the first guy to have a first-rate cocktail program at a boutique hotel in Midtown. In some way, I feel, he legitimized us in the eyes of the media."

Jerri Banks, another prominent mixologist at the time, agreed. "I saw straight white men in five-thousand-dollar suits from Wall Street sipping on this cocktail with kumquats in it," she recalled. "I'm like, 'We've arrived.'"

―――――

KLEMM, WHO HAD HIS OWN likability issues, was a biology major who had worked as a molecular biologist but ended up in New York City, by way of upstate New York and Boston, in 1998. While trying to write a novel, he bartended to pay the bills and slowly taught himself the trade. A friend got him a job at the newly opened Campbell Apartment in 1999. Once the opulent private office of a railroad executive, hidden within the walls of Grand

Central Terminal, it had reopened as a ornate watering hole for well-heeled commuters, the "young and arrogant in that new-money-smell-my-cigar sort of way" crowd, as the *New York Times* put it.

The management cared more about surface values than depth. "They had the Waldorf-Astoria cocktail book and randomly picked ten drinks off that that sounded cool, without giving us the recipes," said Klemm. "As the opening bartenders, we were teaching ourselves the drinks based on the ingredients alone."

It didn't matter—everyone who came in wanted an Amstel Light or Cosmo anyway—but Klemm decided to care. "I thought, *This is kind of cool. We have to do these drinks right. We have to find out.* Half the drinks had orange bitters in them, and no one knew where you could buy orange bitters. So they mixed Cointreau and Angostura together. And there was maraschino liqueur in one drink. I found out that maraschino's a thing, not just the maraschino juice that bartenders are using in this drink. *Maybe I should find it.* So I went down to Astor Wines and bought the one bottle of maraschino they had. I was trying to rebuild those recipes."

At Pico, a Portuguese restaurant in Tribeca that opened in early 2001, Klemm had more license. The restaurant had won three stars from the *New York Times* but was lagging at the bar. Klemm offered a deal: he'd improve the bar if he could create original cocktails. The owners agreed. He mixed lightly sweetened apricot–passion fruit tea with bourbon and club soda, garnished with mint. Refusing to offer a Caipirinha, which he considered too common, he did a Caipirinha variation flavored with cucumber and cumin. For the Collins d'Electra, made with gin and vodka, he created a fresh rosemary syrup. Angolan chiles were part of the Appointment in Angola, a Margarita made with fresh mango puree. With his Anne Hester cocktail, however, he rendered drinkers speechless. Vodka and gin were combined with calendula—the essence of dried marigold petals—and topped with a foam made of grapefruit juice and Campari. "I was trying to create the cocktail equivalent of Proust's madeleine," he told the *Times*.

As the movement that became known as molecular mixology grew, what Klemm did at Pico could be seen as rudimentary. But at the time, almost no one else was doing it. "I got a lot of press," said Klemm. "They were all original. I wanted them to relate to the kitchen. That was the thing that I was doing differently than other people."

Klemm was not shy about his prowess behind the bar, and he quickly developed a reputation as an ornery customer. "He would constantly make fun of how slow I was," recalled Toby Cecchini, owner of Passerby, "so I would not serve him for ages." Phil Ward remembered the staff going on high alert whenever Klemm walked into Flatiron Lounge. "He'd be a very difficult guest," said Chad Solomon, who also worked at Flatiron for a period, "in that he's very opinionated and questioned everything that was being done and not afraid to insult the living daylights out of you."

Klemm made history of sorts, however, when, in 2003, he was taken on as the director of cocktail development for Steve Hanson's sprawling BR Guest restaurant group. It was one of two corporate jobs he had been offered within a matter of weeks. (The other had come from the Smith and Wollensky chain founded by Alan Stillman, who had trained Hanson at the original TGI Fridays.)

Klemm was New York's first corporate cocktail person. It was a turning point. Some colleagues had urged him against it, saying it would stunt his creativity. But privately, they nursed other feelings. Klemm was told "that a lot of people at the time were very pissed that I got this," he said.

Often joining Klemm and Trummer in those early cocktail write-ups was Jerri Banks. Banks was older than her cocktail contemporaries—closer to DeGroff's age than any of his followers—and a rare African-American in the overwhelmingly white mixology world. She was also a tough cookie.

"She's very intense and very specific," said bartender Brian Miller, who worked with her. "She could literally walk by the bar while I was pouring something one-quarter of an ounce and say, 'You poured too much.'" Once, when a pushy customer shook a $20 bill in front of her face, Miller saw her grab the bill, slam it on the bar, and say, "Don't you ever do that again." (A previous such incident had left her with an injured retina.)

The daughter of an NCO who bartended in an officer's club, she came to New York to sell wine for a small French importer, didn't like it, and bounced around for years until Joe Baum hired her as manager of the newly reopened Cellar in the Sky, his windowless, wine-centric restaurant nestled within the bigger Windows on the World on top of the World Trade Center. It was a chi-chi place. There were only thirty-five seats, a private bathroom, and a prix fixe menu. It had opened in the late '70s, but closed after the 1993 terrorist bombings of the center. It closed again in 1998, but put Banks on the map and led to her next job.

Fressen was a hip, club-like restaurant on a desolate block of the Meatpacking District. It had a steel façade, cement walls and floor, and a big central bar. One critic called it a cross between "a minimum-security prison and a utopian factory designed by a Japanese disciple of [Le] Corbusier."

Banks's bosses wanted a scene, and she gave them one—a jungle scene. She bought decorative pots, planted lemon verbena, and placed them on the bar. The verbena was part of the house cocktail, the Fressen Up, a layered drink made with lemon vodka and lemon juice. She went foraging in the farmer's market in Union Square. "Now, you can't go to the Union Square market without finding five, ten bartenders there. Back then, I was basically competing with the sous chefs."

But the Fressen Up wasn't the drink that endured. The Juniperotivo was a gin-lemon juice-mint conflation set apart by a spoonful of pomegranate molasses. It impressed fellow bartenders who would never have thought of using the latter ingredient.

Banks's importance in the cocktail revival would lessen as the years went by, as would Trummer's and Klemm's. But in these early days, their innovative ventures into fresh ingredients, foams, and theatrical pomp would show that the growing cocktail family tree was one of many branches.

XVI. EXCHANGE PROGRAM

ONE OF THE REMARKABLE THINGS about the cocktail renaissance is that it sprouted simultaneously, but largely independently, on three continents. England and America got most of the attention for their strides in mixology. But in a far-off corner of the world, Australia wasn't far behind.

Australia's progress isn't as unlikely as it may first seem, for, as a member of the British Commonwealth, it enjoyed a direct pipeline to the bartending ideas and talents of the UK. Any young Australian with a mind to was welcome to work for a couple of years in the UK.

A lot of people who went on to become some of the most important and influential cocktail bartenders and bar owners in Australia—Naren Young, Michael Madrusan, Sebastian Reaburn—did just that. Moreover, many of the English bartenders who earned their stripes in the London cocktail scene—among them Jason Crawley, Jamie Terrell, and Mike Enright— moved to Australia and stayed, leaving their mark on the country's bars. A London bar or two on your resume almost guaranteed you a prime bartending gig in Sydney or Melbourne. "If you told anyone in Australia you worked in Milk & Honey, bang! You had a job," said London cocktail consultant Angus Winchester.

As a result, Australia's cocktail revival had a distinctly English stamp in its early years.

"That was the paradigm: the Dick Bradsell model," said Reaburn.

That said, Australia's modern cocktail scene was instigated by two men who drew no inspiration from the UK. And, as befits a country that gave the world the platypus, emu, and koala bear, they were a couple of odd ducks.

Vernon Chalker, a flamboyant impresario, opened Melbourne's Gin Palace in 1997. Secreted away on one of Melbourne's many "laneways"— Australian for alley—it dedicated itself solely to gin at a time when the vodka-guzzling masses didn't know a juniper berry from a jujube, and certainly didn't feel they needed them for their Martinis or tonics. A few years later, a young expatriate named Matthew Bax, son of a painter, hating his life as an accountant in Munich, came back to Melbourne to open Der Raum, a place that would eventually hang its bottles from the ceiling by bungee cords and serve deconstructed Sazeracs.

Chalker and Bax hurled themselves into a vacuum. Melbourne was an erstwhile boom town, built on the riches of the Victorian Gold Rush of the 1850s. By the 1880s, it was the richest city in the world, dubbed "Marvelous Melbourne," with an accompanying culture. As in any boom town, the residents enjoyed their food and drink. But an economic bust in the 1890s, followed by World War I and the influenza pandemic of 1918, slowed things down. Following the Second World War, an ill-advised piece of legislation forced pubs to close at 6 p.m., resulting in widespread drunkenness as citizens tried to cram five hours of postwork drinking into one.

An influx of immigration in the 1960s rejuvenated things. Still, there wasn't much of a nightlife along Melbourne's grand Victorian grid come the 1990s. Then change came in the form of large-scale gambling. The Crown Casino was to be Melbourne's first betting emporium, with a wide range of restaurants and bars. The Victoria government wanted the casino, leading to the Liquor Control Reform Act of 1998, which included a "small bar" license. That opened the door to all sorts of smaller entrepreneurs, like Vernon Chalker, who saw the central city's disused laneways as an opportunity.

"From Victorian times, there were lots of small shops on the way to the railway station, on the laneways," he explained. "There were these empty shopfronts just sitting there not being used because people had shopping centers in the suburbs."

When Chalker secured a location on Russell Place, he cast about for a concept. Chalker, like everyone, drank vodka. Vodka was a safe bet. But it had been done; a hotel bar called the Mink Bar, with an enormous range of vodka, had recently opened. So he settled on gin, "exactly for the reason," perversely, that nobody then cared about it or drank it.

"The Martini and the Gin & Tonic are the two best drinks ever made," he reasoned. "Let's work with that. It'll work because it's not trendy." He called it Gin Palace, which he thought sounded funny, fun, and "a bit overblown"—a fair description of Chalker himself, whom Jacob Briars described as "perhaps the world's most camp bartender."

His design brief was equally outlandish. "I wanted it to look like it had always been there," he said. "Imagine a bar in Budapest in the 1890s, the Belle Époque, that was renovated in the 1950s and is still here." The stool-less bar was sleek and modern. Surrounding it, however, were an estate sale's worth of heavy, archaic furniture and overstuffed chairs and couches, arranged in small groups, inviting canoodling and tête-à-têtes.

He bought every gin he could find for the backbar. In 1997, that meant about fifteen, and he had to drive out of his way to get some of those. (Today, Gin Palace carries two hundred gins.) The original cocktail list featured ten Martinis, all $10, drawn from the annals of history and Chalker's own whimsy. There was a 1950s-style dry Martini; another with more vermouth than gin; the Orange Martini, taken from the *Savoy Cocktail Book*; a Fino Martini, made with gin and sherry; two vodka Martinis, one with the Zubrovka, the Polish vodka flavored with bison grass, and garnished with a marinated garlic clove, the other with softer Lukasova potato vodka, the glass lined with white chocolate liqueur and garnished with a chocolate bullet on a toothpick.

All in all, Gin Palace was bizarre. And it was an instant success. Not everyone drank gin. But orders split evenly between vodka and gin, which was remarkable in itself, "because almost every bar would sell 90 percent vodka to gin," said Chalker.

"That was the first time I'd seen anyone use more than a dropper of Noilly Prat," recalled Briars, who was then working at Matterhorn in Wellington, trying to bring craft cocktails to New Zealand. "That was the first time I'd seen anyone use orange bitters."

"Not only was Gin Palace the first cocktail bar, there really wasn't much in the way of independent bars," observed Matthew Bax. "There were pubs and nothing else."

Bax didn't fall in love at Gin Palace. But he fell in love with cocktails while crunching numbers in Munich.

"I was hating the accounting life and trying to paint," he recalled. To curb the boredom, he hung out in bars like Schumann's Cocktail Bar and Havana Bar, a Cuban-style bar where people smoked cigars. "People always drank cocktails. It wasn't an unusual thing. This didn't exist in Australia back then."

He returned to Melbourne and, taking advantage of the new licensing laws, teamed up with a friend to open Der Raum in the blue-collar Richmond neighborhood in 2001, naively thinking the bar would run itself and pay his bills while he painted.

"Of course, it went badly," Bax admitted. "Out of necessity, I was forced to learn how to make drinks." Unable to afford staff, he dismissed them and threw himself into the bar full-time, sleeping there because he didn't have an apartment.

Expecting Der Raum to go under anyway, Bax threw caution to the wind and began experimenting. He put up shutters and blacked out the windows. He heard that the artist Joost Bakker was putting on a show downtown, and he asked to do the drinks for the opening. He served the cocktails in jam jars.

Years later, Bakker did an installation at Der Raum where he hung all the bottles from the ceiling by bungee cords. Bax left them that way. "We had lots of bottles and were running out of room," he said. It was often hellish to serve drinks with such a setup, particularly when bartenders didn't return a bottle to its proper leash, but it gave the bar a distinct identity. (The design has since been copied by bars all over the world.)

So did the drinks. Bax was tutored by bartender Paul Aron, who had worked at the Atlantic Bar & Grill and Che in London. He began to go to the market every day, looking for anything unusual that could be turned into a cocktail.

"The cocktail menu was so wildly complicated," recalled Jacob Briaro. "It was like it had been designed by a conceptual artist."

Bax brought an artist's perspective to both his bar design and his drink design. He injected smoke into drinks, created every possible foam he could think of. It was molecular mixology, inspired in part by El Bulli, the innovative and influential Spanish restaurant. Ryan Clift, chef at Vue de Monde, would come in and they'd mess around with ideas. Ryan turned Bax on to liquid nitrogen, which led to the Frozen Caipirinha, a Der Raum staple.

Der Raum "was probably the pinnacle of the Melbourne scene," in the opinion of Jason Crawley, a London bartender who relocated to Australia. "Massively influential. It was the worst bar in the universe to work in. But they had massive creativity in there. They had an illegal pill press in the back, and they were making absinthe tablets." The pills would be used for a deconstructed Sazerac cocktail, in which a jellied rye would be injected with absinthe.

Three years in, Der Raum finally got some press. It also began to win awards.

Ironically, it was the beginning of the end for Der Raum when Bax tried to move the concept back to Munich, the city where it was born. He was dating a German woman at the time, and the two spent three years putting together a Munich branch of the bar. Then, three months after opening, they broke up, straining the collaboration. Meanwhile, the original Der Raum suffered a scandal: its manager was caught with his hand in the till. It closed in 2012. (Today, the address is the home of Bax's Bar Economico, a "rum shanty bar." Farther inside is the Bar Exuberante, which serves Der Raum sorts of drinks. In Melbourne's downtown, Bax owns the tiny Bar Americano, a exquisite jewel-box aperitivo bar on the Italian model. "He says he's the master of opening up the least profitable bars possible," said Crawley.)

Further cocktail quirkiness opened in 2001 in the bohemian Melbourne neighborhood of Fitzroy. It was born out of heartbreak. Sam Ross's parents got divorced, and he and his sister, Alex, and brother, Toby, convinced their mother to use the divorce settlement to open a cocktail bar. Toby had worked in London and brought back with him the London style of mixology.

The bar they opened, Ginger, is remembered by most who went there as both innovative and odd. The Ross taste for tomfoolery came through in the décor—"Lots of orange plastic; it looked like a psychedelic spaceship," Crawley remembered—and drinks. Sebastian Reaburn, who worked with Toby in London, joined the team in 2002 and became a second mentor to Sam.

"It was very eccentric," recalled Reaburn. "And it was very, very humorous. The cocktail menu read like a comedy script." One year, the Rosses and Raeburn did a cocktail menu in which the common denominator in every drink was Jägermeister. It ran for a week and was never seen again.

Jacob Briars remembered Ginger as a bar drunk on experimentation, a place where "there was no such thing as the idea anything might be wrong." He recalled Ginger using the crystallized sugar that gathered around the edges of liqueurs like Campari and Chartreuse as a cocktail element. "There were drinks with squid ink and totally weird cocktails," said Briars.

That sort of anything-goes frivolity didn't play well with everyone, particularly Sydney bartenders. Sam Ross felt that bias. "There was an element that Ginger wasn't taken seriously because it was so tongue in cheek," said Reaburn. "They thought there should be bits of stuff, like basil, in drinks; it should be rough and ready and fun. And because of that, there was a credibility gap."

But then, there was always a rivalry between Australia's two largest cities.

"Sydney didn't like Melbourne people, Melbourne didn't like Sydney," recalled Mike Enright. "I was English, so I thought, *Who cares?*"

Jason characterized the difference between the two cities this way: "Sydney is the blonde hair and big tits of Australia, and Melbourne is the kind of interesting brunette."

———

UNTIL 2008, SYDNEY'S LICENSING LAWS favored large establishments and deep-pocketed businessmen. The 2000 Summer Olympics shook things up. That "really elevated the hospitality scene," said Linden Pride. "Sydney really changed with the Olympics. A number of new bars opened up, and the city just took off."

Pride and Naren Young were both born and bred in Sydney and attended the same high school, a few years apart. Young had a reputation for headstrong assuredness. "He was notorious in high school, like he is these days," said Pride. "He got dropped from the rugby team and on principle refused to play for the second team."

Like many Australians, both men spent time in London. Pride (the son of a food writer and cookbook author, he had spent his childhood being taken to restaurants his mother was reviewing) worked at Hakkasan, a Chinese restaurant with a cocktail list by Dick Bradsell.

Young had settled on bartending as his future when he was fourteen, after seeing the Tom Cruise movie *Cocktail*. He began learning how to make drinks and would practice throwing bottles around in the backyard. He returned from London with renewed determination to bring craft cocktails to Sydney.

"There was only one bar," he recalled. "It was called the Grand Pacific Blue Room. It was the beacon of celebrities. It was the first bar that had good things in the rail. For me, it was like a myth. You could never get in there." (Young eventually got hired.)

Grand Pacific was reached by a lengthy climb up a circular staircase and past a huge old chandelier, leading to an odd, wedge-shaped space with a long bar. It was a hip-hop bar, with rapping on stage. But it served quality drinks. The English were in charge. Mike Enright, who had moved to Sydney in 1999, managed the place, and he saw in the Blue Room an opportunity to bring craft cocktails to Australia. When his London pal, Jason Crawley, came to Sydney the next year, he hired him.

"It was a revelation," said Pride. "It was a party bar with incredible London-style bartending and cocktails."

Around that time, Young found another way to exert an influence, by becoming the editor of Australia's answer to *Class* magazine, the *Australian Bartender* magazine, which launched in 1999. He remained there for six years, effectively becoming an arbiter of taste for the country's nascent cocktail world, while simultaneously remaining an active player in it.

"Up until then, there was no outlet," said Young. "There was no way for people to communicate, to know what trends were going on. It made everybody take bartending seriously."

His colleagues agree, if sometimes begrudgingly. "He was nearly as big as he thinks he was," joked Jacob Briars. "He was probably the leading figure."

Young found what he calls his "spiritual home" at the Bayswater Brasserie. The restaurant was in the Kings Cross area, a red-light district, and had been open since 1982. According to Young, before he came on, the Bayz, as it was known, was a place where oysters and Champagne were served to Ladies Who Lunch. "The drinks were never that good," he said. "It was Long Island Iced Teas." He hired Bryan Duell, who had worked in Che in London, and beefed up the backbar to four hundred bottles.

"It was a game changer," said Crawley. "It was the second bar [in Sydney] to have a proper cocktail focus." However, "it wasn't a massively fun bar to be in. It was always quite serious. Naren is quite a serious guy. And that emanated through it." The drinks were "good, but complicated." Crawley thought of working there at one point, but decided against it, as every cocktail "was a grand tour of the bar, picking up every fucking bottle. It was crazy."

Pride, meanwhile, was working at China Doll, where he was given free rein and began to bring to Sydney the molecular wizardry that Matthew Bax had to Melbourne.

"I was doing a salt, smoke, and honey Margarita with flame up the cinnamon sticks and a walk through the room with a puff of smoke. I'd do a strawberry Daiquiri with a basil emulsion on top."

XVII. COCKTAILS TO THE MASSES

BACK IN NEW YORK, after Julie Reiner was let go from C3 for getting too much publicity, her next break came from a trio of siblings who were looking to open a new bar in the then-dead Flatiron District. The tip came from Michelle Connolly, who had grown up in Manhattan and knew Reiner from when she managed the Red Room in San Francisco. Alex and Kristina Kossi had, a decade previous, opened up the Zinc Bar on Houston Street, a throwback to the Jazz Age, with live music.

Reiner went to them with her press book, showing off her clippings. The Kossis didn't care. Did she have money? Reiner purchased a partnership with $60,000 borrowed from her parents. "I bought myself a job," Reiner admitted.

They located an old art deco bar that had once been installed at the Ballroom, a Rat Pack hangout, then at Catch a Rising Star, where Robin Williams did lines of coke off it. A 1920s fantasia radiated from that focal point. The walls were covered with pieces of cobalt blue glass. A circular tunnel led to the main bar room (Reiner's idea). "It was like you're transformed as you walk through the tunnel into this place," she said.

Following an eighteen-month build-out, Flatiron Lounge opened in May 2003 as the first mass-appeal craft cocktail lounge in New York. With no PR firm on retainer, Reiner called all the journalists who had written about her at C3. It worked.

"It was cabs pulling up all night long," she remembered. "I don't think we even realized how good a location that was."

Flatiron Lounge stood no chance of becoming Milk & Honey 2. Fashion and music industry people worked in the neighborhood, and they were thirsty for both alcohol and style. "I was dealing with insane volume," said Reiner. "I expected it to be a civilized cocktail bar. But you're four deep in the tunnel."

The cocktail program wasn't overly serious at first. Vodka cocktails were still welcome. If someone ordered a Cosmo, they got a Cosmo. But the bartenders tried to talk them into other things, such as the Persephone. Made of Absolut Courant vodka, cassis, lemon juice, and a little bit of pomegranate juice, it wasn't terribly complex, but it was new and different. And Flatiron sold a ton of them. Other big sellers were the Beijing Peach (jasmine green tea–infused vodka, white peach puree, fresh lime, simple syrup), Mint Jules (muddled mint, simple, Maker's Mark, lime, soda), and the Juniper Breeze (Plymouth gin, elderflower cordial, grapefruit, cranberry, and a splash of lime). The menu's overall personality was light, breezy, and fresh. Dark, boozy drinks were few. Meanwhile, Susan Fedroff, Reiner's business and romantic partner, conceived the idea of cocktail flights—a trio of miniature, thematically linked drinks that led customers down unfamiliar liquid paths: a "Flight to Mexico" with tequila drinks; a "Flight to France" including a French 75. "We wanted people to know what we wanted them to order without saying 'Order this, dummy!'" said Reiner.

The bar "was a huge deal for me and all kinds of people," said Doudoroff, an early habitué. "While there was never anything cutting edge about Flatiron in terms of the state of the art, it was the cutting edge in the state of the market. It was the leading edge of the cocktail thing in New York City, and it reached more people than anything [else] did in relative terms. It brought cocktails to the masses."

Liquor distributors didn't quite know what to make of Flatiron. Simon Ford, then peddling Plymouth gin, remembered meeting Julie when the bar was still under construction. "I walk in, and the guy before me is trying to sell Apple Pucker and some such thing that was not right for her bar," he recalled, "and she was ripping him a new one. It was funny."

New staff was needed, and finding them wasn't easy. She had to train everyone from the ground up. When one left, Reiner was in tears, "because it was years and years of training people." Free pouring quickly gave way to jiggering, then an almost unheard-of practice. But she had no choice. Without jiggers, the cocktails varied from bartender to bartender.

It was on Flatiron's second generation of bartenders that Reiner would impose her training model. She became apt at spotting moldable talent. Katie Stipe was taken on as a server. Six feet tall, blonde, willowy, she looked like the showgirl she was. A Las Vegas native, she had danced on cruise ships and Broadway tours, making side money serving drinks at Campbell Apartment in Grand Central.

"Julie sees a six-foot blonde and says, 'Hey, why the hell not?'" said Stipe. Reiner and company called her Katie the Cheerleader, taunting her with cheers from behind the bar. She got her revenge by collecting more in tips than the bartenders. Eventually, she stepped up to bartender. Her dance training and wingspan came in handy. "It's athletic," she said. "I liked the choreography back there."

Lynnette Marrero, another actress, was working nearby at Cibar. After work, she'd drink at Flatiron. "I decided that was the next place I was going to work," she said. "I went in and stalked Julie for a job."

Reiner's most important hire almost didn't happen. Phil Ward was a tall, rangy, unkempt man with a mullet, who had grown up in stark, near-Dickensian circumstances in the steep riverside inclines of Pittsburgh's Mount Washington neighborhood. He was one of five children of a broken home where, if you wanted something, you had to earn the money to buy it. At twenty-eight, aimless and bored stupid, he took his savings and flew to Rome. Four months later, low on cash, he decided to return. "It was $500 to fly to New York versus

$1,400 to Pittsburgh," he remembered. "OK, I'll fly to New York, visit for a week, then I'll go home and shoot myself." Instead, he took a sublet and found odd jobs as a messenger and waiter. He answered a Craigslist cattle call for a barback at Flatiron. He had no idea what he was walking into.

"I was still drinking Long Island Iced Teas," he said. "I'd go out and have $15 and think, *I'll get two strong ones and I'll be good.*"

Ward was lucky enough to be interviewed by Fedroff that day. "I remember Jules was on one side and Sue was on the other, and I thought, *I hope I get that lady* [Fedroff]. *She's so nice.*" Reiner admits she probably wouldn't have hired Ward. "Sue would talk to a homeless man for fifteen minutes about what his interests were outside panhandling," said Ward. "Jules would look at him for one second and [*brushes hands*]: done with that." (The staff gave the two owners nicknames. Fedroff was "the Creator of False Hopes," and Reiner was "the Destroyer of Dreams.")

Ward set himself to learning the drinks. He wanted to be a bartender. Reiner wasn't interested—he was too rough around the edges, with subpar social skills; his nickname was "Dirty Phil." But Ward got himself noticed.

"He was the best barback ever," admitted Reiner. "He'd hear the order and every glass was lined up behind me. And he'd hand me the next bottle I'd need. And then I'd hire the next guy to bartend, because Phil just didn't have the look. And he would stand behind this guy and say, 'It's half, three-quarter, dash, dash,' because Phil had this crazy memory. It got to the point where I couldn't not make him a bartender." Reiner put him in "the hole," the small service bar on the downstairs level. But he craved the main stage.

According to Reiner, a fellow bartender, John Blue, sat Ward down one day and said, "You want to bartend? Listen, dude. Take a shower, cut your hair, cut the mullet off." He did, and he was in. And then the real work began.

"Julie is a very charming, nice lady," said Phil. "But she'll keep you in your place, too. If she ever knew you were mad at her or upset or something, she would just have no pity. She'd do what you do with a toddler: 'Oh! Does it feel bad? Are you upset?'" Her laugh—the joyful, open-mouthed cackle that seems to have a secret maliciousness at its heart—was the stuff of legend. Once, a very green Brian Miller was working beside Reiner at an event, carving a crate of oranges into elaborate twists. Soon his hands were covered with acid and pulp. "And Julie was just laughing at me," recalled Miller, "that cackling, witch-like laugh. 'Yeah, welcome to the bartending world!'"

With time, Reiner honed her process behind the bar into something both precise and efficient. A Singapore Sling required grabbing too many bottles. So a "sling business" was created, combining the Benedictine and Cherry Herring and whatever else could be put into one vessel. In time, no drink was more than a three-bottle pickup. She started using "cheater bottles," tiny containers of necessary but seldom-used ingredients, like Chartreuse. The ingredients that went together in a drink were grouped next to each other. "I learned this at Flatiron out of necessity, because, holy shit, we're getting killed here," said Reiner. "Either we dumb down our menu—which we really didn't want to do—or we figure out a way to do these complicated cocktails quickly and efficiently."

Other industry people came in to study the model. Doudoroff, a beloved regular on whom bartenders would test new drinks, brought in Romee de Goriainoff, a Parisian who in 2007 would open the Experimental Cocktail Club, the first important modern cocktail bar in Paris. "I don't think it's my favorite bar," said de Goriainoff. "But it's the one I got the most inspiration from. I was blown away by it. I thought it was fascinating."

Also at the bar were Dushan Zaric, bald and serious, and Jason Kosmas, shaggy-haired and grinning, both hailing from Keith McNally's Schiller's Liquor Bar and also veterans of McNally's vodka bar Pravda. "I always thought Dushan was such an odd soul," said Katie Stipe. "He was such a philosopher, really deep and intense. Jay was like a happy, smiley, easy-going guy."

They would combine those traits into one bar when they opened Employees Only.

XVIII. THE MERRY PRANKSTER

IN EARLY 2004, DUSHAN ZARIC and Jason Kosmas left Schiller's, taking Billy Gilroy, the bar manager, with them. Igor Hadzismajlovic, who was from Sarajevo and had worked at Pravda for three years, and Henry LaFargue, a native of New Orleans who also had worked at Pravda, joined them. Keith McNally did not regard this mass exodus with a glad eye. "He was not happy with us," said Kosmas.

They opened Employees Only that fall on Hudson Street in the West Village, inside a former pastry shop.

Employees Only, while one of the earliest of the New York cocktail dens, would always feel like an outlier. Like Angel's Share before it, it drew not on the pre-Prohibition American past (as had Milk & Honey and Flatiron Lounge) but on a foreign model only dimly recognizable to Americans, one reflective of the immigrant character of its founders. Zaric liked M&H style, and EO's curtained, speakeasy façade and minimal signage harkened to it. But he wanted M&H's vibe at Pravda volume. (EO's undulating bar design was something else he took from Pravda.) The jiggered drinks of Flatiron were not for him; EO bartenders would free pour. He also wanted food; he had seen what had happened at Pravda when customers got hungry—they left.

"Jay and I come from a European background," he said, meaning a background where eating and drinking went together. From the first day,

Employees Only distributed homemade chicken soup to anyone still at the bar at closing time.

The white chef's jackets that the bartenders wore were copied from an illustration in Jerry Thomas's *Bon Vivant's Companion* but looked like something out of a European hotel. Continental, too, was the apprentice program, in which a worker—his status stitched upon his jacket—would work for years before being promoted. The system began when management promised a barback, tempted by an outside offer, the next bartending position that opened. It took nine months, but the promise was kept. From then on, the tiered system was institutionalized.

Employees Only workers—overwhelmingly male (yet another leftover from the Old World way of doing things)—were loyal. In an industry where staff barhopping soon became epidemic, no one ever left EO. Several of its bartenders—Dev Johnson and Steve Schneider included—have worked nowhere else.

"We have very little turnover because they feel they had a hand in creating this," said Zaric. "Not just bartenders; my cocktail waitresses, my busboys, they don't leave. These guys, they had no other option, and they have a code, which is: if I've been helped, I'll help you."

"Employees Only started to become this cult of personality," said Charles Hardwick, a bartender who had been trained by Zaric at Pravda, "the personality primarily being Dushan." (Hardwick would later open Blue Owl, an early, influential bar in the East Village.) The customers picked up on that solidarity and contentment. A reporter from the highly focused shopping e-newsletter and website DailyCandy wrote the place up early on, in an item titled "Perfect Bar Found." Women came and, after a few months, men followed. Then it exploded. EO developed a reputation as a party bar, a bar with fun bartenders, a date bar, a bar whose patrons got laid.

What it did not achieve was a reputation for making the best drinks in town, at least among the cocktail elite. They served gin Martinis, and used coupes, and played with infusions, but putting the dot on the i's in daiquiri wasn't their raison d'être the way it was for Sasha Petraske. "We're definitely not the best mixologists," admitted Zaric. "We're not in front of all the new trends and techniques. That's fine. We chose to play a different card in order to provide experience."

Kosmas characterized EO's role in the early cocktail movement in New York as that of "the merry prankster."

"In the beginning, we kind of felt we were outside of that universe," he said. "We weren't jigger pouring. And there was a sense from our side that other people—some of the other cocktail people—looked at us like, 'They can't be really taking their drinks that seriously because people are having too much fun there.'"

The owners cried all the way to the bank. On paper, Employees Only may be the highest-grossing cocktail bar, per square foot, in the country.

XIX. THE WHOLE PACKAGE

PEGU CLUB WAS INEVITABLE. Rainbow Room revived classic cocktails, but it was an elite, expensive aerie with virtually no competition. Many bartenders who would become influential never went there because they considered it a tourist trap and out of their price range. Milk & Honey had brought cocktails from the penthouse down to the dirty streets of the Lower East Side, bringing art, craft, and a hushed, unapologetic seriousness to the bar. Flatiron Lounge had taken that art, toned it down a bit, and given it to the masses. Employees Only took those two blueprints—Milk & Honey's mystique and Flatiron's populism—and redrafted them as a party room. But the cocktail movement hadn't all quite come together in a single accessible, yet haute, media-friendly package.

Pegu was that package: the gelling of a scattershot movement, opening in 2005 at a moment when the whole cocktail thing was still a cool, insider secret, known and appreciated by only a relative few. It was something the media could latch onto with the seriousness it usually reserved for an important new restaurant, and it was fronted by an opinionated figurehead ready for her close-up.

Audrey Saunders had remade herself over the previous decade, throwing herself headlong into the esoteric world of the artisan cocktail, cheerily acting the part of guru DeGroff's gal Friday, and slowly building up a reputation as a bartender and drink creator through stints at Blackbird, Beacon, Tonic, and

Bemelmans. Though she and the public didn't know it yet, she had already created a handful of drinks that would become modern classics, served the world over.

Flatiron was established. The Kossis were interested in opening a third bar. For some time, they had had their eye on a second-floor space across the street from their property Zinc Bar, on Houston Street. It had been a rock club, then a Chinese restaurant. When the eatery closed, they seized their chance.

On a visit to Flatiron Lounge, Saunders met Kevin Kossi and, as is often her wont, she fell into an hours-long conversation. Two weeks later, Julie and Susan were at Bemelmans Bar, pitching the new bar project to Saunders. She was interested, but clear about what she wanted. "My concern was, *Julie, you and I are friends, and when it comes down to it, I want a project where I'm making the calls*," recalled Saunders. That was, at the time, OK by Reiner. "I felt it was too early to put my name on another thing," Reiner said.

Saunders set up shop in the basement of Flatiron, using it as an office, working out her vision on a big Dell computer while the Houston Street space underwent its long construction period. After jettisoning a few other names for the bar (Sun King was an early candidate), she christened it after a favorite cocktail created in the early twentieth century at a British officers' club in Rangoon, a piquant mix of gin, bitters, orange curaçao, and fresh lime juice. It evoked an exotic, Charles Baker-esque world (he was the author of one of her favorite cocktail books), and it expressed her devotion to gin, a then-unfashionable spirit she would trumpet from the soapbox Pegu Club gave her.

Saunders had no doubt the bar would work. "I knew that if I opened a bar called Pegu Club, that bartenders who knew me would get it," she said. "International people would get it. People who hung out on the chat rooms would get it."

She left Bemelmans in January 2005. But the build-out was endless; Pegu didn't open until August. The design drew on old images of the Far East from magazines, old photographs, and the movie *Indochine*. Every detail was worried over. "Just to do the logo alone, my God, that took months!" said Saunders. As she became pressed for time and money toward the end, a few grandiose plans fell by the wayside. An event room in the back, which would have brought in considerable additional income, never happened, nor did a hoped-for New York branch of the Museum of the American Cocktail, a newly founded entity based in New Orleans.

Getting together a staff was considerably easier. Though New York's cocktail universe was still so small as to be near invisible, there was talent out there, and every cocktail bartender wanted to work at Pegu. Saunders was able to cherry-pick the best of the city; no one said no. By the end of 2005, she had assembled the first Murderer's Row of cocktail bartending talent the city had ever known.

"You know how sometimes you go into a bar and you want that person to make your drink and you don't want that other person?" recalled Andrew Knowlton of *Bon Appétit*, who was trying to suss out this whole cocktail phenomenon. "It was never like that. It didn't matter. It was all-stars. Just pick whoever you'd like to make the last shot of a basketball game and they can do it."

Adding to the intimidation level were the uniforms—dress shirts, vests, ties—designed by Kristina Kossi. "I was sick of going to a club and seeing a bartender in a black-collared shirt with a big can opener sticking out of their pocket," said Saunders.

Toby Maloney was chosen to be Pegu's first head bartender. He began working at Flatiron as training, unpacking his private bar tools while Reiner rolled her eyes. Also from M&H was Chad Solomon, who, after a week's work at Flatiron, and a Margarita-fueled meeting with Audrey, was drafted for Houston Street. Phil Ward, the best from-scratch bartender Flatiron had produced, was champing at the bit to join, and Reiner gave her blessing.

Jim Meehan read about Pegu in *New York* magazine; he successfully lured Saunders to Pache, where he was bartending, and sent out one original cocktail after another to their table. As Saunders left, Meehan handed her a printout of the recipes. "They were OK," remembered Saunders, but "I could see he wanted to do what we were doing." They met two weeks later at Bemelmans, and Meehan was hired. However, in the long interim between then and opening, Meehan was promoted to full-time at Gramercy Tavern. He held on to a single shift at Pegu, Mondays, in the opening schedule.

The wild card on that first roster was Brian Miller, who was recommended to Saunders by Jerri Banks. Split from his girlfriend and homeless, sleeping on a leaky air mattress in his brother's studio, he desperately needed the work and squeaked in. Still, he knew he was in over his head. "I had no business being there among that staff," said Miller. "I was by far the least qualified person there."

It was an overwhelmingly male staff, and though female bartenders would sometimes be brought on over the years, it would remain so. Reiner had surrounded herself with both men and women at Flatiron, but Saunders clearly enjoyed being Queen Bee.

The opening cocktail menu at Pegu was a call to arms. There was the namesake drink, redolent of history and botanical rebellion. The very wet, vermouth-heavy Martini with which Petraske had cracked the brains of Milk & Honey barflies was there, renamed Fitty-Fitty, giving it some street swagger. Little Italy, a Manhattan laced with the obscure Italian amaro Cynar, was created for Pegu. Saunders's past creations, like the Gin-Gin Mule, Old Cuban, and Earl Grey Mar-TEA-ni, were given pride of place.

Nothing got onto the menu—classic or original—unless it survived Saunders's rigorous lab testing, which had come a long way since the days of finessing Margaritas measurements on the bar of Pete's Waterfront Ale

House. An eighth of an ounce was the makings of a federal case in Saunders's world. There was perfect, or garbage.

"She is all about the minutiae of the cocktail," observed Reiner. "I certainly like to create cocktails, but I think of things from a broader perspective. She'll make a drink eight hundred times before settling on it, and I'll make it fifteen times before I say, *I think this is good enough*."

"It was very intense," Maloney said of Saunders's never-ending trial-and-error system. "When she decided she wanted to develop a cocktail, she would give you the specs and you would make it. She would walk you through the first one. She would take a sip and put it down, and she'd rattle off some more specs, and you'd make another one. Slightly different. Little tiny tweaks."

One day, they were refining the house recipe for the Ramos Gin Fizz. "I swear we had to make twenty-five of them. Our arms were shaking," said Maloney. Once Saunders tasted each, she went back to the beginning to see how they fared as they warmed. "It was never the twenty-fifth one. It was the twenty-third one. And it was noticeably better. Her palate and the way her mind worked, and the way she could hone in on what she was doing, was breathtaking."

With time, Meehan would spot a flaw at the heart of this method. "The fallacy of this is, we all have different palates," he said. "There is no perfect drink." Still, for 2005, it was revolutionary and, he admits, "That is the way I develop cocktails now."

Saunders's thought process when creating an original drink is well-illustrated in her description of the creation of the Tantris Sidecar, an uncharacteristically complex cocktail for Saunders, and another drink on the opening menu:

"I was looking at my ratios. Say we did three-quarters lemon, one Cointreau, one and a half ounces Cognac. This is where I started to think about how cocktails could be riffed, but to stay within the parameters. Here,

I had three-quarters lemon. I said, OK, let's keep three-quarters, but let's see if we can go half lemon and a quarter pineapple. Then I started thinking in terms of primary acids and secondary acids. The lemon is sharper and the pineapple is flabbier. They contributed different things. Then we had the Cognac. So I said, OK, instead of one and a half Cognac, how about one Cognac and half Calvados. Calvados and pineapple go really well together. With the Cointreau, let's put something interesting in there. I remember seeing pineapple and Chartreuse [as a flavor pairing]. Why not? So then I cut down on the Cointreau and put Chartreuse in there along with it. Then Chartreuse is high octane. So, since we have all these things going on, let's see how it tastes. If I went with all Cointreau, it's too sharp; even though you've got sweetness from the pineapple, there's a lot of alcohol. The only thing you have to soften that all out is a tiny bit of pineapple. And the pineapple wasn't enough to make it feel seamless. So add the simple syrup to add the fat."

In a show of professional force to match that of the mixologists, Pegu's bar stools were quickly occupied by the cream of the young media world. Regulars included Andrew Knowlton, Adam Sachs, and Sam Kinsey of an online thing called eGullet. Knowlton went three or four times a week. "That was the first time I'd go as a grown-up to a bar by myself," he said.

Kinsey said, "To me, the tipping point was basically when Pegu opened. Everybody who was anybody was working here." Kinsey, a trained opera singer with a flop of dark hair and an operatic way of speaking, was invited by Steve Shaw to join his creation, the influential open-forum food website eGullet, where chefs and civilians parried opinions and exchanged ideas. Within that online world, Kinsey claimed cocktails as his turf. He was grateful for Pegu. "Frankly, there wasn't much to say until this place opened."

In the years to come, mixologists would complain about patrons who wanted to talk about nothing but cocktails. But in 2005, such arcane discussions were still fresh. And at Pegu, the enthusiasts and bartenders often talked of nothing else.

"Pegu was different in that by that time cocktails were catching on more," remembered Ward. "There were more nerdier people. There were people who came to Flatiron for cocktails. At Pegu, they were coming for cocktails *and* answers. They wanted to know shit."

Not every questioning know-it-all at the bar was a journalist. Martin Doudoroff followed Ward from Flatiron to Pegu. Matt Massett, a trust-fund kid from New York, and maven of online cocktail chat rooms, was regularly chauffeured from his home in New Jersey to Houston Street, where he got hooked on the Jimmie Roosevelt, a luxe Cognac-Champagne-Chartreuse concoction. And then there were Don and John.

Don Lee and John Deragon were two more refugees from the tech world who, like Doudoroff and Hess, fell willingly down the well of mixology. Deragon was a kid from Bay Ridge, Brooklyn, who abandoned culinary ambitions for the financial safety of computer science. He bet well. He made oodles of money as a senior techie at a string of companies. Don Lee was a Korean-American, short and stocky with a head of impressively thick wavy hair. A man of many interests and pursuits—among them tae kwon do and photography—he nonetheless ended up as an IT adminis-trator. He somehow gained entry to Milk & Honey and, as a Scotch lover, had his world rocked by a Rob Roy. His innately searching personality led him to surf the Internet for cocktail intel and make expeditions to LeNell's boutique liquor shop in Red Hook. Both Deragon and Lee were eGullet regulars, and they finally met at Pegu to swap esoteric bottles. Lee had some bonded Laird's Applejack, which he had rented a car and driven to New Jersey to obtain. John had a bottle of aromatic bitters from Japan.

Don and John became Pegu's Mutt and Jeff, the favorite guinea pigs on which bartenders could test their latest experiments. (This sometimes angered Saunders, whose watchword was consistency; she discouraged ordering "off-menu.")

To supplement their thirst for knowledge, the two began throwing cocktail parties on Friday nights at Lee's Chinatown apartment. A $5 entry fee helped pay for the voluminous amounts of liquor that went into the obscure refreshments. Lee had four kinds of crème de violette when most cocktail bars had none. Soon they were buying lemons and limes by the case. Chad Solomon went to one bash. "I don't know any bar regular who was going to those lengths at that time," he said.

For a time, Deragon catalogued the schedules of every bartender they liked and kept a printout in his pocket. "We're at one bar having a drink," recalled Lee, "and he'd look at the schedule and say, 'It's Thursday. Meehan's at Gramercy.'"

Lee and Deragon got the idea behind Pegu Club immediately and were thus, of course, a pleasure for the bartenders to serve. But not everyone was Don and John. Most patrons were John Does, set in their drinking ways and used to getting what they wanted in any bar they entered. They were interested only in being seen at the new hot spot, not in that hot spot's fancy new menu. These oafs wanted their vodka and tonic, as usual. But, not as usual, they didn't get it at Pegu. They didn't get their Rum & Coke, either, or Vodka and cranberry, or Budweiser. This led to escalating, sometimes cantankerous, and philosophically amusing conversations with the bartender.

"It got so bad in the early days," said Solomon, "Toby started telling people we didn't have any vodka." Or he'd steer them in the direction of a "citrus-botanical-infused vodka" he particularly loved (gin).

Some of the bartenders were a little too eager to *not* give the customer what they wanted. "Right before Pegu opened, Jules and Sue and Michelle had to sit me down because I was getting out of control," admitted Ward. "People would come in and say, 'I'd like a Cosmopolitan.' And I'd say, 'You don't want a Cosmopolitan. There are so many better things to drink.' I was out of my mind. I was fighting with people."

But, overall, Saunders knew her staff were suited to the task. "I could have easily done a vodka drink," she said. "And then what have I accomplished? We had to break the guest's perception that it was always a vodka drink. The common denominator among all those bartenders is they were educators."

Under such pressure, the staff became tight. "There was a lot of camaraderie," remarked Maloney. "It was very much: friendships are best forged on the hinges of hell." Phil, Chad, and Toby all knew each other. Brian Miller was just learning. "The first time I saw Toby he was in a seersucker suit," Miller remembered. "He was the peacock that he was. I went, *That's the coolest guy I've ever seen.*" Phil was another matter. "The first year I worked there, I had no idea whether Phil knew who I was or whether he liked me at all. High praise from Phil was 'That doesn't suck.'"

To school himself, Miller began to keep notebooks—a collection of small, spiral-bound volumes, one for each spirit, in which he inscribed every new cocktail recipe he heard. He would keep them close by him for years. "I let people look at them, but I don't let them have them. I never leave them anyplace. I bring them to work, and I take them back after the shift."

The young Pegu Club, due to the sheer confluence of talents and minds on both sides of the bar, became a chrysalis of ideas and action. It was a place where things would happen, where discoveries were made, where the art was pushed forward. At some point, Audrey asked why she couldn't get Laird's bonded apple brandy, a product far superior to Laird's standard applejack, but not distributed in New York. Soon, Saunders got on the phone with Lisa Laird and leaned on her. "I had to buy sixty cases in order to get it, because it wasn't listed in New York," she recalled.

By early 2006, Chad Solomon's back was giving out, the result of a ruptured disc suffered four years prior. He couldn't shake drinks loaded with big cubes like he used to. "When you're shaking with bigger ice, you don't have the benefit of the ices breaking and diluting quicker," he said. "You're generally shaking the drinks a little longer. It seems intuitive that if I could cheat and get a head start on it—an act of self-preservation on my injury—it would help." He began preparing drinks at Milk & Honey by shaking with no ice. His colleagues saw it not as a cheat, but as an innovative way to better integrate egg and dairy drinks. "I brought it to Pegu and showed people. I remember Meehan put it out there and said 'Chad taught me this.'" Soon the "dry shake" was applied to drinks across the city.

Once the bar was on its feet, the staff was supplemented. Solomon vouched for Jim Kearns, who, with puppy-dog eagerness, had once made Saunders a Manhattan at the Double Seven, a club in the Meatpacking District where Sasha Petraske had consulted.

Sam Ross was a bit more brash. A big noise from Melbourne, where his family's cocktail bar, Ginger, had made an impression, in 2004 he had bought a one-way plane ticket to New York. He knew no one there, and he didn't have a visa. For six months, he couldn't find a single bar that met his standards. Then he sat down at Milk & Honey, ordered a Silver Lining, and decided, *This is where I'm going to work*. He called, got Sasha on the phone, and, after a three-hour lunch, landed the job at Little Branch, another Petraske bar.

"I'm twenty-one. I'm an idiot," admitted Ross. "I've got hair spiked out to here. It was my glamour punk phase." Petraske, Maloney, and Schwartz trained him. He quickly learned that no one knew or cared about his Melbourne reputation. "When I saw these guys doing what they do, I shut my mouth and watched," said Ross.

A weekend man was needed at Pegu, so Maloney brought in Ross. Miller couldn't believe it.

"Sammy showed up like he fell off the set of a Loverboy video in the 1980s," Miller remembered. "He had a Mohawk mullet! He'd show up in acid-washed ripped jeans and ascot and brown leather coat. Like, who is this kid?" (Ross's style was particularly galling to Miller, given that, on

Pegu's first "friends and family" night, he had been sent home to shave off his mustache and soul patch.)

Ross took on the role of Pegu's Puck, paying no allegiance whatsoever to the house rules or hierarchy. When a bartender took a bathroom break, Ross would rearrange the entire well, mixing up the bottles. He'd rile the waitresses up and walk away, knowing Miller would have to deal with their tempers the rest of the night.

As the months and years went by, Pegu was considered the cocktail city on the hill by the press, the bar that bred a generation of top mixologists. Flatiron Lounge was cast in shadow. It continued to do solid business and produce stellar bartenders (Giuseppe Gonzalez and Tonia Guffey among them), but was less discussed, becoming the cocktail world equivalent of Norman Maine (*A Star Is Born*) to Pegu's Vicki Lester.

"What we did at Flatiron gave Pegu a lot of momentum," said Reiner, who said she has no hard feelings. "Yes, there were definitely moments where it wasn't a fair deal. Once Pegu opened, I was kind of out of the picture."

Still, "a lot of the people in the industry knew about the chicken before the egg," she added. "Me being the chicken."

Penicillin

SAM ROSS, 2005, Milk & Honey, New York

2 ounces blended Scotch, such as Famous Grouse

¾ ounce honey-ginger syrup (recipe follows)

¾ ounce fresh lemon juice

¼ ounce Islay single-malt Scotch, preferably Laphroaig 10YO

Candied ginger

No new drink of the twenty-first century has gone further in terms of fame than this complex, spicy, smoky turn on a Whiskey Sour. The Australian Ross created it while at Milk & Honey, just a year after he emigrated to the United States from Melbourne.

"We got one of the earliest shipments of the Compass Box line in New York—Asyla, The Peat Monster, and two others," recalled Ross. "I was playing around. I did a riff on the Gold Rush, which was one of our big sellers," using Asyla. "Now, our ginger juice is sweetened, so it acts like a syrup. I split the sweetening between the two, the ginger and the honey. And it was great. Then I grabbed The Peat Monster—might as well play around with the smoky whiskey. I poured a float on top. That smoke stayed on the top. I preferred to never serve it with a straw. I want that smoke in the nose and that spicy sweet cocktail underneath.

"I went to bed that night not thinking much of it. Like, *That was a good drink.* It wasn't until nine months later, at Little Branch, one of our waitresses, Lucinda Sterling, she came back from a table, and they all wanted Bartender's Choices. She said I should put a Penicillin out because every table needs to experience one of them. It wasn't until she said that, that I was like, *Oh, maybe there's something there.*"

There was something there. In 2007, Sam Ross did some extensive consultancy work in Los Angeles, planting the seed of the drink in bars there. In the years since, the Penicillin has become as close to a household word as any cocktail since the Cosmopolitan. Philip Duff said the first time he had one, it was made for him by Australian bartender Naren Young in Germany, "which gives you an idea of how international it is."

Another measure of the bartending community's familiarity with the potion: you can often get one at cocktail bars that don't even have it on the menu. By 2014, the Penicillin was so well known that some young bartenders assumed it was an old classic from way back.

Combine the blended Scotch with the honey-ginger syrup and lemon juice in a cocktail shaker three-quarters filled with ice. Shake until chilled. Strain into a rocks glass filled with one large cube. Top with the Islay Scotch and garnish with candied ginger.

To make the honey-ginger syrup, combine 1 cup of honey with one 6-inch peeled and sliced piece of ginger root with 1 cup of water in a small pot and bring to a boil. Reduce the heat and simmer for 5 minutes. Refrigerate overnight, then strain, discarding the solids.

XX. THE BALLET DANCER
AND THE MONK

WITH HIS WORK AT ABSINTHE, Marco Dionysus may have been San Francisco's first big mixology prodigy, but in terms of press and publicity, Scott Beattie became the city's first star. Beattie took a very different route than Dionysus, less about classical models and more about what California had to offer here and now.

"I was really influenced a lot by reading Michael Pollan's books," said Beattie. "I was trying first of all to find delicious products, whether herbs or flowers or citrus or spirits—to put a face behind the ingredients I was using."

Beattie wasn't alone. The California style of mixology was, for many years, all about fresh ingredients. It was garden-to-glass. More than that, it was garden *in* a glass, going back to the fresh limes squeezed for every Margarita at the Zuni Café in the 1980s and the fields of mint plucked for Mojitos served at Enrico's.

"Mainly, I picked mint all day long," recalled Thomas Waugh, who, as a young man, worked at Enrico's. "Hours on end. My hands were dyed green."

"In New York, everything came out of bottles," said journalist Camper English. "In San Francisco, everything was made fresh to order." There were no jiggers, no measuring; pours were counted. Freshness prevailed over precision.

"We didn't think a lot about the variance in size between this half lime and that half lime," recalled Beattie. "It was just, 'Oh, this is half a lime. It kinda works, but kinda doesn't.'"

Scott Beattie was born and raised in San Francisco. He studied English literature at Berkeley, supporting himself at Perry's, the famous fern bar, and Postrio, Wolfgang Puck's fine-dining destination. By senior year, he was taken with the restaurant business. He began entering cocktail competitions. When the dot-com bubble burst, he retreated to Napa in 2001 and got a job at a place called Martini House in St. Helena. Beattie's father, who lived there, had a citrus garden at his house, and Scott began infusing vodkas with the fruits. His Bloody Mary was informed by different peppers. "It's kind of an Alice Waters thing," he explained. "You know where the ingredients come from."

Restaurateurs Nick Peyton and Douglas Kean, who had a little place in St. Helena, had become friendly with Beattie. The duo were planning a fine-dining restaurant, Cyrus, in Healdsburg, for 2005. They wanted to have a classic hotel-style bar and asked Beattie to head it. He wrote a forty-page spirits menu, with descriptions of every bottle on backbar, and visited local distilleries. But it wasn't enough.

"Once I really absorbed what they were doing there," said Beattie, "how they were trying to do this restaurant that was going to be as good as The French Laundry, and received the critical reviews to back that up, I started to look at what I was doing, and it was kind of mediocre. I was playing with the big boys here. I've got to bring my A game."

He read more, went to a lot of farmers' markets, and courted the farmers, getting them to grow specific things for him: lemon basil, mint, marigolds. Love Farms, run by Ron and Bibiana Love, became a prime source of ingredients. He found Key lime trees in an alley near a friend's house, kaffir limes at another friend's house, and peach orchards in Healdsburg; wild blackberries grew behind the Cyrus building. Beattie took two hours before each shift collecting the produce for the evening's drinks. "I realized I had access to all this stuff and other people didn't. I was imitating what chefs were doing. It was nothing new. They were getting farmers to grow things for them. They were culinary cocktails." Given the amount of citrus, many of the drinks were sours, and many were made with vodka, a blank canvas that embraced the optimum number of natural flavors.

Had Beattie's creations just been fresh, they might not have garnered attention. But they were also beautiful, framed by wheels of vibrant-colored citrus and festooned with decadent crowns of garnish akin to floral arrangements. "The very first thing that people had when they went into this restaurant was a cocktail, and not only did it have to be delicious, it had to look really good," he said.

Within six months, Beattie was being written up in glowing terms in the *San Francisco Chronicle*. *Gourmet* profiled him, and *Food Arts*. Soon he had a book deal—one of the first mixologists of the modern era to land one.

"Everyone discovered Scott Beattie, who's the most important California-style bartender who's ever been, I think," remembered Camper English. "He still makes these insanely ridiculous cocktails with nine or ten ingredients and six of them are citrus or fresh ingredients. And then vodka or something. He's basically making Chartreuse in a glass with every cocktail."

Bartenders made pilgrimages to Cyrus to admire Beattie's artistry. "Scott Beattie is a wonderful person to be in front of," said San Francisco bartender Neyah White. "Very Zen; 'be here in the moment.' He's the ballet dancer. We're the butchers."

But being a ballet dancer is hard work, and it's not for everybody. And while Beattie's model was brave enough to inspire a school of cocktailing, its followers were, ultimately, few.

"His book [*Artisanal Cocktails*] is basically informational," said English. "You have to get rare peppercorn flowers that bloom once under the blood moon to make the average drink in a Scott Beattie book." Remarked Jeff

Morganthaler, the noted Portland bartender, "Scott Beattie's book. Great book. I haven't made any of those drinks."

Still, if there are any San Francisco bartenders who can be said to have disciples, Beattie is one of them. "There are only a couple of those people," said Martin Cate, owner of Smuggler's Cove. "There's the Thad Vogler school, the Scott Beattie school, and the Eric Adkins school, which is kind of connected to the Thad Vogler school. Those guys have followers. Committed!"

VOGLER'S ANOTHER DIFFICULT SAN FRANCISCO CASE—an unbending political idealist, undeniably influential, but difficult to emulate in practical terms. "He's our local ascetic," bartender and bar owner Scott Baird said. "He's the man of the cloth. He keeps it pure."

And not everyone's cut out to be a monk.

Appropriately for a mixologist compared to a holy man, Vogler doesn't approve of alcohol on its own. The various bars he's worked at, and owned, have actually been restaurants with bars attached.

"Whenever I worked in places that didn't do food, there was a kind of unwholesome quality you'd encounter," said Vogler. "You see someone have a second drink, then a third, then a fourth, and the drinks are delicious. You just see people, young women, just tip over. It would be good if you had food to put in them. It's just more civilized."

Mixologists today have exacting standards when it comes to certain things. They demand quality liquor, fresh ingredients, good ice. Glassware and bar tools are matters of great importance. Presentation should be flawless, and customer service unfailing. But concerning other, arguably weightier matters, the new breed of bartenders often lack principles at all. They'll work for any liquor company that offers a good price, accept trips around the world and lush lodging on the corporate dime, bolster their bars with funding from booze conglomerates. Ethics are often left at the red cordon in the name of hedonism. Compromises and conflicts of interest abound.

In this sense, Vogler is an anomaly. You won't see him on a junket to a distillery and pouring swill at a brand event. The only brand work he does is for liquors he approves of, and that work he does for free every day at his bars. His standards are so bruising that few bottles make the cut. His back-bars are ruthlessly curated down to a few dozen spirits, and chances are you won't recognize many of the labels.

"If a brand is well advertised," he said, "you can almost be sure that it's not very good." He will sometimes eliminate entire types of spirit from his bars because of his suspicions as to their integrity.

"American whiskey is a great example, the conglomeration of it," he argued. "Over the last twenty years, so many times there's been a product that I love that has been bought by an international or a larger domestic group and the product has stopped being what it was." Instead, he focuses on spirits he can trust and control. He travels to France for his beloved Cognac, Armagnac, and Calvados and buys full barrels to use at his bars, eliminating the middle man.

Thad Vogler attended Yale and tried to get out of bartending a couple of times. He was once employed at Oracle, the tech outfit, and during another period he worked in the nonprofit world. But he always returned to restaurants, a business he had come to know while in college in the late 1980s. "My parents are both academics, so there's always a kind of shame about bars," he said.

By the mid-'00s, Vogler had become interested in cocktails. Beginning around that time, he set up the bars at a series of influential restaurants: Slanted Door, Beretta, Heaven's Dog, Presidio Social Club. Generally, his work was appreciated. Sometimes his attitude was not. "I got fired from there because I did an interview with a blogger," he said of Presidio. "I spoke about Diageo and Bacardi and talked about the negative impact they were having on the world of spirits. At the time of an opening, an owner is losing his mind. He's terrified. They all visit his bar. He didn't want to generate ill will in any way."

Slanted Door, Charles Phan's landmark Vietnamese restaurant, was the first time Vogler got attention. The first thing he did was rip out the soda guns.

"They assumed we wanted new ones," said Erik Adkins, a bartender hiree at Slanted Door and Vogler's eventual successor there. "And he said, 'No, that's it, we're good.' The look on their faces."

Nothing got behind the bar without Vogler's say-so. "Everything had a pedigree," recalled Adkins. "Instead of carrying more products, he had less products. Everything had to have a sense of place and time and a link to agriculture." If something he wanted wasn't available, he willed it into existence. "He got Schweppe's Indian Tonic imported into America so he could serve it at Slanted Door and have no high-fructose corn syrup on the menu," said English.

In 2008, at Beretta, a pizzeria in the Mission District, Vogler again paired cocktails with food. His pursuit of perfection took another step.

"In my opinion, Thad Vogler's cocktail menu for Beretta is the best cocktail menu that's ever been put together," said Camper English. "Every drink on it was great. Almost every drink was based on a classic, even when it wasn't apparent. I studied that menu for days. That's when I noticed that every drink had its own sweetener." There was Demerara syrup, honey, maple syrup, grenadine. "It's not just simple syrup."

After Beretta, Vogler started to think about opening his own place. He wrote up a business plan for Bar Agricole. By this time, he had pared his preferences down to the quick—not just the spirits he chose to use, but the drinks. With an anthropologist's zeal—and a rather New York viewpoint— he mainly drew from the late nineteenth century, when American cocktail culture was thriving. He had little interest in wild, modern, kitchen-sink potions. "It's like food," he explained. "If there's a combination you've never tried, odds are that many have tried it and it's not successful. You can defer to the work of those who came before you."

When Bar Agricole opened in 2010, the opening cocktail list was tight, and, he admits, a bit alienating. There were drinks made with brandy and rhum agricole, stuff people were not yet accustomed to drinking; Ti' Punch; an Old-Fashioned stubbornly made with brandy.

This was in keeping with Vogler's my-way-or-the-highway approach. "Most consumers are not wild about agricole rum at the end of the day," commented Martin Cate. "But he's going to push it down your throat."

Each drink had been painstakingly workshopped. "You don't really know a drink until you've made it many, many, many times," said Vogler. He put a Bruce Lee quote on the restaurant's website: "I fear not the man who has practiced 10,000 kicks once, but I fear the man who has practiced one kick 10,000 times."

Bar Agricole's cocktails are routinely cited as perhaps the best in San Francisco. Which is peculiar, since they are like nothing else being mixed in the city, or the nation for that matter. Because of their precise construction and spirit sourcing, drinking a Vogler cocktail is a singular experience. These aren't loosey-goosey, fun drinks. They are very narrowly focused, tight-ass cocktails, usually boozier than the norm, as they shy away from sweetness, both in their application of sweeteners and in the dryness of the spirits. They almost challenge you to like them, insist on their natural flavors. Ascetic is one word for the style. And yet, they are impeccably balanced.

There would be no mistaking a Thad Vogler drink for a Scott Beattie drink. But in one way they are alike, and both identifiably San Francisco artists: sourcing. Beattie knows where every fruit and herb he uses comes from, and Vogler plucks particular spirits as if they were fruits.

XXI. MILK & HONEY WEST

PEGU CLUB'S IMPACT SENT RIPPLES through the U.S. cocktail world: bar people came from all over the country to check out what Saunders and company were doing.

In 2006, Eric Adkins, then working at Slanted Door in San Francisco, visited Pegu. Recognizing Audrey Saunders, he introduced himself. "For about an hour, she proceeded to make my wife and me about ten or twelve cocktails," he remembered. "As we'd sip one, she'd make another. My wife turned to me and said, 'Why don't your drinks taste like this?' I said, 'I don't know.'" He went back to the Bay Area, determined to do better.

Another night, in 2005, a tall, wiry guy named Todd Smith brought a couple of suits into Pegu. They were from San Francisco on a fact-finding bar tour. They liked Pegu, but Milk & Honey made the deepest impression.

Brian Sheehy was not a bartender. He was a hotel man, born in Boston and raised in Ireland. But he and his partners, Dahi Donnelly (a fellow Irishman) and Doug Dalton, would become the most prolific cocktail bar owners in the San Francisco.

The trip to New York convinced Sheehy "to get back to San Francisco as soon as possible and open a speakeasy." He found a space on a seedy corner of the Tenderloin. The bar then there, 501 Club, was so notorious the police had made the owner put a buzzer on the restroom door to flush out drug dealers hiding there. The bar was on the brink of eviction.

Sheehy admits that when he conceived of Bourbon & Branch, he knew next to nothing about cocktails, despite already owning two bars. Todd Smith knew more than something: at the time, he worked the bar at the restaurant Cortez, and he had waited tables at Enrico's when Paul Harrington was bartender at that North Beach icon.

"Todd said there's no way you're going to make this work. It's too small, and it's terrible," Sheehy recalled. But the forward-thinking businessman knew the spaces adjacent to the bar would be vacated soon and the landlord would give him first option. And his experience with the Kimpton Hotel group had taught him how derelict properties could be rejuvenated. (Bill Kimpton was a pioneer in the boutique hotel business, taking over old buildings with character, giving them a cosmetic makeover, and reopening them as chic, European-style lodgings that distinguished themselves in a sea of anonymous chain megahotels.)

As it turned out, backstory-wise, they had hit the jackpot. The address had operated as a speakeasy called the Ipswitch in the 1920s, and then the J. J. Russell Cigar Shop, with a labyrinth of secret exit tunnels and a hidden basement space. "We wanted to open a speakeasy," said Sheehy, "but to have the good fortune to have a speakeasy here, we knew we were onto something good." Architect Andrew Gifford created the dark wooden warrens that make up the bar; glassmaker Ivan Mora fashioned the oft-photographed, much-imitated spiky white chandeliers. Meanwhile, the name, Bourbon & Branch—slang for a whiskey and water—came from Todd Smith. (Being Irish, Sheehy and Donnelly didn't know what the term meant.) Smith may have been inspired by Paul Harrington. "It was always my policy that if someone came in and ordered bourbon and branch, I'd buy him a drink, because I just loved that," Harrington said of his Enrico's days. "When I told Todd that, he said, 'Oh, my God, that's the coolest thing.' That's why Bourbon & Branch is called Bourbon & Branch."

While the bar was 100-percent Milk & Honey in conception, it was all Pegu Club in its staffing, corralling the best bartenders in the city: Jon Santer from Bruno's and Cortez, Dominic Venegas from Range, Neyah White from Nopa, Ryan Fitzgerald of Tres Agaves. Everyone signed on. "We knew that this was going to be 'the school' for a while," explained White.

But past experience was no preparation for the trial that was Bourbon & Branch during its first months in late 2006. The new establishment had the most ambitious cocktail list the city, but a badly designed bar, and a reservation system that made Milk & Honey's look like a model of efficiency. An unexpectedly enthusiastic public response led to a months long spasm of chaos.

"It was a shit show," said Santer. "We didn't have a lot of things we needed. We didn't have an ice machine. We didn't have any prep people. We didn't have a computer system. Everything was handwritten. We didn't have any training. We hadn't made any of the drinks before. We hadn't actually had time to memorize the drinks." And there were a lot of drinks: sixty-seven at the start, plus an extensive bourbon and Scotch list, and beer and wine that absolutely no one wanted.

"We had great bottled wine, great beer," said Santer. "We had tasting notes on everything. And nobody ordered any of that stuff except the cocktails." At Sheehy's previous bar, Swig, he could offer a customer a Manhattan for free and they wouldn't touch it. Now they wouldn't touch anything else.

The physical bar was small and difficult to work in. In retrospect, Smith admitted he would have changed a lot of things. "I'm a big guy. The backbar was too high for anybody but me. Jon Santer is looking at me, like, 'What are you doing?'"

"You enter the bar, there's that first well, right in front of you," explained Santer. "Todd worked that well, which is the personality well. I was at the next well. I was in the speed position. The dishwasher is next to me. If the door to the dishwasher was down, it completely blocked the lane. I could not move. The 'on' switch to the dishwasher was right where my knee was, so if I leaned over to give you a drink, I would turn on the dishwasher and it would spray me with hot water. The glass froster was behind me. We had drawers for garnish, which we would tuck underneath. And there were no barbacks because no barbacks could fit back there."

The ice and produce were kept in refrigerators downstairs, down a flight of stairs. But "there were no stairs between the bottom landing and the basement. So you have to jump down, fill up a tub with all the shit you needed, put it on the landing, press yourself up onto the landing, and then run upstairs. Repeat. It was absurd. It was the hardest bar job ever."

The public didn't know the hell that the bartenders were going through. They just knew they wanted in, and wanted drinks. Getting in, however, wasn't easy. Sheehy had hated waiting for the call from Milk & Honey that said it was OK to come over. His hotel-trained brain set up a reservation system unfamiliar to both bar goers and bartenders, in which seats were reserved for set periods and then released. Smith objected. "I wanted it to be a little more open, more neighborhoody," said Smith. "If we're full, we're full." But the first two weeks, done without a reservation system, were "a complete disaster," said Sheehy, so the staggered reservation setup went into effect. Now it was the press's turn to object. "It was all over the papers," Sheehy recalled. "'Who are these snotty guys opening a reservation-only bar?'"

The ultimate downside of a running a popular reservation-only bar is that, at 6 p.m., when you open, your bar is full. "Then at 6:10, ninety-five drink orders come in at the same time," explained Santer. "So if you're drink number ninety-five, you're waiting a while." That pressure did not let up until closing time.

"The staggering was a fight we had for months," said Venegas. "That was probably one of the most stressful times in my life. We never got a day off. I think we all had nervous breakdowns."

Smith tried to slow down the crush by making the drinks more challenging. That didn't work either. "People were drinking anything. I'd be, like, 'We're going to put a bunch of Scotch drinks on this menu. That will slow it down a bit.' But, no." Sheehy reacted by quickly building out the space in back, called the Library, as a place drinkers could go if they didn't want to give up their place in the main bar on schedule.

"When they initially opened, it was bad for everybody," recalled Camper English. "Thanks to people like me who reported on it, they were crushed from the day they opened. They couldn't handle the speed. They did not keep up with the pace, and drinks would take forty minutes to get there, and people were really unhappy."

The press coverage remained constant. In a small bar where the tip pool at the end of the evening was fairly small, that was one of the biggest dividends for the bartenders. "It was the first time we were in the newspaper on a daily basis," said White. An older bartender remarked to White, "When I was tending bar, the only time a bartender got in the newspaper was if he got arrested."

A more personal sort of notoriety began when the first iPhone was released in 2007. One minute later, the cocktail photo was born, as people tried to capture the exquisitely crafted things they were drinking. "Nobody ever took a picture of a drink I made until Bourbon & Branch," said Santer. "And people religiously did that. I remember how exotic and weird that was. Why would they do that?"

The critical reaction to the bar was mixed. "The cocktails were good," recalled Michael Bauer, longtime restaurant critic at the *San Francisco Chronicle*. "I just found it a bit precious. To me, it just seemed like a rip-off of Milk & Honey."

English, then just embarked on a career as a cocktail journalist—a hitherto unknown profession—was more impressed. "I remember the first sip I had of what they call the house Gimlet," he recalled. "I thought it was so fantastic, I was transported. Todd took the drinks a step apart from the San Francisco style," which was always "garden in a glass."

Two of the popular early hits to emerge from the list, ironically, were created elsewhere. Smith invented the Cucumber Gimlet while at Cortez. And Santer sold the Revolver, his coffee liquor–tinged riff on a Manhattan, at Bruno's. The selling point for the latter, in Neyah White's view, was the flamed orange twist that finished it. "There are a million bourbon drinks," he argued. "Tia Maria? Who gives a shit? *Oh, it's on fire!?*"

Bartenders were also split on the place. Nearly every bartender of note worked there during its first year, and not all of them were impressed. "It was so obviously derivative of Milk & Honey," remembered Marco Dionysus, who put in a few Sunday shifts before the bar started closing on Sundays. "It was kind of gimmicky." Thad Vogler was similarly skeptical. Others were more eager to sign on: Owen Westman, an Australian from Melbourne, did his own version of Sam Ross's Milk & Honey pilgrimage by moving to the United States specifically to work at Bourbon & Branch.

Regardless of all the trouble it took to shift into gear, Bourbon & Branch was the train wreck onto which every other cocktail bar in San Francisco hitched its caboose. The drinking scene was never the same—and it would never be small again.

XXII. THE SCOLDS

ON BOTH U.S. COASTS, the period between 2005 and 2007 was a turning point in terms of cocktail service. Prior to 2005, the serious cocktail drinking community was small and largely knew what they wanted. After 2007, many more customers had been safely indoctrinated into the intricacies of ordering cocktails and the pleasures to be had therein. Between those two dates, however, New York and San Francisco bartenders butted heads with their benighted clientele, and it wasn't always pretty. The stubborn, beer-and-vodka-swilling populace was a bronco that needed to be busted, and the newly swell-headed mixology legions were happy to lay on the spurs.

Like its inspiration, Milk & Honey, Bourbon & Branch had a list of rules. And, like Milk & Honey, the bar posted them in earnest. The first was "Please Speak-Easy." Meaning: be quiet and respectful of what was going on behind the bar. If you weren't, you were shushed, in all seriousness. "I went twice," remembered bartender Scott Baird. "I got shushed the second time."

"Neyah and I were probably the most notorious," admitted Venegas. "The buzz in the bar would get loud, and Neyah and I would just stop what we're doing and go, 'Shhhhhhhh.' It began this thing where people would do it with us." Added Santer, "We were grumpy assholes for sure."

At Pegu Club, there was no shushing, but there was a sometimes adversarial relationship between the bartender and the customer nonetheless, usually resulting from someone ordering something that was pedestrian and off-menu. "We had a thing where we counted how many, 'I'm sorry we don't have that' in a row we could get," said Phil Ward. 'Friday night, three deep at the bar, you have no time, and someone would say 'I'll have a Captain and Coke.' 'We don't have Captain Morgan.' 'OK, just give me a Grey Goose and soda.' 'We don't have Grey Goose.' 'Give me a vodka and cranberry.' 'We don't have cranberry.' It would be up to five or six things."

Ward carried that attitude over to Death & Co, where he was the opening head bartender. One night, chef Philip Kirschen-Clark (who would end up creating food menus for more cocktail bars than any other New York chef) came in and ordered a Plymouth gin Negroni. "Phil looks at me and says, 'Nah, but I'll make you something a little better.' He was really rude. He made a Beefeater one on the rocks. The whole time I was watching him I thought, *This guy is really talented, but he's a fucking asshole.*"

At Drink in Boston, John Gertsen recalibrated patrons' habits by taking their go-to choices away. Not only was there no menu, but there were also no bottles on the backbar. "I don't want bottles behind me," he explained. "I don't want people coming in and saying, 'Oh yeah, there's my favorite brand.' I want it to be about the drink. I want it to be about the experience."

"More than most bars I've been to, they typified that reputation that bartenders would earn over the years of being grumpy and arrogant," observed Camper English of Bourbon & Branch. But he felt it was, at the time, justified and necessary. "People needed to be retrained. People always understood there's a difference between McDonald's and Chez Panisse. No one seemed to think that about bars. The fact that you couldn't get a Cosmopolitan at Bourbon & Branch was really offensive to a lot of people. To this day, people are offended by that. 'What? You don't have Bud Lite? This is the worst bar ever!'"

XXIII. THE JACK ROSE CLUB

BECAUSE THE BOSTON COCKTAIL SCENE was small, it was tight, and a bit incestuous. At one point, nearly all the important players Brother Cleve, Jackson Cannon, Misty Kalkofen—lived in a single house in Somerville, creating, for a time, what must be the densest concentration of mixology talent the cocktail renaissance has ever seen.

"That house was special, man," said Misty Kalkofen. "It was a lot of impromptu stuff. Jackson was still a musician at that time. Bands played in the house. There were a lot of times where Cleve would be coming home from doing a DJ gig at the same time Jackson and I were coming home from bartending, and Cleve would say, 'You want a cocktail?' Next thing you know it's six in the morning and you're still sitting at the kitchen table drinking Buds."

No city had a cooler cocktail godfather than Boston's Brother Cleve. He was born Robert Toomey and grew up in Medford, five miles northwest of downtown Boston. He did a couple of semesters at Berklee College of Music, but dropped out and went on the road as a musician in 1985 and stayed on it much of his life. The quasi-religious name by which everyone knows him came from the Church of the SubGenius, a parody religion founded in Dallas in the late '70s, which worshiped '50s-era square J. R. "Bob" Dobbs, "the world's greatest salesman." The name also derives from an L.A. radio show Toomey did for a time in which he assumed the character of Cleve, a cross between comedian Rudy Ray Moore and evangelist Jimmy Swaggart. Either way, it stuck, and it suited the hep cat who owned it.

Somehow, cocktails followed Cleve no matter what band he was playing in, be it the Del Fuegos or Combustible Edison. Or maybe Cleve followed cocktails. They were in his blood. His grandmother drank Manhattans, his aunt Ward Eights, his mom Daiquiris, his father Rob Roys. Everyone drank. His grandma gave him his first sip of a Manhattan when he was eight. The taste stayed with him. He ordered Manhattans at every bar he bellied up to, which, in the 1980s and 1990s, lent him a certain cachet and class. One such bar was Flat Top Johnny's in Cambridge, where Patrick Sullivan bartended. Sullivan would later remember the Manhattan-loving keyboard player.

Brother Cleve had his "cocktail revelation" in Cleveland in 1985, while on tour with the Del Fuegos. At Shorty's Diner, he picked up the menu and looked at the last page. "Why not try a refreshing cocktail?" it asked. There were a hundred choices.

"I was looking at it thinking, *I thought there were twenty cocktails. What the hell are the rest of these things?* I looked at my bass player and said, 'What the fuck is a Sidecar?'"

So the journey began. He began trying to reconstruct old cocktails at home. Tour dates brought further revelations. At an Italian restaurant in Columbus, a table tent read, "Try our famous Martini: Beefeater, dry vermouth, and orange bitters." Orange bitters? In L.A., in 1994, he met drinks enthusiast Ted Haigh. He went to Haigh's house, drank cocktails, smoked weed, and played Esquivel records.

By that time, he was in Combustible Edison (CE), an ironic, retro-hipster, lounge-music act. Founded in Providence, Rhode Island, and fronted by self-styled characters who called themselves The Millionaire and Lily Banquette, CE took its musical cues from Juan Garcia Esquivel, Martin Denny, and Henry Mancini and its drinking habits from the Rat Pack.

It was music as lifestyle, rebellious in its way as it thumbed its nose at slovenly, overly earnest Grunge slackers. CE was probably the most insistently cocktail-oriented pop group ever. The band had dapper groupies. It even had its own eponymous cocktail, a mix of Campari, lemon juice, and brandy, often set on fire. It was perfect for Cleve.

By the mid-'90s, Cleve was as well known in Boston for cocktail knowledge as he was for music. An article in the *Globe* called him "The Cocktail King of Boston." A year after serving Cleve a Manhattan, Patrick Sullivan showed up at one of Brother's DJ gigs. He had just bought the Windsor Tap, an old "beer and a beating" dive in Somerville. He wanted to turn it into a cocktail bar. Could Cleve help?

It was a risky endeavor. In the late 1990s, the only new bars opening in Boston were Irish pubs. But when the B-Side opened in December 1998, Cleve was behind the bar. The menu included just a few drinks: Martini, Manhattan, Stardust, Hemingway Daiquiri, Bobby Burns, Sidecar. But it filled a need. The place flooded with punk rockers, bike messengers, MIT and Harvard people, even some of the old dive customers. "It was busy," said Sullivan. "We were getting our asses handed to us on a nightly basis." They needed another bartender. Cleve said, "I know the girl."

Misty Kalkofen was an ex-Harvard divinity school student from Wisconsin who had taken a break from her studies to earn cash as a waitress. She knew Cleve from the clubs, and met him again at Lizard Lounge, where she quickly moved from server to bartender. Cleve presided over a weekly party called "Saturnalia," doing double duty DJ'ing and writing the cocktail menu. Cleve took her under his wing, schooling her during the off hours.

When B-Side opened, Kalkofen was in Key West, trying to earn money to pay off her student loans. She hated it. When Sullivan called her, she flew back on a Wednesday and was behind the bar at B-Side on Thursday. "Misty showed up wearing her Margaritaville apron," Sullivan remembered.

The B-Side became the place where the scattered cocktail nerds of Boston found each other. John Gertsen, a one-time would-be actor, was then a chef at Stan Frankenthaler's Salamander restaurant. Gertsen's order was Punt e Mes with grapefruit juice, a liquid dog whistle that got Kalkofen's attention. "You're one of only three people who drink out of this bottle," she said, meaning the then-obscure Italian vermouth, "so I'm going to talk to you now."

Kalkofen, who began dating Cannon while at B-Side, was the catalyst behind the Somerville house. Her landlord, who owned the house, liked her, so he asked her to find people for the upstairs apartment. She invited Cleve and his wife, Diane, who moved in in 1999. Both installed impressive bars, stocked with Havana Club rum, Amer Picon from France, and rare fernets. All their stocks combined, the house was the best bar in town. And it soon hosted the best party in town: the Jack Rose Society.

When Jackson Cannon was a dyslexic kid, struggling to read, his father read Hemingway's *The Sun Also Rises* to him. When they got to the part where Jake Barnes is drinking a Jack Rose, Jackson asked his father what that was. "I remember him saying he didn't really know," recalled Cannon. "'It's a classic cocktail. I think it has grenadine and apple brandy.'"

Years later, Cannon was trying to master the Jack Rose. It was 2004, and he saw the cocktail as the key to winning a position as bar manager at a sprawling new place near Fenway Park called Eastern Standard. (The bar was built on the bones of the gritty old Rathskeller, a famous venue known at "The Rat," where Cleve had played.) "I wanted to get the Jack Rose thing down," he recalled. "I had tried to make it. But we were using Rose's grenadine." One day he found a recipe for grenadine syrup in an old book, and realized it was made with pomegranate—a simple fact forgotten by most bartenders through decades of lapsed education. "The day I saw it, I just dropped the book." He began making his own grenadine syrup.

His plan was to bring the perfect Jack Rose to his Eastern Standard interview as a sort of signature drink for the place. One night, the house turned full-blown mixology lab. Jamie Bissonnette, who would become the opening chef at Eastern Standard, came over. "He and Misty and I got all our cocktail books together, which is a lot, and tried every recipe for the Jack Rose," said Cleve. "There were twenty-five or twenty-eight of them. And we made them all one night. Misty kept very copious notes on them all."

There was much disagreement, but the winning recipe (for Cannon, anyway) was 1½ ounces applejack, ¾ ounce lemon, ½ ounce grenadine. "At that point, we started the Jack Rose Society," said Cleve.

The society met several more times. On each occasion, they dusted off an old cocktail, testing every recipe for it they could find. One night it was a forgotten tiki classic, the Suffering Bastard. Another, it was the Ward Eight, the closest Boston comes to a famous hometown creation. ("We all basically agreed that the Ward Eight was a lousy drink," recalled Cleve.)

At one meeting, they were joined by a journalist from *Boston* magazine, who had gotten wind of the ritual. After the article came out, their cocktail clique was locally famous. "All of a sudden we're in magazines," recalled John Gertsen. "People are writing about us."

The Jack Rose Society did not last; when Misty and Jackson broke up, the group disbanded. But the Boston cocktail scene was off and running. Eastern Standard opened with six cocktails on the menu. It was twelve after a couple of months. Eventually, it grew to fifty drinks.

The place was huge and did great volume, yet the drinks rolled out fine-tuned and pristine. "I was in there with Audrey Saunders one day," said Liza Weisstuch, a Boston-based cocktail journalist, "and she said 'I have never seen bartenders do what they're doing at this scale, and with this consistency.' It was just packed all the time."

———

SADLY, FOR BEING THE NATION'S CAPITAL, Washington, DC, had very little in the way of a cocktail culture. It had no Cleve, no DeGroff, no nothing. It had only Todd Thrasher, who was doing many of the things that his brothers in arm garters were doing across the country, and often doing them earlier. But no one knew, for he was doing them across the Potomac, in Arlington and Alexandria, where nobody went except to retire for the evening. To a certain extent, people still don't go, even though his secreted, upstairs bar PX, which opened in 2005, ranks as one of the oldest serious cocktail bars in the United States.

"No one comes to my bar," said Thrasher. "I'm four miles outside Washington. It's forever."

Thrasher's interest in drinks came early. In 1991, when he was barely drinking age, he made the pilgrimage to the Rainbow Room to see DeGroff in action. He attended the first Tales of the Cocktail convention in New Orleans in 2002 just to check it out. Still, his ambitions never ranged far beyond northeastern Virginia. He was an Arlington boy, and today he still lives within a few miles of his childhood home. All his bars are in either Alexandria or Arlington. More than any other major figure in the cocktail world, he's a townie. But he's a townie who was pickling his own pearl onions for Gibsons, making his own tonic syrup with unrefined quinine for Gin & Tonics, and playing around with foam and smoke in cocktails long before most anyone.

"I was completely alone," he said. "There was no community. To this day there's still not a lot of community for me, because I'm here and they're there."

He had dropped out of college in 1991, and the Carlyle Grand Café provided his schooling thereafter. He made Kamikazes, Woo-woos, Shooters, Fuzzy Navels, and Martinis and flipped through the *Mr. Boston Official Bartender's Guide* he found behind the bar. In 1996, he wandered into Café Atlántico, run by an unknown chef named José Andrés. They composed a list of five Latin cocktails: Caipirihna, Caipiroska, Mojito, Pisco Sour, and Shoofly, a traditional Bolivian drink. "People ordered them all the time," Thrasher recalled. "It was insane."

In 1999, Michael Batterberry from *Food Arts* magazine dined there. He had cocktails with dinner, including the Nuevo Mojito, a mint-infused Bacardi Limon with a crown of mint-lemon-lime foam. "It was a cocktail that got mixed in your mouth," explained Thrasher. "He had two of them." A month later, *Food Arts* interviewed Thrasher and asked for a photograph of the cocktail for Batterberry's article. "That article had a profound effect on me. I thought, *Oh, I'm good at this*."

In 2002, he left Andres to open Restaurant Eve with chef Cathal Armstrong and his wife, Meshelle, in Alexandria. That hadn't been the plan. The plan was for Todd and his wife to sell their condo, get off the grid, and scuba dive for the rest of their lives. A previous partnership with a chef to open a restaurant had gone south, and bolting city life was the Thrasher reaction, along with growing a beard. But Armstrong asked for a little help with the wine list before Todd took the plunge. Thrasher said OK, but wanted no money. Then he helped with the cocktail list. Here, the house-made tonic came into play, and a Bloody Mary made with tomato water. Then he became general manager. Again, a critic, Tom Sietsema, came and spotlighted the cocktails, a thing that wasn't done. The Thrashers' condo didn't sell. He shaved off his beard. "Now we own five restaurants together."

The next was PX, Thrasher's showcase. The Armstrongs wanted to open a fish-and-chips place and were considering an old 1800s building in downtown Alexandria. The owners mentioned there was a second floor. "We walked upstairs and literally it looked like all the walls had been whitewashed by Mark Twain or something. Broken mirrors, old mirrors. It was an apartment, but it was also a booking parlor. The guy who owned it ran a card game for years." Later, Thrasher found out his dad used to play cards there.

The team stripped the walls and put in a bar and some furniture. Meshelle gave it a Victorian look. PX could have been written off as another Milk & Honey speakeasy knockoff, except that Thrasher had never seen Milk & Honey.

"Before we opened PX, I'd never been to a bar of that style," he said. "I had no idea what that style of bar was. The only idea I had was what my grandfather told me. He was from the Midwest, and he would go to Chicago and go to those types of bars."

———

THRASHER'S ONLY HOPE OF NOT toiling in cocktail isolation was a self-described "shiftless loser" named Derek Brown.

"I think my greatest ambition was to write an anarchist zine," Brown remembered.

Born in DC and raised in Maryland, he got a job at Rocky's Café to get through college. Then someone came in and asked for a Sazerac. "That's was the weirdest thing I'd ever heard in my life," recalled Brown. "I never heard a stranger thing come out of a person's mouth. They could have said 'Xanadu.' That started me on a weird search."

He read Williams Grimes's book and learned the history of the American bartender. He moved on to Palena and, armed with a killer Sazerac (made with Peychaud's smuggled in from New Orleans), convinced chef Frank Ruta to let him do a cocktail menu. Emboldened, he and a friend started a blog called "DC Drinks." But then he shifted to wine. In 2007, he became sommelier at the restaurant Komi, working with Johnny Monis. *Wine & Spirits* named him a rising sommelier.

One drunken night, Thrasher met Brown at a sort of wake for a wine retailer they both knew named Mike Tilch. They were both drinking absinthe that Tilch had smuggled in from Czechoslovakia.

"I said, 'Why aren't you doing cocktails anymore?!'" Thrasher recalled.

Brown's version: "Todd just kind of harangued me for being a sommelier."

So Brown changed. He opened the clandestine cocktail club Hummingbird to Mars. Rules, garters, carved ice, the works. Then Eric Hilton, a local restaurateur, asked Brown to open a cocktail bar with him. The Gibson, a speakeasy, became DC's first stand-alone craft cocktail bar. After a year, he was given the chance to open Passenger in 2009. Inside, as a bar within a bar, he created the Columbia Room, an intimate, ten-seat, seasonal, menu-less, reservation-only rectangle devoted to classics and interpretations thereof.

His brother, Tom Brown, who reigned over Passenger, couldn't have cared less. "He's older," said Derek. "He's that old school of bartender. He's the kind of curmudgeonly bartender you love. If you're a jerk, he's going to tell you off."

The Columbia Room was about as hoity-toity a cocktail joint as power-mad DC had seen. In the end, Brown overshadowed Thrasher's achievements, largely owing to his bars being in the District. When President Obama needed a mixologist for a few holiday events in 2009, he called Brown.

XXIV. THE ENTREPRENEURS

FOLLOWING THE SUCCESS OF MILK & HONEY, Sasha Petraske embarked on a business model he would adhere to for more than a decade: finding bartender-partners to open new bars at a rapid rate, with some of the proceeds funneled back to keep the ever-money-losing M&H afloat. His first such enterprise, opened in 2005, was the East Side Company, a narrow, low-ceilinged basement space a few blocks from M&H. The idea was a more consumer-friendly rendition of the speakeasy—Milk & Honey Lite. The venture went south quickly. "It was the same drinks, but with DJs; a semi-club," said Petraske. Few who worked there have anything good to say about the place, including Petraske, who split with his partners fairly soon after the place opened. The joint limped along until 2009.

Little Branch, which also opened in 2005, was ultimately the most lasting of the post-M&H projects. But its start was rocky. The space was Milk & Honey–improbable: an oddly shaped underground lair inside a narrow brick wedge of a building in the West Village. Petraske thought of it as "my last chance to open a bar in my neighborhood." The bar benefitted from the central location. It would become his most profitable tavern.

The building had been home to a bar that "was three kinds of illegal," said Joseph Schwartz, but it was getting shut down. A regular at Milk & Honey lived above it, and brought his landlord in to meet Petraske. Schwartz was invited to partner and run the place. Little Branch was still small, but bigger than Milk & Honey. It was designed to be more accessible. There was a doorman, and usually a line, but no reservation system. And there was an actual menu: short, sweet, but with choices.

M&H bartender Christy Pope had the genius idea of taking "bartender's choice"—a nonchoice choice that happened every night at M&H, placing the next drink in the bartender's hands—and putting it on the menu. A year later, every New York cocktail bar had a bartender's choice on its menu.

Aussie Sam Ross, still pining for a position at M&H, nonetheless accepted shifts at Little Branch, as did Michael McIlroy, an Irishman who, like Ross, moved to New York in 2004 on a wing and a prayer. ("I knocked on the door at Milk & Honey and said, 'Could I have a job?'" recalled McIlroy.) The two would in time become twins, the Mickey and Sammy Show, a couple of glad-handing, arrogant, likeable scamps, one of the tightest partnerships in the bar world.

Little Branch opened June 2, 2005. On July 27, it closed. A water main break had flooded the space, ruining the floor and the bar Petraske had built. It didn't reopen until December. The gap in activity didn't matter. There were still lines every night.

———

THROUGH 2006, THE COCKTAIL MOVEMENT in New York had largely been driven by bartenders: Dale DeGroff, Julie Reiner, Sasha Petraske, Audrey Saunders, the Employees Only boys. But after the opening of Pegu Club, that changed. Entrepreneurs lifted their noses from the tufted mint of their juleps and smelled money. In 2007, a failed artist, an heir to a mattress fortune, and a hot dog king would open, within weeks—and within blocks of one another—two East Village bars that would kick the cocktail boom into a high gear from which it would not decelerate.

Ravi DeRossi (born Ravi Lalchandani) grew up in Hell's Kitchen. His mother was Sicilian, his father Indian. The family moved to Boulder,

Colorado, when he was twelve. But, by his own account, Ravi was not a good kid, and he moved out when he was thirteen.

Eventually, under a pseudonym, he embarked on a full-time career as an artist, executing huge paintings. According to DeRossi, he found success overseas. "I was getting $20,000, $30,000, $40,000 a pop," he attested. "There was a lot of press. I never showed in this country. I showed all over Western Europe."

It all came crashing down in 2001. "I was living like a rock star," said DeRossi. "I had a show in Florence, and I knew I was going to sell out. I'd sold out so many shows in a row. I never knew how much money was coming in. I had this manager. He would pay some bills and give me an allowance." The Florence show was set for September 10. People put down deposits on every work. Then 9/11 happened. In the economic and travel downturn and uncertainty that swiftly followed, "Everybody backed out." Soon, his manager told him he was broke. (DeRossi is the only source to this part of his life, which, he says, is the way he likes it.)

DeRossi eventually returned to Boulder and helped out at a gourmet deli his mother and sister had opened. Ravi and his sister worked hard at the business. After two years, DeRossi had twenty-six employees. He sold the business for ten times the initial investment.

He moved back to New York. His initial plan was to produce a play he had written while in Boulder. But an investor bailed out, so he thought, "While I'm in New York City, let me just open up a little business so I'm not just spending all this money I just made."

DeRossi opened a small coffee bar and antique shop on East 7th Street. It was a tiny place, and quickly started bleeding money. So he applied for a wine license, and the Bourgeois Pig became a wine bar. One of his regulars was a slim, dark-haired young man named Dave Kaplan. He lived next door.

Kaplan and DeRossi had some common interests. Kaplan had trained as an artist in Rochester, New York. He'd done large-scale installation pieces in the vein of Damien Hirst (such as an elk's heart encased in resin). Also like DeRossi, Kaplan had some money to burn. Kaplan's family, on his father's side, had once owned the Sealy mattress company. He wanted to open a bar. While knowing nothing about the business, Kaplan had toyed around with cocktails. In Rochester, he'd put $20,000 down, bought a 1890s house, and built a bar in the front parlor. He had two different beers on tap, and tried to make every drink in the *Mr. Boston* manual.

Kaplan began to check out Milk & Honey, Flatiron Lounge, Pegu Club, and Angel's Share. He took DeRossi along.

"Dave comes to me and says, 'I want to open a bar, too,'" remembered DeRossi. "He was covered in tattoos. Young kid. Twenty-four. Loved him to death. I said, 'It takes money to open a bar. It's not going to be cheap.' He said, 'OK, no problem.'"

DeRossi wasn't exactly sold on the cocktail thing, but it was his nature to be swayed from passion to passion.

"I think Ravi likes everything," theorized Kaplan. "He's a sort of manic, excitable guy."

"I have a problem," admitted DeRossi. "I have a super obsessive-compulsive personality. I think it's showed in that I've opened fourteen bars."

DeRossi found a space on East 6th Street, an Indian restaurant with a liquor license. Kaplan came up with the grim name Death & Co. A girl-friend had given him a decoupage platter from the temperance movement illustrating the "Devil's Toboggan Ride." Beneath that were the words "Death & Co, Proprietors." Kaplan designed the place as well, going for a "sort of edgy New York feel," including dark-stained wood panels, antique mirrors, banquets, black granite tables, and a bar topped with white marble. A heavy wooden door marked by the smallest of signs led to a Milk & Honey–type curtain. It was a dark, slightly garish cave. Chill and cool, it oozed exclusivity.

Now the two just needed some people who knew how to make drinks.

———

AFTER TWO YEARS AT PEGU CLUB, everybody was ready to leave. Audrey Saunders had turned her drink slingers into the best cocktail bartenders in town. She was a great mentor, a frequent inspiration, but a severe taskmaster.

After Toby Maloney left, Phil Ward assumed the mantle of head bartender. His skills had grown immeasurably. He could turn out a good new cocktail with a flick of a mixing tin. But Pegu was the Saunders Show, and bartenders took a supporting role. Ward no longer saw himself that way.

"That was the weird thing," Ward recalled. "I was unhappy at the best bar in New York City. I really wanted to do something smaller and cocktall-centric. At Pegu, we made probably the best drinks in the city. But it just turned into mass transit. I was tired of it. It made me creatively crimped."

Ward wasn't alone. "We would stand around and smoke cigarettes and talk about how, on our own terms, we were all thinking of leaving at the same time," remembered Brian Miller. "It wasn't planned. It was kismet."

Opportunity came in the form a Craigslist want ad posted by David Kaplan. "I'd never met Phil," said Kaplan. "I didn't know any bartenders in the industry. Phil's an odd duck. He wrote, 'I've been head bartender at two of the city's leading cocktail bars. Let me know if you'd like to meet.' He didn't say the places. Very cryptic."

By both men's accounts, it was Ward who interviewed Kaplan. Kaplan gave him a questionnaire to fill out. At the end, it asked him to name as many bitters brands as he knew. "Nobody could name any bitters," said Kaplan. "Phil named at least fourteen. That kind of ended any questions I would ask him. And then Phil started asking me everything. 'What's your ice situation? What kind of glassware do you have?'"

"I went back and interviewed him like three times," recalled Ward. "I wanted to see if he was serious. It was a crazy decision. I was the head bartender at the most renowned bar in New York, and I'm going to go over here and take a chance on this goddamn bar? When I found out Dave was only twenty-five, I almost shit myself."

Seeking brothers in arms, Ward reached out to Miller, who was ready to jump. Not too long after, Jim Kearns followed. At Pegu, it was a mass exodus.

"We all gave notice at about the same time," said Miller. "And Audrey was pretty upset. She took it personally, and it wasn't personal. We were ready to move on."

"Oh my God, it kicked me," Saunders said. "How do you run a place with three bartenders going over to Death & Co?" A period ensued in which Saunders froze out Ward and Miller, refusing to speak to them. For Kaplan, whom she didn't know, she had no words.

"Audrey kind of had it in for me for years for 'taking' them," said Kaplan. "For years. She would say that to anyone: that I stole them, poached them, whatever. We had it out a few years ago at Tales. She made some comment to me at the Olde Absinthe House. I said, 'Audrey, really, you know this is clean. You know they answered an ad and they left of their own account.' She said, 'Let's take this outside.' I thought, *I'm going to get punched by Audrey Saunders. This is not going to go well for me.* We ended up having a very sweet, sobbing heart-to-heart."

"I don't think I was at all easy to work for at that time, those early years," admitted Saunders. "Having to launch this and having to teach and having to deal with the media. It was huge pressure on [my] shoulders. I wanted to change things. I wanted to change drinking history. This is the revolution. I knew that if we didn't do it right then people would be, 'Oh, it wasn't all that.'"

For years, Saunders refused to visit Death & Co. Reiner—Ward and Miller's other godmother—wasn't as rigid. But neither was she unaffected by the defection. The first time she saw Ward and Miller behind the bar at Death & Co, she burst into tears.

XXV. SOMEWHERE IN
EASTERN EUROPE

IN 2008, SIMON FORD CONVINCED Ann Rogers—founder of Tales
of the Cocktail, the annual cocktail convention held every summer in New
Orleans—that what Tales needed was an awards show that honored members of the industry. She called them the Spirited Awards. There were a
variety of award categories honoring cocktail bartenders, menus, and bars,
of both the domestic and international variety. The first ceremony was held
at the Harrah's casino. When it came time to name the recipient of Best
Cocktail Menu, the winner was a bar called Paparazzi.

Two months later, a package arrived in Bratislava, Slovakia, for Stanislav
Vadrna. Many weeks earlier, having read about the Spirited Awards online,
on a whim he had mailed the menu he created for Paparazzi to Rogers. He
didn't know his bar had won until he opened his mail.

"He was a man in the wilderness," said Eben Klemm, a lone soul collecting information about Dale DeGroff, about New York and London cocktail
trends, about anything he could lay his hands on. Of all the crucibles of the
cocktail revival the world over, the prize for obscure and improbable must
go to Vadrna, who created a destination cocktail bar in a country that was
just a few years old, and trained a group of bartenders who, in the 2010s,
would make an impact on the London cocktail world, and disseminate a
Japanese style of bartending all but unknown to Western bartenders.

He was born in Ternava, a city of four hundred thousand near the border with Hungary, then part of Czechoslovakia. By age six, he had decided to become an actor, but he also enjoyed studying the barmaids and waiters in the bars and trains he visited in the company of his libertine grandfather. To him, they, too, seemed like a kind of actor.

When his parents wouldn't back his acting dreams, he went to catering school, hoping to score a waiter job on the Orient Express. He bounced back to acting, performing naked, while working in pubs for money, and studying photography in art school.

In 1994, he saw the Tom Cruise film *Cocktail*, and his years of indecision ended. "It changed my life," he said. "If someone who is now around forty years old would say, 'Oh, fuck the *Cocktail* movie,' I will laugh in his face. I know there are thousands of bartenders who worked at TGI Fridays who were influenced by this movie."

The next day, he walked into the local pub he worked in, in the village of Zemné (population: two thousand-plus), and asked the boss to buy him a cocktail shaker.

In the late 1990s, there was a cocktail bar boom in Prague. Vadrna wanted to work at Tretter's New York Cocktail Bar. He had long dreadlocks at the time, and Tretter's was a formal place. What about the hair? asked the owner. He trimmed it back a bit. Every weekend, he took the train five hours to Prague to barback at Tretter's, and then went back to Slovakia, where he ran a restaurant during the week.

In 2002, he started at Paparazzi, first as a bartender, then head bartender, then bar manager. Czech bars at the time were influenced by Charles Schumann and his Munich cocktail bar, and Paparazzi followed suit, serving Daiquiris, Margaritas, Piña Coladas, and High Societys (gin, Campari, peach liqueur, and fresh pink grapefruit juice).

With every trip Vadrna took, Paparazzi's menu evolved. After a visit to London, he threw out the bar's thick glassware and simple garnishes, and incorporated tropical fruits imported from Holland. After a four-month stay in New York, during which he worked beside Eben Freeman at Lexington Bar & Books, he began making drinks using the fat-washing technique Freeman had taught him. Paparazzi's cocktail style became a mélange of London and New York.

When not traveling, he haunted Internet cafés. "I was interested not in what's going on in Europe, but what's going on in London and New York." He saw photos of Sasha Petraske, Gary Regan, and Albert Trummer and translated articles from English to Slovak.

His feverish pursuit of cocktail knowledge knew no bounds. He went to New York to attend Regan's "Cocktails in the Country" confab in 2005. After a night of drinking, he had a heart attack crossing a street in Times Square. He was sent to Bellevue. Because of his condition, doctors ordered him to postpone his flight back to Europe. But nothing kept him from going to Regan's upstate symposium. (He never told Regan what had happened, but he did write down Regan as his emergency contact at the hospital.)

Vadrna stayed at Paparazzi until 2009. During that time, he trained Marian Beke (who would work at Nightjar in London), Rastislav Cerven (Connaught Hotel), Wendy Stoklasovska (Connaught), and others. "All these people went through my hands," said Vadrna.

No trip Vadrna took, however, influenced him as much as the one to Tokyo. For ten days he studied Kazuo Uyeda, a Japanese bartender with a cult-like following. To Stanislav, it was "everything. I said to myself, *This is what I've been looking for for years*."

Vadrna became the conduit of the Japanese style. He shared it with Eben Freeman, who shared it with New York. The bartending community ate it up. But, perhaps inevitably, a lot was lost in translation, most significantly the misunderstood Japanese technique known as the "hard shake." An intricate, repetitive combination of horizontal and vertical moves, it was posited as a somehow better method of chilling and integrating ingredients.

"I don't think the guy from Japan ever said his shake was better," said Eben Klemm (who, unlike his fellow Eben, was not a believer). "He never said it was a superior shake, except that it was the show his customers liked. It was his interpreters who decided when he called it the hard shake it was better. He was the mysterious man from the Orient. Cocktail history had been covered in confusion for so long, when people discovered things they're so excited they want it to be true."

The obsession over Japanese bartending and the hard shake reached a crescendo in 2010, when cocktail book publisher Greg Boehm, who had visited Uyeda at his bar in Tokyo, flew the man to New York for a two-day symposium. The event was attended by nearly every bartender of note in New York, and some from outside the city, each paying $400 for the privilege, and many of them highly suspicious of their ticket's true worth.

Uyeda spoke next to no English. A translator was used, and some were offended by what they thought were Uyeda's condescending remarks.

"People got angry because he said 'Nobody can do the hard shake but me,'" said Boehm. "But what he was trying to say was, 'Based on the human anatomy, everyone is different. I can't do your shake. I can do my shake.' People took it to mean, 'I'm better.'"

Vadrna thought the event was a disaster. "It was the biggest mistake," he said. "You cannot train like that, with 150 people in the room. We are talking about skeptical bartenders. This is New York City."

Looking to dispel the mystique of the hard shake, Klemm, Dave Arnold, and Toby Cecchini staged an experiment at Pegu Club in which they shook cocktails in a variety of ways to see if technique made any difference. Their findings—that there was essentially no difference at all—were printed in the *New York Times* in an article Cecchini wrote. "That article made a lot of people upset," recalled Klemm.

"They made it an American- versus Japanese-style thing," said Sean Kenyon, who became the leading player in the Denver cocktail community, and was at the seminar. "I was really angry. I thought a lot of the comments by the American bartenders were in poor taste. He wasn't saying Japanese bartending was the right or only way. He was just expressing his way."

From Vadrna, Kenyon adopted the idea of the actual cocktail being a small part of the taste of the cocktail. "This was all Stanislav. Uyeda said the same."

Nonetheless, the Uyeda event exposed many American bartenders to a Japanese-style bartender first hand. Thanks to Boehm and Vadrna, some of the fog surrounding the style was dissipated, and mixologists had a new set of tools and techniques to draw on.

The year after Papparatri won its Spirited Award, the ceremony produced another surprise victor. The tiny Le Lion Bar de Paris in Hamburg, Germany, was named World's Best New Cocktail Bar. It was the creation of Jörg Meyer and Rainer Wendt. Meyer's influences were obvious. The first tiny Le Lion—secreted away on a second floor, with a low ceiling, seven barstools and operating without a license—was Hamburg's own Milk & Honey, which Meyer had learned about and studied on the Internet.

"I was digging everything in the New York and London cocktail scene," recalled Meyer. "But I mainly fell in love with a gentleman named Sasha Petraske. I fell in love with the way he did a bar: classy, not pretentious, quality, no PR, no bullshit, ice, good drinks, proper people, have to behave a little bit."

When Le Lion became too popular, Meyer moved it to a larger, legal space. The world found it. It was mentioned in *Australian Bartender* magazine. "Suddenly, we're on every list on the planet."

Its reputation was secured when Meyer created the Gin Basil Smash, a riff on Dale DeGroff's Whiskey Smash, which he had drunk at Pegu Club. "After a few weeks it was all over Germany," said Meyer, who has since seen it in France, Italy, Great Britain, Netherlands, Hong Kong, and Shanghai. Meyer knows on what side his bread is buttered. Today, the sign outside the bar reads, "The Cradle of the Gin Basil Smash."

Gin Basil Smash

JÖRG MEYER, 2008, Le Lion, Hamburg, Germany

Handful of basil leaves, plus more for garnish

2 ounces gin

1 ounce fresh lemon juice

¾ ounce simple syrup

Jörg Meyer, while creating a summer drinks menu, was inspired by Dale DeGroff's Whiskey Smash, which Meyer had drunk at Pegu Club. The smash category of drinks was unknown in Germany. He later wrote about the drink on his blog, and through that portal word of it spread. It has never gained much traction in the United States, however.

Muddle the handful of basil leaves at the bottom of a cocktail shaker. Add the other ingredients and ice. Shake vigorously until chilled. Double strain into an Old-Fashioned glass filled with ice. Garnish with the remaining basil leaves.

XXVI. THE GOLDEN ERA

AFTER BOURBON & BRANCH, there was no going back. The cocktail movement flowered in full in San Francisco, not just for the bartenders, but for the public and the media, too. New bars were wanted, and they came about. As ever, there was no one figurehead. "It was a lot of little leaders," said Paul Clarke. "It was more of a collegial thing. People all band together, whether it's Beretta or Smuggler's Cove or Heaven's Dog."

The late '00s were a time of intense creativity for bartenders. "This was the golden age," recalled Neyah White. "We could talk about what we wanted out of a drink instead of going, 'OK, what can I do with this product?' That was the big shift. Get an idea in your head, and shoot for it."

The California style still prevailed: fresh produce, squeezing citrus *à la minute*, adjusting each drink to taste. Perhaps no bar personified that style more than Cantina, which opened in 2007 and was run by a charismatic, garrulous one-time aspiring actor and playwright named Duggan McDonnell.

"He was one of the first startenders in San Francisco," recalled Camper English. "Duggan became famous at Frisson. He had a squid ink Martini on the menu, and it got press around the world."

At Frisson, McDonnell used essences, bitters, and syrups in his cocktails. "Really, I was just a year ahead of everybody," he said. The press paid attention, and he knew what to give them. "Being a writer, I hope I know how to give a good quote," he said.

He left Frisson in 2006 after two years, and after a while opened Cantina. "The concept was and is cocktails made in a very California, San-Francentric sort of way," he said. "What that means is using spirits that have a historical precedence here. That means Latin America, things that come from the Pacific: tequila, mezcal, pisco, to a certain extent rum, and spirits made in California. And that's what I stocked."

The opening cocktail list had a Pisco Punch, mezcal cocktails, and a five-spice Margarita with agave nectar. "I used to lived in North Beach," said McDonnell. "I walked into Chinatown. San Francisco is this culinary infusion of Latin America and Asia. That's what the five-spice Margarita is. It's really a product of its place. You couldn't think of it in Cleveland. This city was leading in terms of experimentation with agave cocktails, much before the rest of the country and the rest of the world. We didn't lead with gin or bourbon." He would go on to produce his own line of Piscos.

Dominic Venegas, who had worked at Bourbon & Branch, helped McDonnell open Cantina. Then he moved on to Range, a new restaurant run by husband-and-wife chefs Phil and Cameron West. It was a small place, but it won a Michelin star. And a long list of quality bartenders passed through it, including Brooke Arthur, Jon Santer, Neyah White, Ryan Fitzgerald, and a young Thomas Waugh, who had already put in time at Enrico's and the Starlight Room.

"The owners [of Range] were among the first in San Francisco who cared about having a good cocktail program," said Waugh. The bar offered a cocktail of the day, with a new potion invented every twenty-four hours. (Out of that experiment came the 1794, a Venegas drink made of rye, Campari, and sweet vermouth whose fame spread quickly until White figured out it had existed for nearly a century under the name Boulevardier.)

"The owner walks in with a bag of kumquats, so you made a drink with kumquats," recalled Arthur. "Regulars would come in just to have the cocktail of the day."

Neyah White—another Bourbon & Branch refugee who had been working in bars and restaurants since he was a teenager, managing places as
disparate as a Cheesecake Factory in DC and Bacar, where Venegas and
Fitzgerald worked—finally found a forum at Nopa, a large restaurant named
after its neighborhood that needed a bar manager. Jonny Raglin, who had
worked at Absinthe, had done the initial cocktail program.

"I thought I understood busy," said White. "This was the perfect syn-
ergy of a really tight ship, family owned, amazing food, and rock-and-roll
busy. It was everything I wanted."

White took over. He did the liquor ordering himself, and stopped buying what he felt he could make better himself: bitters, cassis, and other
liqueurs. During the Angostura shortage of 2009, when the vital bitters
were hard to find, White didn't have a problem. "Nobody could make a
Manhattan in San Francisco," he said. "I ran a Manhattan menu with eight
different versions, using my homemade bitters."

The restaurant was designed to be a place where people in the industry went to eat and drink. So White's work was noticed. For the Grilled
Peach Old-Fashioned, the fruit was muddled with rum and left in the
glass, with ice packed on top. He went through buckets of basil making
the Washhouse, the popular basil Gimlet, using only basil from a favorite
farmer. When that farmer didn't have basil, White didn't make the drink.
Very San Francisco.

White's principled creativity could be a bit priggish. "Somebody would
ask him 'How much Benedictine goes in this cocktail?'" recalled bartender
Daniel Shoemaker, who would open the Teardrop Lounge in Portland.
"And he'd say, 'As much as the cocktail wants.' And he meant it. That's how
he trained people."

Greg Lindgren saw what was going on around him. Enrico's was having
luck with Mojitos and other cocktails, so when he opened his third bar, Rye,
in late 2006 he decided to pull the trigger on craft cocktails.

Rye did well, but its true impact on the San Francisco bartending community came with its monthly Monday cocktail contest. Each bout centered on a specific ingredient, provided by a liquor sponsor. The winning cocktail won a place on the menu for a month. Thus the Rye menu ended up being an all-star list. Mixologists used the competition as a way to cut their teeth, try out new ideas, and just congregate.

"Some did it like training," remember Lindgren. "They did the contest for six months and never won. Then they went out and won every contest that had significance."

Waugh left Range to go to Alembic, a small bar in the then-uncharted Upper Haight territory run by bar manager Daniel Hyatt. Alembic's cocktails hewed to the classics, but Hyatt played around with molecular techniques; under the bar were whipped cream chargers and a vacuum sealer.

"He puts things together that I would never think to put together," said Scott Baird. "He'll stir a tequila drink with a vermouth and garnish it with a sliced radish. And it works beautifully."

"Alembic was fun," said Waugh. "It was stuff behind stuff behind stuff. You had to get the ladder out. It would get raucous in there."

Waugh was a Californian, the son of teetotalling Christians, and a fairly aimless soul until he fell into bartending. Despite this unprepossessing background, everyone who encountered him remembered him the same way.

"Cocky," said Venegas, who worked with him at Range. "He's always been ahead of the curve as far as what he wanted to do."

"Great palate, solid bartender," said Eric Adkins. "Definitely, I would say he was very New York."

And New York is where he went. In 2007, Daniel Hyatt got a call from Phil Ward at Death & Co. St. Germain liqueur was sponsoring a bartender exchange. Was he interested? Hyatt backed out at the last moment and sent Waugh. After the stint, David Kaplan asked Waugh if he wanted to come back. "It was a loose offer," said Waugh. "I took it as flattery." But he had been impressed by what he had seen in New York. "I thought it was way cooler than anything that was going on in San Francisco. People were doing their research and working harder. I went back to San Francisco wanting to wear a vest and a tie to work. I was fired up."

So when Ward, anxious to take a month off to vacation with his girl-friend, asked him to be there in two weeks, Waugh's heart started pounding. "Phil called me one day out of the blue and said, 'Do you really want to move to New York, or are you just flaky, San Francisco bullshit?'"

Waugh's move made sense to Camper English. "He was unhappy in San Francisco, and it showed," said English. "I could find a nicer way of saying this, but he was always complaining. When he left, he was up and coming. Then he went to New York and was instantly a superstar. The first time I saw him in New York, he was a super happy person."

He had reason to be. He was fresh blood in a city bursting with cocktail bars and hungry for new talent. Bar owners fought over him. "He was like LeBron James," recalled Brian Miller. "*Who's going to hire this guy?* He was new and fresh and had really good ideas. He looked at cocktails differently."

Venegas eventually moved to New York as well, which also gave him some perspective on the two cities' differences. "In New York, things got done faster," he said. "In San Francisco, people talk about it more before it gets done. Here, it's action. It happens. And there's a lot of respect for the classics. There was more of people coming in and saying, 'Can I get a Brooklyn cocktail? Can I get a Hanky Panky?' You can do that in San Francisco, but it's like, 'Oh, man, I have to look that up.' Here, everyone knows."

There's a different way of looking at that hidebound adherence to the cocktail canon, however, and English isn't as complimentary.

"Every drink requires adjusting to taste," he argued. "You can't just have a robot pour things out of bottles like you do in New York. You need to understand that limes change over the course of the day. Therefore, the drinks at the beginning of your shift have to be made differently than the drinks at the end of your shift, because the citrus keeps changing. It's a moving target. Everyone in San Francisco seemed to understand that, and no one in New York seemed to understand that."

XXVII. OLD HOTELS, NEW BLOOD

UNTIL DICK BRADSELL AND OLIVER PEYTON and the private after-hours clubs came along, London hotels had kept London cocktail culture alive, with Peter Dorelli holding up standards at the American Bar at the Savoy and Salvatore Calabrese gaining attention at a series of hotel bars, first at the Duke. It was classy and traditional, but also stale and utterly lacking in innovation.

After cocktail attitudes were shaken up by chic, stylish bars like the Atlantic Bar & Grill and LAB, London hoteliers had to change their ways. The success of the Met Bar in the Metropolitan Hotel showed what a trendy boîte could do for a lodging's reputation. And just as the old hotel bars had depended on the style and work habits of Italian immigrants, the new, reimagined hotel bars again turned to Europe for their staff.

Eric Lorincz was a Czech who had worked at the Greenwich Cocktail Bar in Prague and taken a master class with Stanislav Vadrna. After the Czech Republic admittance into the EU eliminated the need for a travel visa, he went to London and got a job at the Attica Club in SoHo. He took what he had learned on trips to Tokyo with Vadrna, studying the polished style of Japanese bartenders, and brought it to the Purple Bar, a tiny members-only place inside the Sanderson, a boutique hotel in the West End. After some effort, he found a big block of ice like those he had seen in Japan and began chipping away at it at the Purple. He worked with jiggers and three-piece cocktail shakers from Japan, aiming to make his cocktails taste the same every single time. *Class* publisher Simon Difford came in and was dumbfounded. Loricz was nominated for a Tales of the Cocktail Spirited Award in 2008.

Lorincz learned that the Connaught, a posh hotel in Mayfair, was closing down for refurbishment, and the new bar manager wanted him to be part of the new team. He was tempted, but wanted to work there only if the rest of the bartenders were as serious as he was. Agostino Perrone, too, had been approached. Perrone wasn't a hotel type; he had worked at LAB, and at Notting Hill's edgy Montgomery Place and Trailer Happiness. But it was a measure of the Connaught's commitment to upgrading their bar that they courted the Italian.

"At that time, the creative process in hotels was in a secondary position behind style, details, and a luxurious guest experience," said Perrone. "The Connaught wanted to inject the innovation of the global trend of cocktails as one of the main objectives of the Connaught Bar. They asked to have the world's best hotel bar." Once Perrone signed on, Lorincz followed.

The Connaught bar was covered in oak paneling and silver-leaf mirrors and hand-dyed leather by David Collins, who was famous for having designed Madonna's apartment. It reopened to the public in 2008.

The bar quickly became known for two signature drinks. The Bloody Mary required chiles from India and a celery foam. The Martini was prepared from a trolley that was wheeled from table to table—a nod to the Duke's famous Martini cart. But customers customized their drink by choosing from six different bitters. "I wanted to do the whole ritual," said Lorincz. "In Japan, they did the full ceremony, full on."

Young, trend-seeking Londoners were so set in their ideas of what a hotel bar was that it did not occur to them to be curious about the revamped Connaught. "For six months when we opened, no one even knew there was such a bar," said Lorincz. "They remembered an old bar with a fireplace, no music, grannies smoking cigars and drinking whiskeys."

But eventually the public noticed and the Connaught became chic. And it changed the perceptions of bartenders as well. The brash young mixologists, who had wanted nothing to do with the dusty ways of London hotel bars, now saw them as an option.

Alex Kratena was also a Czech. Seized with wanderlust, he worked in New York, Maryland, Barcelona, Tokyo, and Oslo before finally moving to London in 2007. He got a job at a French restaurant around the corner from the Langham Hotel on Regent Street. Soon he heard the hotel was looking for a senior bartender. The Langham's bar had been a sleepy place called the Checker Bar, a gentleman's club type establishment with leather chairs and a fireplace. Designer David Collins, the same Irishman who transformed the Connaught Bar, did away with that. The posh new Artesian Bar opened in 2008.

The Artesian took even longer than the Connaught to get noticed, though it would eventually throw shade on every other bar in London.

"Half of London thought the hotel was closed, because there's just a small entrance," recalled Kratena. The delay allowed him to focus, however, and take considerable time over each cocktail on the menu. The Artesian would ultimately become known for a kind of theatricality peculiar to London bartending, where every drink is accompanied by a show.

The Forever Young cocktail is a representative Artesian libation. It was created by Simone Carponale, an Italian recruited by Kratena. The cocktail, made of vodka, vermouth, eucalyptus, maraschino, and citrus, is served in a silver cup hidden behind a small mirror, and accessed through a straw that pierces the looking glass. One must constantly gaze at one's image in order to enjoy the drink. It was inspired partly by Oscar Wilde's *The Picture of Dorian Gray* and partly by the kind of people that patronize Artesian.

"Regent Street is a shopping street," said Carponale. "We look into the shopping window because we can see each other, like a mirror." As with many other Artesian cocktails, the staff collaborates far in advance of the menu release, with glass makers and other artisans commissioned to achieve the desired result.

Similar theatrics can be witnessed at Nightjar, an intensely self-serious, reservation-only cocktail bar in Shoreditch where drinks arrive in wooden boxes and owl-shaped pitchers, and drinkers are discouraged from distracting the bartenders. The bar's linchpin when it opened was Marian Beke, a Slovak who had worked with Perrone at Montgomery Place.

Lorincz eventually moved on from the Connaught to the most storied stage in London bartending, the American Bar at the Savoy. When it comes time to give out awards, the Artesian, American Bar, and Nightbar are regular recipients. Today, London bartenders joke about the Czech-Slovak mafia.

"I think some people thought we were controlling the jobs in some of the good bars," said Kratena. "I think Czech and Slovaks, generally, are hard workers. We don't tend to complain. We look for solutions."

Philip Duff noted that Erik and Marian had been feted bartenders in eastern Europe, but when they came to London, they took jobs as cleaners in nightclubs and worked their way up. "They're just hungry, is what it is."

And in today's cocktail world, filled with opportunities, new hungry workers are never in short supply. "I asked Alex who scares him," said Duff. "He said, 'The guys from Nepal. They're terrifying. They're going to run the Artesian in a few years.'"

XXVIII. DON'T CALL IT MOLECULAR

THERE IS NO QUICKER WAY to get someone on the wrong side of the craft cocktail movement than to bring up molecular mixology. The term inspires invective and mockery, from both those who practice it and the consumers and media who are skeptical of its value. Wrongly or rightly, it remains the most derided of the many cocktail trends of the last twenty years, the straw man of mixology detractors and the hot potato of mixology advocates. But it is also one of the most persistent of creative paths.

Its initial heyday was brief and intense. Improbably, it arose somewhat independently in several corners of the world, creating a crescendo big enough that in October 2005 cocktail consultant Philip Duff was able to put together a two-day molecular mixology summit in Paris. Invited were Tony Conigliaro and Wayne Collins of London; Eben Klemm, Audrey Saunders, and Eben Freeman of New York; Linden Pride of Sydney; and Colin Field of Paris, all of whom met with Hervé This, the chef who is considered the father of molecular gastronomy. (The event, held at the Ritz Hotel, was sponsored by Bols, the Dutch genever company for whom Duff worked.)

Among the drinks demonstrated was Freeman's Gin & Tonic, in which a canapé of Gin & Tonic–infused jelly was served on a sugared lime chip, fizzing with bicarbonate of soda and citric acid.

Duff made DVDs of the event and distributed them. One got into the hands of a Canadian named Jamie Boudreau.

Boudreau was a braggadocious sort with a mixed bag of a past. The product of teen parents who had split up, he was in and out of their custody and in and out of school for much of his youth and young adulthood. He was a theatre major for while, and he tried out for the 1996 beach volleyball Olympic team. He also threw dinner parties that were often more like cocktail parties. In 2006, he started a cocktail blog and made contact with Drinkboy founder Robert Hess and London bartender Tony Conigliaro. Molecular mixology seemed a good fit for Lumière, then quite possibly the most acclaimed restaurant in Canada; Boudreau was bar manager there.

"I realized it would bring in business," he said of molecular cocktails. His love affair with the approach, however, didn't last long. "While a lot of them, I maintain, were very good, a lot of them were technique driven. I quickly realized that the modernist technique is only good if they order a second one. If they don't have a second one, how good really is it?"

Linden Pride, too, eventually left the genre behind. "A lot of molecular technique back then was about turning liquids into nonliquids," he recalled. "And when you're out for a drink, you want a liquid. I didn't see the integrity in the molecular stuff. I found it gimmicky."

Pride thinks the movement, for all the heat it took, nonetheless had a positive legacy in terms of bartender prestige. "It's broadened the public's awareness of what cocktail culture is," he said. "The PR agencies would always latch on to this molecular thing. It was something to talk about. These bartenders were shooting forward in terms of their kudos. More and more people began talking about cocktails. It increased our audience. I think it attracted a lot more youngsters into the industry, made it more sexy."

The innovations didn't go away, either. Not every cocktail bar put a molecular drink on its menu. But a few bars built entirely around the concept arose and were of such quality that they stuck around. Their success was always owing to the passion of the true-believer founders at their center: Tony Congliaro of 69 Colebrooke Row in London, Dave Arnold of Booker

& Dax in New York City, and chef Grant Achatz and his various bartender lieutenants at Aviary in Chicago. None of these three men think of the other bars as being in the same category. But that's one of the two characteristics that bind the molecular artisans together: they don't like to be pigeonholed, and they all hate the term "molecular mixology."

———

THE COCKTAIL REVOLUTION BROUGHT SCIENCE to the coupe, where it had never found a footing before. But it didn't bring any scientists. Instead it brought a few spirited Mad Hobbyists Without Degree who advanced the cause through sheer curiosity and chutzpah, hacking away at any hint of a path through the woods of liquid knowledge.

"We don't have the Harold McGee of spirits," said Eben Klemm, naming the author of the seminal work *On Food and Cooking: The Science and Lore of the Kitchen*. "We don't know the chemistry of the things we're working with. We're making these crazy claims about products that are unverifiable. We need to study the basic science of ice, water, and alcohol. We need to find out what's going on. Dave Arnold began with shaking. It had been so fetishized. It was such bullshit."

Dave Arnold got a bachelor's degree in philosophy from Yale and an MFA in performance sculpture from Columbia. Proof of the latter focus can be found on the wall of Booker & Dax, his bar in the East Village, where he does not bartend but cooks up outlier techniques for those who do. On that wall is a giant blowup of a man shielding himself from a torrent of flame. The man is Arnold, and the photograph depicts a trial run of a performance piece he workshopped called St. George Fighting the Dragon. He was burned badly and went to the hospital. His wife nursed him for three weeks, and promised to leave him if he ever tried it again.

Arnold hasn't learned his lesson. One of the gizmos that Booker & Dax bartenders are required to use is a red-hot poker that looks like a fire iron that has been resting in the flames. They pick the long weapon up like a sword and insert it into a drink to heat it up. The poker, which he custom-made, was modeled after the hot irons early American innkeepers would stick into customers' cups to heat up their drinks. It all looks very dangerous and well beyond the regulations of the Department of Health. But it's the kind of thing Arnold does, the kind of thing that has made his reputation.

Other drinks are made with a roto evaparator, or rotovap, a device used to distill and extract flavors. His first rotovap was a used one he bought on eBay because the French Culinary Institute (FCI), where he was working, refused to invest in one. He got it to work somehow. "If I'm denied something, I go apeshit," he said. (The FCI finally gave him a new one because he was going to do a demonstration on TV.)

Arnold, though now well into middle age, is boyish looking, and there's a kid-like "why not?" enthusiasm in everything he does. There's also a craziness that makes you wonder if you're dealing with a charlatan. He'll put a penny on every railroad track just to see what happens. He once built a periscope for deep-fry camera work. He never used it, a fact that disappoints him. But through sheer perseverance and devil-may-care experimentation, he became the behind-the-scenes answer man for the cocktail world during the aughts.

In 1998, he and his wife lived in an illegal loft in a twenty-story building on 38th Street between Eighth and Ninth Avenues. He had rented it as a commercial space for a handbag company with his wife. But he knew they were also going to live there, and he convinced the landlord to put in a bathroom and shower, purportedly because he needed them to develop photographs. A bed was stowed in a space in back; the kitchen was enclosed in a four-foot-high cabinet. There was no heat, so he installed a gas burner. They wore parkas in the winter. Only one other person lived in the building. Hookers did tricks in the hall. There were drugs.

Arnold began messing around with kitchen equipment, at first in service of his art. He tried to make a puffing gun (an imposing metal contraption that makes cheese puffs or puffed cereal), and he took an old Blodgett confection oven and cut the sides out and pasted glass on it so he could shoot into it. The idea was to do the bombing of Nagasaki in gingerbread.

Once he realized no one was ever going to enter the loft, so long as he never answered the telephone or the door, he outfitted the space much like a commercial kitchen. He found a deli slicer on the street and fixed it. He went to restaurant auctions. He bought an espresso machine and a deep fryer. He got a two-door deli case for $60. "It was a life-changing moment," he recalled. He threw a party, for which he found he could fit two hams, a turkey, four cases of beer, four cases of seltzer, and a case of Champagne in the fridge with room to spare.

Eventually, he hatched the idea of forming a Museum of Food and Drink, and realized it was what he needed to devote himself to. He didn't have friends in the food industry, but his wife's sister, Maile Carpenter, did. (Carpenter would eventually become editor-in-chief of the *Food Network* magazine.) Through her, he met Dana Corwin, editor of *Food & Wine*, food writer Jeffrey Steingarten, and chef Wylie Dufresne, of WD-50 fame.

He started working at the FCI when writer Michael Batterberry, editor of *Food Arts*, told founder Dorothy Cann Hamilton to hire him. His function was amorphous. He was to come up with new ideas and then teach those ideas. His blog, *Cooking Issues*, was a record of those demonstrations.

Arnold's role in the cocktail world was equally difficult to define. When the Japanese hard shake method of mixing cocktails became a curiosity in the late '00s, he conducted a series of tests to see if the technique made any difference in the quality and coldness of drinks. (It didn't, he concluded.) And he takes some credit for making forced carbonation one of the popular tools now used by bartenders.

Arnold stayed a behind-the-scenes character—a kind of unseen Bond "Q" of the cocktail world—until he teamed up with restaurateur David Chang to open a bar at the back of Chang's Ssäm Bar in the East Village in

2012. Here he put into practice all his research. His intention had always been that every bizarre technique he cooked up should not just be intriguing or eye-catching, but actually improve and refine the quality of cocktails. At Booker & Dax, he was able to put them all to the test in a very public way. Some drinks were chilled on the spot with a shot of liquid nitrogen. Manhattans were premixed, diluted, and bottled, to eliminate variation and cut down on prep time.

"I don't think we should be in a business of pushing outside people's comfort zones here," he told the *New York Times* at the time. "I'm more interested in slam-dunk delicious. I want you to feel happy to be here. I don't want you to feel like a lab rat we're testing on."

Not many bars followed his example. It was just too much. Of the few cocktail dens that could be compared to Booker & Dax, there is 69 Colebrooke Row in north London, the cornerstone of Tony Conigliaro's lab-born liquid work. Though they couldn't be more different in terms of personality, Conigliaro and Arnold are often paired as twin totems of molecular cocktail wizardry. (If you were looking for a rotovap in the '00s, they were the two men to go to.)

"His approach is very different," said Arnold. "He's more a nuance and melody man. He's more a conductor. I've got a much more American attitude toward what I'm doing. I always joke with him he's too interested in subtleties. I want a hammer."

Unlike Arnold, Conigliaro has put in considerable hours behind the bar, initially under the wing of Dick Bradsell. Indeed, he is probably Bradsell's best-known protégé, though their approaches are poles apart.

"What he's done is beyond me," said Bradsell. "He didn't do all that stuff he does now when he worked for me. When I met Tony, he was working in a coffee shop."

Conigliaro's destiny found him earlier than he knew. Born and bred in London, he was sometimes babysat by the family of Fausto Dorelli, the brother of famed Savoy bartender Peter Dorelli. He studied art history, painting, photography, and the like, but became disillusioned with it, so he took a job cleaning glasses in a bar in the late 1990s. When the owner's girl-friend asked for a Park Avenue cocktail and Tony knew how to mix one, his boss put him behind the bar.

He first met Bradsell when the older man ordered a Margarita from him at Ricky Ticks, a bar Conigliaro worked at in Brighton. He knew of Bradsell's reputation, having frequented Fred's Club. Bradsell offered him a job at Match in SoHo. Thereafter he trailed Bradsell from consulting job to consulting job: Detroit, Hakkasan, the Lonsdale. "It was kind of like the Traveling Wilburys," Tony remembered. "We went from one bar to another. We just did openings for about two years."

He began to get attention on his own at Isola, a 2001 effort by Oliver Peyton modeled on New York's Four Seasons. "I wanted another advance-ment in cocktails, and I thought he would bring something fresh to it," explained Peyton. "He went to a lot of trouble in terms of the cocktails."

Yes, he did. "We literally lived in that place," said Conigliaro. "Oliver would have murdered us if he knew we were living downstairs. To get in the kitchen, we had to get there before the chefs arrived, to get the space we needed to make the ingredients. Sometimes we had to get there 5 or 6 in the morning, so it wasn't convenient to even go home. In the summer, there were times we slept in Hyde Park. We'd go under a tree, sleep for a few hours, and then go back. It was bonkers. We knew that this was our opportunity."

He created Bellinis of different flavors, which changed seasonally. He infused vermouth with truffles and employed a solera system, and he used the results to make a Martini. (Across the ocean around the same time, Albert Trummer was doing something similar at Town in New York.) The drink cost fourteen pounds, but Isola sold bucketloads of them. Simultaneously, he trolled bookshops for old cocktail books and began writ-ing for *Theme* magazine. While working at Roka, a Japanese restaurant in

London's Fitzrovia neighborhood, he began traveling to Japan and visiting the small bars there.

In 2009, he opened his own small bar, on a shoestring budget, in a corner ground-floor place on a side street in far-off Islington, where there was no cocktail action whatsoever. Upstairs was the Drink Factory, where he would develop the techniques and ingredients that would be incorporated into the cocktails. The shelves of the Factory are filled with things like botanicals sent from gin distillers, various teas, moss, clay, and beaver glands. A perfume library is kept for inspiration and scent reference points. Flowers are stored in the freezer. Some drinks are developed over a course of weeks; other take years.

Conigliaro is a patient man. He was the first to toy with aged cocktails, putting Manhattans and El Presidentes in glass vessels for years to see how they evolved. "I'd been trying to float this idea to my customers at Roka for years," he said. "And nobody paid a bit of attention to it. No one was interested. When we opened 69, the context was right for that. All of a sudden, all the stuff building up exploded." (Jeffrey Morganthaler, a Portland, Oregon, bartender, tasted one of Conigliaro's bottled cocktails while on a London visit. It inspired him to barrel-age Negronis and other drinks at Clyde Common, his Portland bar. The experiments proved wildly successful. They spawned a world-wide cottage industry of barrel-aged cocktails and forged Morganthaler's reputation as a bartender influencer virtually overnight.)

The lab and the bar were a study in contrasts. The Drink Factory looked just like what it was—a lab, with strange bottles and odd pieces of equipment in every corner. The bar, however, looked like a bar, and a very elegant, Jazz Age boîte at that. It is an expression of Conigliaro's artsy roots. If ever there were a cocktail bar that came close to functioning like an art gallery, it's 69 Colebrooke Row. Everything is curated, everything directed. With his slim build and dark, intense looks, Conigliaro even looks more like a gallery owner than a bartender.

A William Klein photo of two Italian baristas in Rome joking around with one another was his chief inspiration. "You knew these two guys. They would make you the best coffee, and they'd make it bloody fast, but also there'd be this level of cheekiness and banter. The place almost had to look like a stage set from a 1950s film noir. It was about people coming into a stage set and rather than the décor being the main feature, the customer was the main feature. You became the actor when you came in."

The original drink list was only twelve drinks long. Only the ingredients were listed. The upstairs experiments that had gone into the cocktails were kept upstairs. "We very rarely talked about the drink unless people asked us," said Conigliaro. And people didn't ask much.

———

EBEN FREEMAN HAD BEEN A BARTENDER longer than Sasha Petraske or Audrey Saunders or Julie Reiner or anyone who was becoming famous during the cocktail boom. And in 2007 (the same year PDT and Death & Co opened), he finally got his moment at a restaurant called Tailor. It wasn't a long moment, but it blazed brightly for a time.

Freeman had grown up on the Lower East Side, not far from Milk & Honey. Like Petraske, he was a true New Yorker: eccentric, opinionated, simultaneously idealistic and cynical. His mother, a writer, and father, a sculptor, had split. He went to NYU, hoping to make it as an actor, but didn't graduate, and he kept taking jobs in wine shops, restaurants, and bars, among then a West Indian restaurant in the West Village, an East Village dive bar, a department store restaurant, a Brooklyn beer bar, and the Spring Lounge in SoHo.

In 2002, he finally opened his own bar, with two of the owners of Spring Lounge. They called it the Collins Bar. It was on Eighth Avenue right in the thick of Hell's Kitchen. The space was a sketchy piece of property. It had been Little Annie's Full Moon Saloon, which the *Village Voice* had called "a pimp hangout so unsavory that even the most seasoned slumming debauchee dared not enter it." The sounds of porn seeped through the walls from the peep house next door. Eben came to know the various titles; he heard them several times a day.

Freeman gave the sliver of a place an art deco façade, a mid-century bar he found upstate, a great jukebox, a wide beer selection, and customer service out of keeping with the area. But it was a losing battle. He took a side job at Palladin to make ends meet, but he figured out that, under the terms of his agreement, it would take another five years to just pay back the investment. Eventually, his partners bought him out.

After he abandoned Collins Bar, he worked at Eleven Madison Park; Fanelli's, the timeless SoHo corner tavern; Red Cat, where the *Times* gave him his first mention in the press; and WD-50, the trail-blazing Lower East Side restaurant run by Dewey Dufresne and spotlighting the kitchen wizardry of his son, Wylie.

At WD-50, Eben began to find himself as a different sort of mixologist, collaborating with Dufresne and pastry chef Sam Mason on cocktail ideas that landed halfway between the backbar and the kitchen. (He had first met both men at Palladin.)

"I saw it as my job to adapt the language of the kitchen," said Freeman. The kitchen was known for molecular gastronomy. So whatever techniques were being used by Dufresne and Mason, he tried to find an application in cocktails, be it foams or carbonation or turning liquids into gels, powders, or papers.

"Eben is a bit of a chameleon in the best sense of the word," observed Jim Meehan, who counts Freeman as an early mentor. "When he goes to work for a chef, he's good about adopting their philosophy and cuisine."

For the Royal Blush, a Gimlet in which some cherry puree is floated on top, Freeman found that when he added Champagne, the drink changed from green to red. "Unintentionally, this became a molecular cocktail," he said. "That drink was huge. That drink made that restaurant a lot of money." The Pimm's Pony, a take on a Pimm's Cup, featured Pimm's, gin, and 7-Up in a short glass covered with cucumber foam.

"One of my first memorable cocktail experiences was at WD-50," recalled Philip Kirschen-Clark, who worked at the restaurant for a time. "I had a Violet Gin Fizz from him. I talked about that drink to anyone who would listen."

"They were delicious," Don Lee remembered. Freeman tested Lee on some drinks that never made it onto the menu. One technique that was sidelined was fat-washing, in which a liquid would be chilled with the fat of meat or butter. When the grease was later scraped away, the remaining liquid retained the fat's flavor. It was something Freeman picked up from Mason. "The idea of putting bacon fat into bourbon was born there," said Freeman, "but it wasn't something that I ever served." Lee ran with it, creating the Benton's Old-Fashioned and selling thousands of them at PDT.

Freeman remembers turning more to Mason for help in creating cocktails. "There is a natural affinity between the bar and the pastry arts," he said. "Sam was just a more open guy."

"My knowledge was based in flavor and manipulating flavor," said Mason. "He had this extreme knowledge of the cocktail world and what he wanted to do with it. He would just point me in a direction and I'd make it happen."

"That's where I really perfected my craft," said Freeman. "It's where I became the complete bartender."

When the restaurant opened, many of the critics praised the drink and dessert menus. Freeman remembers bartenders from Milk & Honey and other places hanging out at WD-50's bar to check out what he was up to.

"At first they were really happy with the attention that I received," said Freeman of the Dufresnes, "but later it became an issue." After three years, he left. The bar continued, run by a series of very capable and talented bartenders. But it never again enjoyed the attention it had under Freeman. "I've been surprised how little attention it's gotten since," said Dufresne shortly before WD-50 finally closed in 2014. "You're talking about an eight-year period where we didn't just stop making good drinks. But there wasn't much chatter about the cocktails."

Freeman worked at the Austrian restaurant Wallsé and Bar & Books on the Upper East Side, but kept in touch with Mason, who was putting together his own restaurant in SoHo. When Tailor was almost ready, he pulled Freeman in.

Freeman was given the downstairs bar. Whatever experiments he had tried at WD-50, he doubled down on at Tailor. The Bazooka, an infusion of bubble gum and vodka, mixed with a house sour mix, was made to taste like the gum it was named after. Fat-washing returned, and this time the drinks were put on the menu. When Mason considered making Sambuca gummy bears, Freeman convinced him to substitute absinthe. Like many of Tailor's cocktails, the gimmick quickly went viral in the Internet. The most popular drink, however, was The Waylon, a simple whiskey and Coke, in which Freeman took a smoking technique Mason was applying to ice cream and used it to smoke cola with cherry wood and alderwood. Freeman served the highball out of a soda gun.

"He definitely adulterated cocktails to the nth degree," recalled Mason. "It got even crazier at Tailor."

Bartender Alex Day began working at Tailor and Death & Co at the same time. He had two very different experiences.

"The expectation at Death & Co was get the drink right, do it fast, and don't watch Phil Ward, because he's sloppy, but he still makes better drinks than you," said Day. "At Tailor, Eben was very much into methodical technique. I think he realizes that some of the paths he has gone down don't necessarily result in the result he wanted. But the path down there is just as important. The time to do it is worth it intellectually."

The press, too, realized Freeman was doing something different from the purists at Pegu Club and Death & Co, and they ate it up. "It was extraordinary what happened and I still can't say that I understand it," said Freeman. "Chefs were coming in who were excited about a beverage director. I was in *Wired* and *Vibe* magazine—so far outside of my sphere. It was unreal. Part of that was that I was where I was at the time. I'm not going to say I didn't have talent, but if I hadn't had Sam with me at that time, I wouldn't have had those interesting ideas."

And this time, the chef didn't mind. "He was obviously who I wanted on that project," said Mason. "It was my restaurant. Any positive vibes were appreciated. I do find that a lot more people went to Tailor for the bar. If Tailor was a destination, it was for the bar. I would go down there, and some of the biggest mixologists were always hanging out."

The restaurant never achieved parity with the bar. The food got mixed reviews. Tailor's odd location on a side street and its difficult, bilevel floor plan exacerbated matters. Internet food coverage was in its early days, and the blogs tracked every misstep. Freeman left months before Tailor finally closed in late 2009.

Freeman went on to work as beverage director for chef Michael White's sprawling restaurant empire and then AvroKO, another big group. He hasn't suffered. But there's a general feeling that had Tailor endured, his position in the cocktail world would be more exalted. Instead, as the fates played out, he ended up playing Tesla to a group of more savvy Edisons.

"There are few people's menus that have made me as professionally envious as have his menus," said Eben Klemm. "He has done more great things than almost everybody. I believe he is the master of spectacular failures."

"I do not think he gets his due," said Day. "He knows that he is a smart guy, and put together some great things, and probably set the foundation for a lot of innovation, and Eben is not shy about saying that. And I think that can be a very off-putting thing in a culture that likes the 'bro' element of it all. There are plenty of examples around town of bartenders who really like their insular dude culture, and Eben doesn't really fit into that world, because he lives half in the kitchen and half in the bar and isn't afraid to say, 'You guys are fucking idiots. Be a professional.'"

GRANT ACHATZ GOT THE IDEA for Aviary in 2008, before 69 Colebrooke Row, Tailor, and Booker & Dax existed. But he and his anointed lieutenant, Craig Schoettler, spent years workshopping the cocktails with such scientific intensity that the bar (if you could call it that) didn't open in Chicago's Fulton River District neighborhood until spring 2011.

"El Bulli was doing some frozen and edible cocktails," said Achatz, mentioning his world-renowned temple of molecular gastronomy. "We wanted to blend technique modernity with tradition in a way we thought hadn't been done yet."

Achatz was an anomaly: a hotshot chef who was actually interested in cocktails rather than disdainful. He nurtured this attitude on his own, for certainly his mentor, Charlie Trotter, hadn't instilled in him a love of the bar.

"Several famous chefs banned bars in their restaurants," he said. "They made a strong statement that high-proof spirits dull the palate. 'They kill our food.' Trotter was very vocal about that in the early '90s. At the time, I bought into that philosophy."

From the start, Achatz didn't see Aviary as his entrée into the cocktail world, but as a drinking version of his restaurant Alinea. "We aligned ourselves with ourselves," he said. "You like Alinea, you're going to like this." Therefore, it made sense to put Schoettler, a cook at Alinea with no bartending experience, in charge of the program. Schoettler, unfamiliar with the cocktail canon, acquired his knowledge from the ground up, studying each classic, and injecting the tricks of the trade from the culinary world into mixology.

No Aviary drink was an easygoing affair. Custom glassware and gadgetry were commissioned for many of the creations, which arrived at the table like science projects, smoking and fizzing and taking unexpected forms. The Ooolong cocktail was served in a sort of coffee percolater. The mix of pear brandy, gin, water, citric acid, and sugar was heated up in a glass container filled with pistachio, applewood, Oolong tea, orange and lemon peel, and brown sugar. Thus briefly infused, the liquid flowed back down as a complete cocktail, tasting and smelling of potpourri. The drink Cranberry was composed of 1,500 quarter-inch frozen spheres of cranberry juice, icing down a blend of bourbon, ginger, orange, and chervil foam.

The ultimate Aviary cocktail was perhaps In the Rock, an Old-Fashioned suspended within a partially frozen orb of ice sitting in a rocks glass. The egg was pierced by a circular sling of sorts that was attached to the top of the glass. Pull back the ball bearing at the center and *crack!*—the cocktail flowed out into the glass, and what was once in the rock was now on the rocks. Moreover, all these drinks were experienced at the table; there was no bar to belly up to; the bartender stations, in a separate part of the room, resembled lab stations.

The mixology crowd in Chicago received Aviary rather coolly at first.

"There were mixed feelings about it," said Charles Joly, who would succeed Schoettler as head bartender at Aviary—and become famous for it. "You need to sit through the experience to understand it. I didn't go there that often. What made it not a bar is it lacked a sense of hospitality."

The drafting of Joly, Achatz admitted, altered Aviary's approach 180 degrees. "Charles is super spirit forward in his knowledge and a classic uber-professional bartender," he said. "We had to talk him into our world." The drinks were just as bizarre, but now they came with a bartender joke and a chat.

Barrel-Aged Negroni

JEFFREY MORGANTHALER, 2009, Clyde Common, Portland, Oregon

1 gallon gin, preferably Beefeater

1 gallon sweet vermouth, preferably Cinzano

1 gallon Campari

Orange twist, for garnish

An unusual modern classic, in that it's not the cocktail that's new, but the way it is made. Tony Conigliaro, the London bartender, was a pioneer in the process of aging cocktails when, in 2004, he started putting classic drinks in glass vessels to rest for years. But it was the brash Portland, Oregon, bartender Jeffrey Morganthaler who took the idea to the bank. Morganthaler tasted one of Conigiliaro's aged Manhattans at 69 Colebrooke Row in London. Being an impatient American, when he returned home, he instead put his cocktails in small barrels, which rushed the aging process. He tried everything from the Deshler to a Trident, but scored the biggest hit with an aged Negroni. Many followed his lead, and by 2010 barrel-aged cocktails were on menus all over the planet. Many think of the trend as pure gimmickry. But advocates say barrel-aged cocktails are more mellow and possess deeper flavor. The process works best on the Negroni, where it tames and integrates the various bontanical notes found in the gin, Campari, and sweet vermouth.

Combine the gin, vermouth, and Campari in a large foodsafe bucket. Funnel into a small oak barrel of roughly three gallons capacity. Seal. Let sit for seven weeks, periodically taste-testing the mixture after two weeks. Strain several times through cheesecloth to capture bits of wood and sediment. Store in a glass bottle. Pour three ounces into a rocks glass filled with one large ice cube. Garnish with the orange twist.

XXIX. BRINGING IT ALL HOME

IF YOUR AIM WAS TO HIDE your business from customers, you could scarcely have done better than the location LeNell Smothers chose for her wine and liquor store in 2003. It was nearly on the Brooklyn waterfront, at the end of Van Brunt Street, in remote Red Hook. To say the shop was isolated was putting it mildly.

But people found LeNell's anyway. Cocktail bartenders especially. For she crammed her shop with what they needed. All sorts of bourbon, including brands not distributed in New York; rye, when no one had rye, including Red Hook Rye, made from barrels she hand-selected during trips to Kentucky; amaros from Italy and cachaça from Brazil; the then-exotic gins Hendrick's, from Scotland, and Aviation, from Oregon. She flouted local liquor laws and carried Peychaud's and Underberg bitters (considered food products and therefore the stuff of grocery stores). When Bitter Truth bitters from Germany became available, she was the first to carry them.

St. John Frizell, just then getting into cocktails, moved to Red Hook in 2002. He had a copy of Charles H. Baker Jr.'s *The Gentleman's Companion* and was trying to create the cocktails in it. "All the stuff that he had in the book, she carried for some reason," he said. "I didn't realize how good I had it."

Don Lee got in the habit of renting Zip Cars, driving out to Red Hook, and loading up. "It was the mecca of cocktail stuff before anyone had anything," he said. "It was just a pain in the ass to get out to."

LeNell Smothers, a fiery Alabamian, knew what she was about. "With my Southern background, bourbon had to play a major role," she explained. "I also knew how hard it was to find many items if you were into classic cocktails."

Many of the things she had in stock were readily available, but most liquor stores just didn't bother with such esoteric stuff that didn't move quickly off the shelves.

"Other friends in the business were more worried about buying massive cases of Hennessy to get a good price," she said. "I was chasing down odd-ball cases of amaros, like Amaro Cora." (The closest San Francisco came to a LeNell's was John Walker & Co., which opened in 1933 and lasted until 2011. When bartender Dominic Venegas worked there as spirits buyer in the '00s, Walker became a destination shop for mixologists, the first place in town to carry new and rare spirits.)

LeNell's quickly developed a reputation as a destination store. By the end of 2005, the *New York Times* had written up the place several times. For the booze-conscious, it was instantly legendary, as was its owner, though often as much for her cantankerous personality as for her inventory.

Damon Boelte remembers walking in for the first time and seeing the Red Hook Rye, wrapped in tissue paper. "I wanted to see the bottle," he recalled. "I started taking the paper off. She said, 'Excuse me! What the hell do you think you're doing?!' I got yelled at by LeNell immediately." (Smothers later hired Boelte, who went on to design the cocktail programs at Brooklyn's Prime Meats and Grand Army.)

Getting upbraided by the proprietor became almost a rite of passage for the store's devotees.

"The first time, she ripped me apart and made me want to cry," said Eric Seed, the importer of rare elixirs. There to hawk his pine liqueur, he was berated by LeNell for selling his wares at Astor Wine & Spirits, a huge Manhattan shop. She raged, "They're the devil! They kill my business!"

Smothers's liquor store lasted a mere six years. When Red Hook's fortunes rose (partly due to businesses like hers), her landlord refused to renew her lease. But it had its impact. By the time it shuttered, other New York stores learned they had to carry what mixologists and mixology nerds wanted. You could buy rye anywhere.

"Anyone in the world where I go, I can tell them where I work as far as bars," said Boelte. "But when I tell them I worked at this place, LeNell's, the reaction is, 'Oh my God, you worked at LeNell's!'"

———

THE VOYAGE OF DISCOVERY for mixologists and cocktail enthusiasts in the early years of the drinks revival followed a pattern. You pick up a pre-Prohibition cocktail book in a used book store or on eBay. You page through it and alight upon an unfamiliar cocktail and decide to make it. Then you stop, because you can't make it. What is all this stuff? Orange bitters? Swedish punch? Forbidden Fruit? Old Tom gin? You call liquor stores. No one carries it. No one even knows what it is.

Post-Prohibition, many classic cocktails faded from the bartender's repertoire because the tools needed to make them were no long made or imported. Or, worse, the base spirits had been so degraded in both proof and recipe that the end result didn't come close to the taste of the original drink. Every young bartender trying to do the cocktail thing around 2000 was working with a half-empty toolbox. They wanted to make a Brooklyn cocktail but had no Amer Picon. They wanted to make Manhattans and Old-Fashioneds with decent rye, but there was little rye on the market. They wanted to make every drink that called for absinthe, but absinthe had been banned in the United States since 1915 (or so it was thought at the time). Headstrong mixologists don't like it when they can't get stuff.

"In the 1990s, we had these obsessions—orange bitters, crème de violette," said Martin Doudoroff. "Rye whiskey was an obsession. Absinthe.

The unobtainable was a big obsession." A few smart people listened and got the bartenders what they wanted, both boutique craft distillers and big booze concerns.

"When I first jumped into the game, in 2004, you'd see a backbar that was replications of the same stew," said rare spirits importer Eric Seed. "You'd see twenty-plus vodkas. Where you see gin, they're all London dry. To a big distributor, that's a screaming success. They've sold brands."

Eric Seed may be the most mild-mannered person in the cocktail industry. He is a soft-spoken, slightly built Midwesterner in a world of brassy characters. But there was nothing safe or boring about his business. Over the past decade, a visit by Seed to a cocktail bar was always an occasion. One never knew what arcane spirit he would pull from his bag. Would it be Allspice Dram or Velvet Falernum, potions that make certain tiki drinks possible? An unfamiliar aperitivo from Milan or Turin? An obscure line of vermouths from France's only appellation dedicated to vermouth?

Seed started off modestly, with an Alpine pine liqueur, a niche product if ever there was one. He had discovered the liqueur while studying in Austria and thought he could sell it among the ski towns of Colorado.

He went to Austria to find an example. He ended up bringing over a pine liqueur called Zirbenz that had been made for two centuries. In a nod to this early focus, he called his company Haus Alpenz. He could afford to buy only a pallet of sixty cases. None of the big distributors were interested, so he contracted a one-man wine outfit to distribute it. It was sold as an après ski tradition. The product struggled, but there were places where it did well.

Sean Kenyon, an early mixologist in Denver, took on Zirbenz at Steuben's, where he then worked. "I was like, 'Who is this bookworm?'" recalled Kenyon. "He has amazing things."

With the Alpine liqueur under his belt, he went to Of Grain & Grape, the best liquor store in Aspen, and asked them what they would be interested in carrying. This would become his modus operandi, the flip side of the usual importer/distributor pitch of "This is what we have. Will you take it?" Seed perceived a cocktail culture cropping up on the coasts and asked bartenders in San Francisco and New York what he should be importing or creating. Cocktail historian David Wondrich wanted a serious, funky Jamaican rum for punches. Bartender Jim Meehan asked for Batavia Arrack, a rum-like spirit from Indonesia, traditionally used in punches. Crème de violette, needed for Aviation cocktails, was a common demand.

Seed primarily brought in products that existed but weren't available in the United States. But some spirits and liqueurs no longer existed at all. They were just gone, and it was up to adventuresome distillers to haul them back from the grave. A few had the will, but not the know-how.

For that, they often turned to historian David Wondrich, who had the directions but couldn't drive the car. Tad Seestredt, an old friend of Wondrich's, had founded Ransom Wine and Spirits in Oregon. He wanted to make a gin. Wondrich advised him to instead make an Old Tom gin, a sweeter style of the spirit once popular in the nineteenth century and used for making the Martinez and Tom Collins. He did. They later collaborated on The Emerald, a whiskey made from an old Irish mashbill Wondrich had found.

Pierre Ferrand, a small cognac producer, consulted Wondrich in the making of a number of spirits, including a Cognac and curaçao in keeping with pre-Prohibition styles, and a pineapple rum, a spirit popular in England and the United States in the 1700s and 1800s. (Wondrich did not profit, except in terms of publicity, from the projects. "I don't want to be tied to them," he said. "I don't want responsibility. I did it for the PR and the fun, to get products I wouldn't otherwise be able to get.")

Wondrich didn't ask Rob Cooper to make an elderflower liqueur. No one did. In fact, nobody in twenty-first-century America felt the need for an elderflower liqueur. (Few outside Austrian Albert Trummer even knew what it was.) But that didn't stop Cooper from making what would become the breakout liqueur of the cocktail revival.

Cooper was a booze scion. His family owned the venerable Philadelphia-based Charles Jacquin et Cie liqueur company. (Their archaic Rock and Rye, filled with pickled fruit, could be spotted on a bottom shelf in some liquor shops.) He entered the company as a young man. During a 2001 trip to London, inspiration struck when he saw a bartender use some housemade elderflower syrup in a cocktail. The unusual, floral flavor was familiar to Europeans, but unknown to Americans. He began toying around with prototypes.

"My dad would come into the room and say, 'Are you still working on that flower shit?'" he recalled. When he had the formula and stylish, Art Deco packaging worked out, his dad was still uninterested, so Rob asked to leave the company. "He said, 'I'll hire you back in a year when you fail.'"

St. Germain was launched in 2007, the year Death & Co and PDT opened in New York. "It was lucky timing," admitted Cooper. "They wanted something different they could work with that had integrity." He went down to Tales of the Cocktail and hawked his invention in the lobby of the Hotel Monteleone, further spreading the word. He also helped pioneer a new sort of carnival-esque direct marketing to bartenders.

"We were in lockstep with the bartender, trying to do crazy creative things that are a dime a dozen today," Cooper said, "like taking a bunch of bartenders out to Montauk for the night, or doing events where we'd get a bus and give people flasks of St. Germain cocktails." He also hired a couple of well-known bartenders as brand ambassadors.

Within a year or two, St. Germain was everywhere, on every important backbar and seemingly in every other cocktail. It was used so widely that people began to refer to it, somewhat derisively, as "bartender's ketchup."

Cooper went on to introduce other needed bar liqueurs like Crème Yvette, a proprietary violet liqueur, and Slow and Low, a form of the ubiquitous nineteenth-century tipple Rock and Rye. None reached the heights of St. Germain (which he eventually sold to Bacardi for what was rumored to be seven figures).

What Seed didn't import, and distillers like Cooper didn't make, other freelance fanatics took care of. Bitters was a nearly extinct category. There had once been hundreds of brands. That was now down to two, Angostura (needed for Old-Fashioneds and Manhattans) and Peychaud's (for Sazeracs). Bitters were critical to the creation of cocktails; they were, after all, what made cocktails *cocktails*, according to the first printed definition of the term. Most vexing was the absence of orange bitters, which were called for in many pre-Prohibition drinks, including the Martini. A few sleuths had found out that Fee Brothers in Rochester still made a version.

Writer Gary Regan did not know about Fee's. So he opened Jerry Thomas's nineteenth-century cocktail book and followed the recipe found there. "I made that," he recalled. "I wasn't real happy. I kept playing with the formula." He supplied Dale DeGroff at the Rainbow Room with the potion he finally settled on. Later, he contacted the Sazerac Company, which made Peychaud's, about bottling the bitters commercially. Regan's orange bitters debuted in 2005. Bartenders snatched it up, effectively making Regan a household name in bars across the United States.

Regan soon had competition. By 2010, bitters had become a cottage industry, taken up by every cocktail fancier who wanted to get in the game. Because they required no still, they became "the vodka of the craft cocktail world," in David Wondrich's words, because "anyone can make them." Bitters brands sprang up like so many hot sauces: Bitter End, Bittermens, Berg & Hauck, Bittercube, Hella Bitters, Miracle Mile. DeGroff came out with a signature bitters. The mighty giant Angostura was stirred out of its slumber long enough to put out its own orange bitters. Darcy O'Neill, a bartender and chemist in Canada, recreated Abbott's bitters, a once-famous brand. A distiller in California created a rival version. The new flavors were all over the place: hopped grapefruit, lavender, celery, rhubarb, spiced chocolate. Within a few years' time, bartenders who had been bitters-starved were forced to reserve a fair amount of bartop real estate to the tiny bottles.

The holy grail of lost cocktail ingredients, however, was absinthe. "The green fairy" had a twin reputation, one part romantic, one part dangerous, both parts tantalizing. The high-proof herbal liqueur had been the preferred drink of beau monde France, depicted in paintings by Degas and Picasso. But it was also characterized, in an effective smear campaign by French wine makers, as the devil in a bottle, a drink that ruined lives and drove men to madness. It was effectively banned in the United States in 1915, and those who loved their absinthe frappes or Sazeracs (many of them living in New Orleans) had to resort to anise-flavored substitutes like Herbsaint.

Gone for nearly a century, absinthe cast a magical spell over the cocktail-minded, including one curious research scientist in the Louisiana petroleum industry. In 1993, Ted Breaux heard a lab colleague refer to it as "that green liqueur that made people crazy." He was intrigued. He bought Barnaby Conrad III's book *Absinthe* and read it three times, even going so far as to contact the author.

He tried to distill his own. But then he got his hands on two bottles of vintage, unopened absinthe. "These were the Rosetta stones," he recalled. "I tasted them. *OK, this is a lot better than what I'm doing.*"

The knock against absinthe was always that it contained thujone, a chemical compound found in many plants, which led to hallucinations and violent behavior. Breaux had the tools to analyze this widely held assumption. Breaux found nothing poisonous in the absinthe he had. He sent it to a third-party lab; they also found nothing.

"There's nothing wrong with this stuff at all," Breaux concluded. "This is all socio-economic-political bullshit." In 2008, he coauthored a couple of scientific studies, maintaining that absinthe was not hallucinogenic.

"I came at this from a very oblique angle," recalled Breaux. "I was not in the cocktail world at all. This was about absinthe and chemistry and history. It seemed there was an injustice, and I wanted to set that record straight."

The next step in Breaux's obsession was to make an absinthe. Since it was still forbidden in America, he went to France to the Combier distillery, which had been designed by Alexandre Gustav Eiffel. "It's like Captain Nemo walking into the Nautilus," he said of the place. In 2004, he began producing Jade Nouveau Orleans. Amounts were small, a couple thousand cases a year, and sold mainly online.

An article about Breaux in *New York* magazine brought him to the attention of Viridian Spirits, who asked him to collaborate on an absinthe. With Viridian's legal resources and Breaux's science, they were able to finally beat down the long-standing U.S. ban in March 2007. (It turned out the spirit had actually been technically legal for years, if it was produced with an acceptably low thujone level.) Viridian and Breaux's Lucid became the first-mass market new brand of absinthe in the United States in a century. Dozens of other new labels followed. Mixologists were ecstatic.

"In the 1930 *Savoy Cocktail Book*, there were more than a hundred cocktails that called for it," noted Breaux. "That was a big get."

Some overestimated the appeal of the newly available elixir. Sasha Petraske opened a dedicated absinthe bar called White Star on the Lower East Side. It folded quickly. Absinthe was too singular a spirit to ever again become as popular as it had been in late-nineteenth-century France. But it did take a place of honor on the backbar at cocktail dens and did not relinquish it.

As the cocktail tide rose, some bartenders tired of waiting for microdistillers to create the products they wanted, or for megadistillers to bring back the ones that had been discontinued. Instead, they went into the distilling business themselves. One of the first was Ryan Magarian, a bartender and cocktail consultant in the Pacific Northwest.

In 2005, he met Christian Krogstad, who had just founded House Spirits in Oregon. They decided to collaborate on a new gin that would appeal to bartenders. At a time when new gins were about as common as

California condors, Aviation gin caught bartenders' attention. "I feel what we did with Aviation was create the template [for a bartender crossing over into the distilling business], which a lot of people followed," said Magarian. Mixologists who followed Margarian's example included Chicago bartender Adam Seger, Southern Wine & Spirits rep Allen Katz, Leeds bartender Jake Burger, and Dushan Zaric and Jason Kosmas of Employees Only.

SOME BARTENDERS AND COCKTAIL MAVENS were too ambitious to be contained by the creation of a single bottling. They resolved to stump not for just one brand of a spirit, but for a whole spirit category.

The aborning mixologists of the late '90s and early '00s entered a world where only a few spirits enjoyed widespread acceptance. Vodka was king. Scotch was esteemed. But bourbon was underestimated; gin old-fashioned. Cognac was associated with gentlemen's clubs on one hand, and hip-hop circles on the other. Tequila was viewed with near contempt as a destructive rotgut, and mezcal and rye were a mystery. Each had to be resurrected and restored to constructive use—and each was.

Gin was the first neglected spirit to be dusted off and honored. The Martini fad of the 1990s had prolonged the notion that vodka Martinis were OK. Gin evangelists like Audrey Saunders made it clear that was *not* cool. (Indeed, simply calling a vodka Martini a Martini was not cool.) And the return from oblivion of drinks like the Last Word, Aviation, Pegu Club, Negroni, and many more made gin a vital player again. Large distillers responded by giving their venerable old brands (Beefeater, Plymouth, and so on) a makeover. Small distillers responded by flooding the market with new gins within a matter of a few years.

Gin, at least, had plenty of brands out there that needed but to be dis-covered again. When rye fell out of favor after Prohibition, the spirit all but up and died. There were very few straight ryes left—Jim Beam, Wild

Turkey, Old Overholt—should anyone care to find them. Most American whiskey distillers devoted one day a year to distilling rye, if that. There was no money in it.

"I was always trying to promote rye," said David Wondrich. "It was a lost cause for years." He knew Heaven Hill, a Kentucky distiller, made a bonded rye called Rittenhouse, the name being an old Pennsylvania brand. He called the distiller and said that, if they shipped a couple of cases, he could get it carried in a Brooklyn bar where he handled the cocktail list.

Slowly, Kentucky began to catch on. Wild Turkey and Beam began to release new rye bottlings. And new craft distillers and nondistilling producers (who bought whiskey made by others and bottled it under their own name) started to release ryes before they even thought of a bourbon. From 2009 to 2014, rye sales increased by more than 500 percent.

Like rye, tequila had a reputation as a wicked spirit, the kind that got you drunk in a way that was somehow worse than the drunk you got from other spirits. It was the drink of green and immature college kids, a dare drink that was commonly ingested through an adolescent ritual involving salt and a lime wedge. No one thought of it as artisanal, as the product born of long traditions and skilled labor, as something you might sip and savor. And no one thought of it as a cocktail base outside of the ubiquitous Margarita, most of those consumed frozen.

Julio Bermejo in San Francisco and Tomas Estes had done their part to open bartenders' eyes to the allure and artistry of tequila at their separate perches in San Francisco and London. Henry Bessant, the cocktail consultant, also played a role in turning young bartenders on to tequila. And a few bars and restaurants, such as Green and Red in London, Tres Agaves in San Francisco, and Mayahuel in New York, offered extensive tequila lists.

Mayahuel, co-owned by Phil Ward, opened in April 2009. Among the bottles on the backbar were the entire line of Del Maguay single-village mezcals. It wasn't difficult for any bartender interested in mezcal to learn more about the spirit; you just had to know Ron Cooper, the creator of the Del Maguay line.

Cooper was an artist who lived in New Mexico. In 1990, he began an art project that involved creating fifty blue bottles and then filling them with different mezcals. He went to Oaxaca and began visiting farmers making small productions of mezcals in a painstaking, old-fashioned way, with horse-drawn mills. It was stuff that never left the immediate vicinity. The mezcals were better than any he had ever tasted before. As a side mission, he decided to bring a few of them into the United States. He started with Chichicapa and San Luis del Rio, named after the Oaxacan villages where they were made.

Soon, he connected with Steve Olson, a sommelier with plenty of restaurant and bar experience and lots of connections. The liquid impressed; it was strikingly different from the rotgot-with-the-worm-inside spirit that most bartenders knew. Slowly, the mezcals—expensive and in limited supply—were placed in select bars. Mixologists found them useful as a way to introduce a smoky note into a cocktail, rendering the flavor more complex. But many just preferred to drink it straight. By 2010, mezcal had taken its place next to rye as one of the cool, obscure spirits favored by bartenders and dedicated drinkers.

À *La Louisiane*

Classic

¾ ounce rye

¾ ounce Benedictine

¾ ounce sweet
vermouth

3 dashes absinthe

3 dashes Peychaud's
bitters

Cherry, for garnish

A cocktail created at the New Orleans Restaurant de la Louisiane, it is a blend of rye, sweet vermouth, Benedictine, Peychaud's bitters, and absinthe. Following the nationwide adoption of better-known New Orleans drinks like the Sazerac and Ramos Gin Fizz, more obscure cocktails from the city's past like this one rode on their coattails. The cocktail was discovered by most bartenders in the 1938 volume *Famous New Orleans Drinks and How to Mix 'Em*; some increase the amount of rye.

Combine all the ingredients except the cherry in a mixing glass three-quarters filled with ice. Stir until chilled. Strain into a chilled coupe glass. Garnish with the cherry.

Aviation

Classic

---

2 ounces gin

¾ ounce fresh
lemon juice

½ ounce maraschino
liqueur

Barspoon of crème
de violette or Crème
Yvette

A pre-Prohibition gin drink reclaimed by gin-mad
bartenders in the early years of the renaissance, and an
early calling-card cocktail for the in-the-know crowd. Its
supporters love it madly. Its detractors claim its pivotal
ingredient—crème de violette—causes it to taste of
hand soap.

Combine all the ingredients in cocktail shaker three-
quarters filled with ice. Shake until chilled. Strain into
a coupe glass.

Boulevardier

Classic

---

1 ounce bourbon

1 ounce sweet vermouth

1 ounce Campari

Orange peel, for garnish

A variation on the Negroni that calls for whiskey instead of gin, this drink dates to the 1920s, when it was listed as but a footnote in Harry McElhone's *Barflies and Cocktails*, and credited to Erskine Gwynne, an expatriate writer and socialite who founded a magazine by the same name. As the Negroni grew in popularity in the '00s, the Boulevardier naturally followed it, finding a particular champion in bartender Toby Cecchini.

Combine all the ingredients except the orange peel in a mixing glass three-quarters filled with ice. Stir until chilled. Strain into a coupe glass. Garnish with the orange peel.

Hanky Panky

Classic

1½ ounces gin

1½ ounces sweet vermouth

2 dashes Fernet Branca

Orange twist, for garnish

This creation of Ada Coleman, who tended bar at London's Savoy Hotel in the early 1900s, became a darling of young mixologists owing to its early and unusual use of Fernet Branca.

Combine all the ingredients except the orange twist in a mixing glass three-quarters filled with ice. Stir until chilled. Strain into a chilled coupe glass. Garnish with the orange twist.

New York Sour

Classic

---

2 ounces rye

1 ounce fresh lemon juice

¾ ounce simple syrup

½ ounce red wine

Simply a Whiskey Sour with a float of red wine on top, this previously little-known, nineteenth-century drink has been championed by several prominent mixologists, including Julie Reiner.

Combine all the ingredients except the wine in a cocktail shaker three-quarters filled with ice. Shake until chilled. Strain into an Old-Fashioned glass filled with ice. Carefully pour the wine over the back of the barspoon so it floats on top of the drink.

Remember the Maine

Classic

---

2 ounces rye

¾ ounce sweet vermouth

¼ ounce Cherry Heering

½ barspoon absinthe

Cherry, for garnish

A creation of mid-twentieth-century cocktail writer Charles Baker Jr., whose reputation was revived largely through the efforts of bartender-historian St. John Frizell, this is basically a Manhattan laced with Cherry Heering and absinthe.

Combine all the ingredients except the cherry in a mixing glass three-quarters filled with ice. Stir until chilled. Strain into a chilled cocktail glass. Garnish with the cherry.

Vieux Carre

Classic

¾ ounce rye

¾ ounce Cognac

¾ ounce sweet vermouth

1 barspoon Benedictine

2 dashes Peychaud's bitters

2 dashes Angostura bitters

The cocktail revival has been very good for the reputation of lost New Orleans drinks, particularly the brown and boozy ones. This one was created at the Hotel Monteleone's Carousel Bar, and varies only slightly from the À La Louisiane.

Combine all the ingredients in a mixing glass three-quarters filled with ice. Stir until chilled. Strain into a chilled Old-Fashioned glass filled with ice.

XXX. TAKING BACK TIKI

RUM ARGUABLY TOOK THE LONGEST to emerge from the drinking shadows. It had been America's first unofficial national spirit, but it hadn't enjoyed a place of honor in U.S. drinking habits since the demise of tiki bar culture. Wayne Curtis's seminal history, *And a Bottle of Rum,* spurred new interest in the spirit. And advocates like Ed Hamilton—who spent twenty years sailing around the Caribbean, learning about every rum made on the islands, before he began importing his first bottles—certainly helped the cause. But before mixologists were going to warm up to rum, tiki's reputation had to be repaired.

"Craft cocktail people in 2002, 2004 didn't want to touch tiki with a ten-foot pole," said Jeff Berry. "It was the worst thing you could do if you're trying to do the lost art of the cocktail and present it to customers as worth their time. They don't want any slushy drinks on their menu."

Jeff Berry reversed that bias. If it took an army of amateur historians and professional bartenders to bring pre-Prohibition cocktail styles back from the dead, the return of tiki can largely be credited to this single, dogged, quasi-masochistic individual. Without Jeff Berry's diligence in tracking down former barkeeps from Trader Vic's and Don the Beachcomber and prying from them the drink recipes secreted in their brains, the tiki revival that began in the late 2000s simply wouldn't have occurred.

Beginning in 1998 with a volume called *Beachbum Berry's Grog Log*—published by Slave Labor Graphics and available mainly in comic book stores—Berry has steadily produced a modern library of tiki scholarship, with titles like *Intoxica!* and *Sippin' Safari*. His canon culminated in 2013 in the coffee table–worthy *Potions of the Caribbean* (his only hardcover release to date).

Like the warm-climate drinking fantasy he inhabits, Berry is a product of Hollywood. His father and mother, both Jewish, were from the Bronx and Brooklyn, respectively, but in the late 1960s they moved to California, where Berry was raised mainly in the San Fernando Valley.

"The food of my people was Chinese food," he said. "In the mid-'60s, the tiki craze had peaked at such a point that regular old-school Cantonese restaurants figured out that they were already serving Polynesian food, which is just Chinese food under different names. All they had to do to cash in on the trend was to retrofit their restaurants with décor."

When he was eight, his folks took him to Ah Fong's, a joint owned by Benson Fong, who played the "Number Three Son" in the Charlie Chan film series of the 1940s. The people around him were drinking flaming punches and sipping Navy Grogs through ice cones. "It was a complete Disneyworld when I walked in there. My parents were there just for the chow mein. I wanted to *live* there. It had been art-directed to a T."

When he turned twenty-one in 1979, he visited tiki bars on his own and began to get nosy. "I went to the Tiki-Ti," he said, referring to the legendary tiki relic that still does business today on Sunset Boulevard. "I would ask Ray, the old guy behind the bar, 'What's in this drink?' and no matter what the drink, he would say, 'Rum and fruit juice.' I ran into that everywhere I went. 'Rum and fruit juice.'"

Ray Buhen, who once bartended at the original Don the Beachcomber in the 1930s, was only acting on ingrained instincts. His former boss, Donn Beach, had told him never to reveal trade secrets, lest they be adopted by competing tiki bars. For this reason, many of the recipes of tiki's golden age—including the Zombie—were shrouded in mystery by the time Berry started asking questions. (Buhen died in 1999.)

As the remaining tiki palaces in Los Angeles began to vanish one by one, Berry tried making the drinks he loved at home, using the 1972 edition of *Trader Vic's Bartender Guide*—just about the only tiki cocktail book one could buy back them. During the day, he began breaking into the movie business in various marginal ways, writing coming attractions and movie poster copy. (He wrote the famous tagline "The family comedy without the family" for *Home Alone*.)

"All through the 1980s, I thought I was the only guy in the world who had any interest not only in tiki drinks but in all these old restaurants," he recalled. "I was working completely in isolation."

That changed when, in 1990, he met his future wife, Annene Kaye, a music critic who wrote for *Crawdaddy!* Through her, he met other tiki-heads who dotted the fringes of the film industry like so many islands in a South Pacific archipelago. Annene took him to a party in the Silver Lake neighborhood, where he met a Chicago actor named Charles Schneider who was also into tiki. He urged Berry to contact Sven Kirsten, a German-born cinematographer and director of music videos whose mania for tiki culture found full expression through his 2000 *Book of Tiki*.

"I went to Sven's house," Berry remembered. "He had a huge loose-leaf folder of lost tiki culture. We were like dogs sniffing each other out." They began hanging out at the Tiki-Ti and Madame Wu's in Santa Monica, where Tony Ramos, another Beachcomber veteran, served them peerless Fogcutters.

Through Kirsten, Berry inevitably met Ted Haigh. Gregarious and bombastic, Haigh was the opposite of Berry, and Berry's skeleton key into the tiki secrets of the past.

"Drinking with Ted Haigh in bars was a nightmare," recalled Berry. "He'd walk in, didn't know the bartender from Adam, put the cocktail books down and say, 'Excuse me,' in his best Jimmy Stewart voice, 'Can you make me a Corpse Reviver, No. 2?' The guys would look at him. Some of them would try. Some of them would just say no. He had nothing but chutzpah."

But it worked. When Berry walked into a tiki bar alone, he got "rum and fruit juice." When he went with Haigh, he walked away with a recipe.

"The first Don the Beachcomber recipes I got were because of Ted," admitted Berry.

Haigh put Berry in touch with Stephen Remsberg, a soft-spoken, courtly New Orleans lawyer who happened to own the most expansive collection of old and rare rums in the country. Like Berry, he had long loved and frequented the old tiki bars and tried to recreate the drinks at home. The difference was that Remsberg actually had the exact rums needed for the project.

Berry had a friend who had a place in Venice and threw luaus. At one, Berry was the designated punch maker. People would ask how he made the drinks, so he put together a little photocopied thing to hand out to people. The pamphlet found its way to Slave Labor Graphics, a comic book company in San Jose. They asked Berry to do a book version of it. It came out in 1998. "The only place you could get that book was in comic book stores. It was the only non–comic book they had."

While putting the book together, he began calling himself "Beachbum." Berry had a love of font. He liked the font used for a restaurant called Beachbum Burt's. "It was a beautiful font. It was as if it were drawn in the sand with Robinson Crusoe's walking stick." He tried cutting up the letters to make them spell Jeff Berry, but couldn't manage it. "Finally, I said why not just call it *Beachbum Berry's Grog Log?*"

Eventually, he adopted that name. "It was much easier for me be a character when giving a talk or doing an interview." (The cocktail cognoscenti's fetish for self-administered nicknames knows no bounds.)

More books followed. As the years went by, Berry became something of a rolling rum ball, spending his off-hours looking at microfilm in libraries and hunting down former Beachcomber and Vic barmen in unlikely places, gathering ferns and Falernum recipes as he went. His research roughly coincided with the digging that classic cocktail historians were doing around the same time. But for many years, the mavens of the Manhattan and other pre-Prohibition elixirs paid him little heed. So he took his tiki talents to Europe, lecturing in Belfast, Italy, and Germany. "I felt like the Dexter Gordon of the cocktail world," he said. "The U.S. doesn't want me! I'll go to Europe."

London began toying with tiki at bars like Trailer Happiness and Maliki. "They didn't have the preconception that we have in the States," explained Berry. "They never experienced the devolution of tiki in the '70s, '80s, and '90s. To them, it was all just drinks.

"The whole tiki revival was happening almost independently of the craft cocktail revival on parallel tracks," he continued, "and I always thought *never the twain shall meet.*"

But they did meet. By the time he first visited Death & Co, the serious-minded East Village cocktail bar, in 2008, New York attitudes had changed, and he was treated like visiting royalty. Eventually, other bars came around to the idea of tiki being a respectable form of mixology, if fresh juices, quality rums, and accurate recipes were used. Brian Miller, doing consulting work with Lynnette Marrero for Elettaria in 2008, gave the New York Indian restaurant a tiki drink list and large rum selection. He used Berry's book as a source.

"Personally, I think New York was shamed into putting these drinks on their menus," argued Berry. "New York bartenders who wanted to expand their horizons would go to Berlin and London. They came back and saw possibilities."

Once mixologists finally embraced tiki as a respectable branch of the cocktail family tree, they went whole hog, but with mixed results. Smuggler's Cove, which opened in San Francisco in 2009, and Three Dots and a Dash, in Chicago in 2013, were ambitious, sprawling affairs, and both were near-instant successes out of the gate. Ninety-three percent of the sales at Smuggler's were rum. Three Dots sold six thousand drinks a week in its first year.

Both owed a debt to Berry. Martin Cate, who opened Forbidden Island in Alameda, California, in 2006 before creating Smuggler's Cove, read Berry's books cover to cover. Paul McGee, the abundantly bewhiskered brain behind Three Dots and a Dash, actually named his bar after a lost tiki drink whose recipe Berry had uncovered.

However, America's cocktail capital, New York, stumbled. Three tiki bars opened in quick succession in 2010—Lani Kai, Painkiller, and Hurricane Club. Within three years, all had gone dark. The tropical booze ethos in Gotham fell back on a smattering of "tiki nights" at a half-dozen scattered bars.

Berry witnessed this revolution with both pleasure and a little resentment, like an inventor watching corporate titans get rich off his innovations. "Eighty percent of these bars, if it weren't for my books, they wouldn't have a bar," he remarked.

Jungle Bird

Classic

1½ ounces blackstrap rum, preferably Cruzan

1½ ounces pineapple juice

¾ ounce Campari

½ ounce simple syrup

½ ounce fresh lime juice

Pineapple wedge, for garnish

An obscure tiki drink uncovered by Jeff Berry, the Jungle Bird was invented at the Kuala Lumpur Hilton in 1978. The drink quickly found favor with mixologists, owing to the presence of Campari in the recipe—a rarity in the tiki world. Bartender Giuseppe Gonzalez tweaked the original formula, replacing Jamaican rum with more intense blackstrap rum, thus hitting on the specs most bartenders came to adopt.

Combine all the ingredients except the pineapple wedge in a cocktail shaker three-quarters filled with ice. Shake until chilled. Strain into a rocks glass containing one large ice cube. (Some bartenders prefer to use a copper mug, the kind typically reserved for Moscow Mules.) Garnish with the pineapple wedge.

Suffering Bastard

Classic

1 ounce brandy

1 ounce gin

1 ounce lime cordial

1 dash Angostura
bitters

4 ounces chilled
ginger beer

Mint sprig, for
garnish

Orange wheel, for
garnish

A quasi-tikiesque long drink created by barman Joe Scialom at the famous Shepheard Hotel in Cairo in the late '40s as a sort of hangover cure for his guests. It was all but forgotten when tiki scholar Jeff Berry began championing the drink.

Combine all the ingredients except the garnishes in a rocks glass filled with ice. Stir until chilled. Garnish with the mint sprig and orange wheel.

XXXI. THE BIG TIME

DEATH & CO'S OPENING BARTENDERS couldn't have been happier. Their new home was a fresh breed of cocktail bar. At Flatiron Lounge and Pegu Club, a bartender-owner had been in charge. But Death & Co was run by the cocktail bartenders themselves. Dave Kaplan and Ravi DeRossi were happy to step back and let the animals run the zoo.

"It was so nice," recalled Ward, "because when we first opened we had carte blanche to do whatever the hell we wanted." Along with Brian Miller, his Sancho Panza, Ward had Joaquín Simó. A smiling, polished former religion major with a lean resume, Simó was half Ecuadorian, half Cuban, and raised in Miami. Simó was no Phil Ward in terms of experience or skill. But then again, he was no Ward in other ways as well. Brimming with gracious charm, his bow tie, suspenders, and hair always just so, Simó quickly became known to D&Co patrons as "the nice one."

Death & Co needed a nice one. The cocktails were good from the get-go, and the service was professional. But the Bartender-Is-Always-Right era only intensified there, and there was no Julie Reiner or Audrey Saunders to rein in the haughtiness.

Simó didn't know what to make of Ward. "Phil was, at that point, terrifying," said Simó. "The kind of guy who, if you ask a question, he'll just stare at you as if he's wondering whether to step on you like a bug or if you're worthy of a response." But, like many others before him, Simó put up with the personality out of respect for the skill.

"The thing about Phil is, he understands relative weight in cocktails," he continued. According to Simó, a lot of Ward's Mr. Potato Head drinks—that is, drinks in which new ingredients are applied to an existing, proven drink template—work so well because Ward has a unique ability to weigh ingredients in his head. "You could hand him a bottle of product he'd never used before, and within ten minutes he'd give you seven really beautifully balanced cocktails with it. It was mind-blowing to watch."

Death & Co became known for its lengthy menus, with dozens of drinks divided by spirit base. But its first list had only seven drinks. It quickly grew, however, and grew boozier, moving away from the juices and gins of Pegu.

"When Pegu Club first opened, most of the cocktail revival's cocktails were sours of one kind or another," observed Kinsey. "At some point, Audrey said, 'I get it, these kind of things are cool, but what about these brown, bittered drinks?' Then Phil leaves and that becomes the whole aesthetic of Death & Co." Led by Death & Co, brown, boozy, bitter, and stirred would come to be the New York cocktail aesthetic in the final years of the 2000s' first decade. Riffs on classic whiskey drinks like the Old-Fashioned and Manhattan abounded. The style would eventually spread to London, San Francisco, and beyond.

Soon enough, Death & Co added a new arrow to its quiver. Kaplan and Ward flew to London to inspect the drinks scene. They visited Hawksmoor, a steak place in Whitechapel where Nick Strangeway was in charge of the bar. To distinguish the place, he had bought vintage glassware on eBay and served a punch of the day, as well as cocktails. He chose punch to make a political point.

"I thought the drinks we were making in England were exciting," said Strangeway. "Yet we were still slightly bashed by America by the fact that they invented the cocktail. I used to deliberately try to provoke people. 'Fuck you and your cocktail. We invented the punch!'"

Kaplan and Ward were duly rebuked. They decided to introduce punch at Death & Co, thus kicking off what would grow into a punch craze in America (helped along greatly by David Wondrich's book *Punch: The Delights (and Dangers) of the Flowing Bowl*).

At the start, almost all the drinks on the D&Co menu were Ward's. That was not surprising. As head bartender, he basically played Caesar at the bar's menu tastings, where bartenders offered up their new creations for judgment.

"Phil was always the biggest gun," said Thomas Waugh. "He never deleted any of his drinks, even if they weren't the most popular in the tastings." The menu tastings were hilarious, dramatic, messy affairs. "It would end with somebody crying and running out," said Waugh. "The poor bastards who had to work that night were sloshed."

"Say you have seven drinks you were planning on presenting," said Simó, describing a typical tasting. "Two, maybe three of them are rock solid. You've already tasted them with most of your staff. A couple are works in progress: 'I'm close, but I don't know how to make it pop.' Then there were always a couple like, 'I have this idea. Let's see if we can make a couple passes and work our way through it.' By the time everyone got through all that, we were all pretty tanked. And then Phil would go up last. By then, everyone was fairly drunk, so it was hard to have constructive criticism."

The drinks that made the cut in those early days were fairly unimpeachable in terms of balance, invention, and flavor. They also may have been among the least cost-efficient cocktails in history. Kaplan never told the bartenders "no" when it came to ingredients.

"We had remarkable freedom," said Simó. "'You want to mix with a $50 bottle of Japanese whiskey? You just throw it in a cocktail! It's delicious!' We were basically accountable to ourselves, and we had the highest possible standards."

The freedom of the staff and the excellence of the drinks aside, Death & Co's first year was tumultuous, and the bar teetered on the brink for what seemed like forever. An article in the *New York Times* Styles section, running soon after the bar opened, ensured a steady flow of business. The press focused on the cocktails. The wine program, once a big part of the vision for the bar, was a dud and quickly 86'd. Back of house was a mess. "We had very little left in the coffers," said Kaplan. "We didn't have a point of sale when we opened. We did everything in triplicate."

Patrons loved the place. But the surrounding community did not, particularly one man, Joe Hurley, who lived above the bar. Ward pointed out the irony that Hurley belonged to an Irish drinking band called Rogue's March whose most popular song was "Shut Up and Drink." A host of legal challenges threatened the bar's very existence.

"We had to live through it," said Ward. "We were the most civilized bar that probably ever opened in the East Village in the history of the world. Then we almost had our license revoked and had to close at midnight. That was a pretty good buzzkill. We were throwing a full bar out every night, because we had to close at 12."

Cops came in every night, waved to the bartenders, took a music-level measurement, and left. "It was disgusting," said Ward.

DON LEE AND JOHN DERAGON, playing "follow the bartender," became as common a sight at Death & Co as they had been at Pegu.

Six months in, Ward asked Don and John if they would take over the bar for a night. Ward wanted to hold a staff party. It was an insane proposal. But there were no civilians in New York who knew more about cocktails than Lee and Deragon.

Jim Meehan came in the night the duo worked, "specifically to see the train wreck," according to Deragon. With him was a man named Brian Shebairo, the owner of Crif Dogs, a hip wiener shop nearby. Deragon made Shebairo a Daiquiri, made with contraband Havana Club rum, that blew him away. When Don and John failed to crash and burn behind the bar, Meehan thought they had something. He asked if they'd be interested in working at a new venture he and Shebairo were working on, a place called PDT.

PDT began as a simple consulting job for Meehan, who was working at both Gramercy Tavern and Pegu Club. Shebairo's partner had heard of Meehan from St. John Frizell, another Pegu Club bartender. Shebairo was taking over Jenny's Bubble Tea Lounge, which was next door to Crif Dogs on St. Mark's Place, and he wanted to turn it into a bar. Shebairo offered Meehan profit-sharing in both PDT and Crif Dogs at the eleventh hour. But Meehan wasn't interested. "I said, 'I'm not going to leave Pegu and Gramercy to be your profit-sharing manager. I will stay to be your consultant.'"

But events changed his mind. At Gramercy one day, he spotted a young bartender screwing up a Martinez for one of his cocktail geek regulars. "I lost my shit," admitted Meehan. That was a no-no in Danny Meyer's hospitality book. "If this guy had ordered chicken when the guest had ordered steak, we wouldn't be having this conversation. But because this is a cocktail, something [management] thinks is not important, I was terminated," said Meehan.

"He was as passionate as anyone I'd ever seen," recalled Meyer. "He was 100-percent interested in what he was putting in the glass, and I'd say 100-percent interested in 50 percent of the people he was serving."

In retrospect, Meehan pretty much agrees. "You never get fired for what you actually did," he said. "Ultimately, when I look back at it, I was let go because my zeal to make Gramercy's cocktail program as good as its food and wine alienated key members of its team."

That left Pegu Club. Meehan was the last original bartender on staff. But one day, while on a Partida tequila junket in Las Vegas, he failed to cover his Monday shift at the bar. He caught a red-eye and walked in three hours late for his shift. Saunders had had to cover. "She never yelled about it, we never talked about it," said Meehan. "She was obviously pissed. At that point, I realized my extracurricular activities were getting in the way of my being able to be a team member. It was time to move on." (Like Ward and Miller before him, Meehan would endure a couple of years where he and Saunders were not on speaking terms.)

Originally, Shebairo planned to open a rock-and-roll bar, a psychic match to the rough-and-tumble Crif Dogs. But he sensed that cocktails were ascendant and sought out Meehan. The bar's setup was basically in place when Meehan arrived. "Jim came in and basically said, 'Wrong, wrong, wrong,'" said Shebairo. "I was like, 'Wow, we just hired this guy and he already cost me $14,000.'" The soda guns were out. So was the ice machine. New speed racks and ice bins were needed. The phone booth door—arguably the most famous bar entrance in the world—was Shebairo's idea. "A little *Get Smart*," he called it.

Initially, Meehan put the bar largely in the hands of Don Lee and John Deragon. It was an odd move, but, having witnessed firsthand what had happened at Pegu Club, he didn't want to be seen as a poacher himself.

"Death & Co had always been the New York Yankees," Meehan said. "It's always been a team built on free agency. There's never been a farm team at Death & Co. The key was to find a staff I didn't steal from someone else. There's where Don and John came in." He also hired David Slape from Slanted Door in San Francisco. "It was the Australia of bartenders, people who were rejected or didn't fit in or didn't have enough shifts—that was my opening team."

Lee and Deragon were left to their own devices. "They worked their asses off," recalled Shebairo. "They dedicated a lot of time, a lot of energy, a lot of creativeness into PDT."

They worked Monday night, an off night in the industry, and thus became popular with fellow bartenders. "They thought it was funny," said Lee. "'Hey, our regulars are bartending at this place!'" Chef Wylie Dufresne had a standing Friday night date there with his wife. David Chang was a regular.

"When it first opened, it was John Deragon and Don Lee," recalled David Wondrich. "Those guys are so unique. They were big personalities in their way."

But the team wasn't just a novelty. Influenced by the work of chefs Dufresne, Chang, and Sam Mason, they began tinkering with fat-washing and infusions. "After tasting Wylie's popcorn soup, I thought, *Why can't we make cocktails out of popcorn?*" said Lee. He butter-fat-washed white rum that had been infused with popcorn. The drink tasted like a date at the movies. Out of this period came PDT's most famous drink. Benton's flavorful country bacon from Tennessee was then an ingredient found in many dishes at Chang's Momofuku Ssäm Bar. The restaurant let Lee have their leftover bacon fat. Lee, who was a regular at WD-50, was inspired by its barman, Eben Freeman, to create the Benton's Old-Fashioned, a Four Roses bourbon Old-Fashioned fat-washed with the bacon fat.

Some experiments didn't work. They once tried to carbonate cherries. The bottle blew up and cherries flew all over the bar. But people came in just to see what Don and John were up to. It was a cocktail-world sideshow that was sometimes more interesting than what was going on in the center ring. "At that time, you went to Pegu for classics, Death & Co for more modern classics, and you came to PDT for the experimental," said Lee.

For other staff members, it was all a bit confusing. "For the whole beginning, it was really unclear what it was going to be in many ways," recalled bartender Michael Madrusan. "Jim was only supposed to be a consultant. Nobody enjoyed being told what to do by somebody like Don. Don was somebody who had no stripes. He was a customer."

Lee and Deragon did it mainly for fun, working for hourly wages and what tips there were. They still had their outside lives. With Gramercy and Pegu behind him, Meehan came back as a full-time manager. The by-the-book Meehan didn't always see eye to eye with the loose-limbed Lee and Deragon. "We'd get used to doing things a certain way," explained Deragon. "And the parents come home and you get yelled at. But you say, 'Look, it's working.'"

"I think we were too powerful a team," continued Deragon. "I think there was a little bit of Jim [that] was afraid of the chaos we were causing. Around the same time, there was a shortage of senior bartenders, and they wanted to spread us out."

Madrusan has happy, however. "When Jim came back, I feel like it really took," he said. "It was a little bit aimless in the beginning. PDT would not be where it is if Jim didn't come back and steer it in the right direction." (More than any other bar that played a major role in the cocktail revival, PDT's origin story is tangled and confused, replete with conflicting accounts.)

From then on PDT became "back-up band and solo artist," in Wondrich's words. Meehan became the face of PDT and, in time, the face of New York mixology. More than the bartenders who came before him, or any of his mentors, he played the press and career-building games impeccably, ever professional, positive, and ready with a quote.

"He deserves it," said Shebairo. "He worked his ass off for it. He's been able to create another whole life outside of it because of it. He's turned it into a way bigger thing than the bar. He's turned himself into a brand."

The bar itself became synonymous with the speakeasy style of cocktail bar, even more so than Milk & Honey. Meehan fielded press queries about the speakeasy movement. At first, he didn't want any part of the pigeonholing. But then he pivoted.

"Identity is equal parts what you think of yourself and what others think of you," said Meehan. "If all these great publications want to call us a speakeasy, maybe we should figure out how we're a speakeasy and how we aren't. That's when I started saying, 'We're a modern speakeasy.'"

PDT and Meehan also benefitted in framing themselves as the tonal opposite of Milk & Honey. "Sasha was incredibly exclusive and never, ever spoke to the media," said Meehan. "I, on the other hand, love speaking to the media. I've always been a ham for a microphone or press request. Some people found it so contradictory that this neo-speakeasy would do interviews or allow photographs. A lot of the success of PDT had to do with Sasha's complete Draconinan unwillingness to talk about what he did. I benefitted greatly from Sasha's silence."

Oaxaca Old-Fashioned

PHIL WARD, 2007, Death & Co, New York

1½ ounces El Tesoro reposado tequila

½ ounce Del Maguey San Luis Del Rio mezcal

2 dashes Angostura bitters

1 barspoon agave nectar

Orange twist, for garnish

This is the drink that opened the American mixology world's eyes to the potential of using tequila and mezcal in cocktails. According to Angus Winchester, British bartenders were making Old-Fashioneds with tequila much earlier. But if they were, the drinks were thrown down the gullet unnamed and unsung, and they likely didn't contain mezcal. Ward called it his eureka moment when he figured out, regarding mezcal, "this shit works." It has inspired countless imitations, with different names, but essentially the same recipe.

Combine all the ingredients except the orange twist in an Old-Fashioned glass filled with one large ice cube. Stir until chilled. Top with a flamed orange twist, then drop the twist into the drink.

Benton's Old-Fashioned

DON LEE, 2007, PDT, New York

---

2 ounces Benton's bacon fat-washed Four Roses bourbon (recipe follows)

¼ ounce Grade B maple syrup

2 dashes Angostura bitters

Large piece of orange zest, for garnish

Contrary to some claims, Don Lee did not invent fat-washing spirits, as it pertains to cocktails. But he did invent the drink that made fat-washing famous.

"They were using Benton's bacon in almost every dish at Momofuku," he said, referencing the famous country bacon made in Tennessee. "One day, Tien Ho, who was a regular of ours at PDT, said, 'I've got all this bacon fat. I don't know what to do with it.'" Lee did. A regular at WD-50, he had sampled some of Eben Freeman's experiments with fat-washing—the process of mixing a melted fat with a liquor, freezing the mixture, then skimming away the fat, thus adding the savory flavors to the spirit. "They were delicious," Lee recalled. "He had never put any of them on the menu, though. I think partly, it was, 'This is a huge hassle to do and I don't know what the customer backlash would be.' We didn't know any better at PDT. So we just put it on the menu."

The Benton's Old-Fashioned became PDT's best-known and best-selling cocktail. Despite the labor involved in creating it, you'll find Benton's Old-Fashioned on menus beyond PDT. It also inspired a whole genre of cocktails, with liquors being fat-washed with every meat and nut under the sun. The drink comes with an Achilles' heel, though: it has to be made with Benton's bacon. "Ninety-nine percent of the time when someone had that drink and said it wasn't good, it's because it wasn't made with Benton's," said Lee.

While Lee is proud of the cocktail, the multitalented man is also a bit haunted by it. "For me, it kills me that that's the drink that probably follows me to the grave," he said.

———

Combine all the ingredients except the orange zest in an Old-Fashioned glass filled with one large ice cube. Stir until chilled. Twist the orange zest over the drink and drop it into the glass.

———

To make the fat-washed bourbon, warm 1½ ounces bacon fat in a small saucepan over low heat, stirring until it is melted, about 5 minutes. Combine the melted fat with 750 milliliters of bourbon in a large freezer-safe container and stir. Cover and let sit at room temperature for 4 hours, then place the container in the freezer for 2 hours. Remove the solid fat from the surface of the bourbon and discard. Strain the bourbon through a terry-cloth towel or a double layer of cheesecloth into a bottle and store in the refrigerator for up to 2 months.

XXXII. OTHER CITIES, OTHER BARS

IF YOU STUCK AROUND as a bartender long enough at Milk & Honey, Sasha Petraske sent you out into the world to open your own Milk & Honey. Some of these Milk & Honeys were in New York and went by a different name. Joseph Schwartz, an early M&H bartender, opened Little Branch. Richie Boccato, who began as a doorman at Little Branch, graduating to bartender, partnered with Petraske on Dutch Kills, the first major craft cocktail bar in Queens. Lucinda Sterling, another bartender, opened Middle Branch in Midtown with him. Petraske would eventually hand over the Milk & Honey space to its longtime bartending team, Sam Ross and Michael McIlroy, who turned it into Attaboy, a bar not very different from Milk & Honey aside from a more open, egalitarian atmosphere. Part of this pollination policy was Petraske's make-it-up-as-you-go business model, in which each new venture was meant to help pay for the previous ones. And part of it was his socialist viewpoint that his loyal employees should do as well as he did, or, as was often the case, better.

"My partners have all done well," Petraske quipped. "It's just the things I'm in charge of that have lost money."

When New York was saturated, he started thinking past the Hudson River. The first target was Los Angeles. Eric Alperin, a tall, handsome actor who had pulled shifts at Milk & Honey and Little Branch, was chosen for the expedition. While searching for the right location, he got a job at Osteria Mozza, a Mario Batali restaurant.

Los Angeles was not without a few decent cocktail programs. But, oddly enough, they were the work of Sam Ross, who had gotten there before Alperin. In 2007, L.A. restaurateur David Myers, had hired Ross to consult on Comme Ça, a new French-style brasserie he was opening in West Hollywood.

"The cocktail scene in L.A. was fairly nonexistent," recalled Ross. He trained the staff on the short, but serious cocktail list, which included the M&H staple Gold Rush and his own drink, the Penicillin, the smoky Whiskey Sour riff that he invented at Milk & Honey. That staff included bartenders who would go on to become name mixologists as the L.A. cocktail scene matured. When they moved on to open other bars, they took the Penicillin with them. Within a few years, the cocktail became one of the best-known new drinks in the country.

Alperin and Petraske didn't know Los Angeles or where to look. But while Alperin was at Osteria Mozza, he met a man who did.

Cedd Moses was a hip cat. Born in Virginia but raised in Los Angeles, he was the son of artist Ed Moses. As a kid, he was surrounded by artists and musicians. Early on, he came to understand he had a brilliant analytical mind. He could spot patterns and outcomes others couldn't. He used that mind to handicap horse races. Because he needed adult accompaniment to attend the races, a high school teacher sometimes snuck him out of class. There, he met the poet Charles Bukowski, who later took an of-drinking-age Moses to some of the bars he would eventually own. For a time in the early 1980s, Moses dated Bukowski's daughter. She finally dumped him. "She said I was too much like her father," he said. "I wasn't too insulted by that."

Attending UCLA, he breezed through with a double major in mechanical engineering and computer science. His betting had started to affect the odds of Santa Anita, so he went into the stock market instead. He ran mutual funds and hedge funds during the 1980s and 1990s and made a pile of money. By the late 1990s, he was burned out and sold his company.

He turned to real estate. Through his bar hopping and restaurant going, he had come to love the seedy urban heart of Los Angeles. But downtown was dead. "I came downtown with a vision of opening ten bars and revitalizing downtown and cocktail culture in Los Angeles," he recalled. "As an Angeleno, I take a lot of pride in Los Angeles, and I had a love for all the architecture and old buildings downtown. I had a vision for that area coming back and making it a cultural center again."

He started buying up real estate. Properties were inexpensive. "Everyone at the time thought I was insane." He set up a company, The Proprietors 213. Golden Gopher was his first bar. But it was Seven Grand, in early 2007, that made the difference.

"To me, the big turning point came when Seven Grand opened," said Chuck Taggart, one of L.A.'s early layman cocktail enthusiasts. "It wasn't the first, but it seemed to launch so many others." Seven Grand was primarily a whiskey bar, but it attracted talent. Marco Tellos, Chris Bostick, Aidan Demerest, and many more promising bartenders worked there.

Moses and Petraske were a good match. Petraske had the cocktail acumen that Moses admired, while Moses had the real estate connections Petraske needed. Moses introduced Petraske and Alperin to Cole's, a joint he had once drunk at with Bukowski. The place had a lot of history. Established in 1908, it boasted of having originated the French dip sandwich. But it wasn't wearing its century in business well. There was a urine stench. The sewer system was backing up. "When I first went back in the kitchen," said Moses, "I regretted ever having eaten French dips. There was a man cutting the meat under the asbestos." But Petraske loved the romance and history of the place.

The old kitchen was ripped out, and that back room became The Varnish, a speakeasy and the first out-and-out modern craft cocktail bar in Los Angeles. You walked through Cole's to a door at the rear to enter. As at Milk & Honey, it was a closed-off incubator of decorum and cool. The décor was dark wood and tables. The cocktail list was classic and short, with a focus on bartender's choice. Alperin culled the best talent in the city for his opening staff: Tellos, Bostick, Mattie Eggleston, Chris Ojeda.

All the attention the new place might have needed came when Jonathan Gold, the local legendary restaurant critic, dropped a huge piece called "The New Cocktailians," in which The Varnish figured prominently.

"We got hit really hard and a lot of attention, and cocktails were part of L.A. all of a sudden," recalled Alperin. "That enfranchised everybody."

Moses kept opening bars: the Edison in 2008, Las Perlas in 2009. When David Kaplan and Alex Day of Death & Co fame came west, he did the same thing for them he had done for Petraske, and together they opened Honeycut, a disco/cocktail bar mashup. Because of all of the New York players involved, the L.A. scene had a Gotham feel during its first years.

———

PETRASKE NEVER COLLABORATED on a bar with Toby Maloney, one of his first hires at Milk & Honey. But Maloney opened his own Milk & Honey in Chicago anyway. It was called The Violet Hour.

By 2007, Maloney had a lot of influences to draw on. "I would put it halfway between Sasha and Julie Reiner," he said of The Violet Hour. "Audrey Saunders could be seen in that area as well. A lot of thought toward ice and technique, everything fresh, everything measured right."

The Violet Hour opened in the rising hipster neighborhood of Wicker Park. The owner was Terry Alexander, who had employed Maloney as an oyster shucker and bartender at his restaurant Soul Kitchen in the early 1990s. Since then, Alexander kept walking into bars where Maloney worked. It seemed kismet. The interior design was based on the idea of ice, with various shades of chilly blue. Curtains and small arrangements of long-backed chairs chopped up the sprawling space. The bar was forty-four feet long. "Even Pegu wasn't that big," noted Maloney. "It was basically four Milk & Honey bars stacked next to each other." Its rules of etiquette also outdid Milk & Honey. No cell phones, no baseball caps, no O-bombs, no Budweiser, "and finally, please do not bring anyone to The Violet Hour that you wouldn't bring to your mother's house for Sunday dinner."

Chicago wasn't exactly ready for this sort of nose-in-the-air thing. It still hewed close to its brash and brawny origins. It was beer and whiskey and nothing fancy. There were a few places that took cocktails seriously. Matchbox, an odd little wedge-shaped dive, worked with egg whites and used fresh juice in its sugar-rimmed Gimlets. Adam Seger—who had made his mark at Louisville's historic Seelbach Hotel by resurrecting its long-lost house cocktail—was working with herbs and homemade bitters at Nacional 27.

Seger was the first cocktail pro Bridget Alpert met when she moved to Chicago. Alcohol was in Alpert's blood. She grew up south of Chicago, where her mother, grandmother, and great-great aunt owned a bar. Her father's side of the family had made bathtub gin. She got the cocktail bug from Tony Abou-Ganim while working on the opening bar team at the Bellagio in Las Vegas. When Alpert moved back to Illinois in 2005, Tony and Francesco Lafranconi, of the huge distributor Southern Wine & Spirits, had recommended her for a position at Southern's Illinois office.

Alpert faced the same problem in Chicago that the Italian-born Lafranconi had faced when he first moved to Las Vegas: before she could sell bartenders on cocktails, she had to educate them. "I was coming to Chicago with a muddler," she recalled. "I was telling bartenders, 'We need to be measuring stuff.' It was really hard." She started an Academy of Fine Spirits and Service, modeled on Lafanconi's Vegas school. Charles Joly, who would later become the most famous cocktail bartender Chicago has produced to date, was in the second group of students.

"I didn't have any place to go and learn in Chicago," said Joly. "The academy taught me how to taste and open my palate. It wasn't like New York where you could work under Toby or go to Milk & Honey. I was really on my own. I bought books and read them."

Like Alpert, Joly was an Illinois native, growing up around the Comiskey Park neighborhood. There was nothing in his upbringing that would indicate his rosy future. After his parents divorced, shortly after he was born, he and his sister became wards of the court until his grandmother adopted them. Money was always scarce. In 1999, after meeting an old high school friend at a huge dance club called Crowbar, he began barbacking there. He got his first bartending gig at Bigwig and hooked in with the place's owners, who went on to open several other places in Chicago, Milwaukee, and Charlotte, eventually becoming general manager of the group. The last bar they opened together was The Drawing Room.

Lynn House was in Alpert's third session. She, Joly, and Debbie Peek (who would eventually take over Alpert's academy) formed the opening crew at The Drawing Room. It opened a month after The Violet Hour. Suddenly, Chicago had a cocktail scene.

There was some pushback from the public. The Violet Hour had no olives, had no vodka, and served drinks in small coupes with a sidecar. But Maloney had already been through the wars at Milk & Honey and Pegu Club. He was battle-hardened. "In the beginning, we had to be serious," he said. "I cringe at some of the things I did back then, like not making a vodka Martini because I thought it was beneath me. Without that rather militant seriousness, I don't think you would be able to have this."

Part of the resistance was that Chicagoans recognized the bar wasn't really something of their own. "The Violet Hour is definitely a New York style bar," said Joly. "People in Chicago either loved The Violet Hour or they hated it. The Midwest wasn't quite ready to deal with the rules."

But some industry people were more than ready. The crew from Grant Achatz's restaurant Alinea would hang out. Mike Ryan, who had taken Alpert's course and was trying to make things happen at the bar at Otom, remembered his impressions on first walking in. "This was the first place I had seen that was really committing to the concept. We've always had an egalitarian ethic at our bars here in Chicago. These guys were like, no, it really is our way or the highway." (Maloney hired Ryan in 2008.)

Like The Violet Hour, The Drawing Room was hard to find. It was below ground, with a door hidden in plain sight on busy, touristy Rush Street. The space had challenges. It was a tiny bar. Joly crammed liquor bottles into every corner he could find. Plush and elegant, it fought against the noise emanating from a nearby nightclub.

"It was a lot of growing together at the same time, as we were discovering what the beast was," recalled House. "When you're down in a cave, the outside world is out there."

While shooting for the same stars, the two bars were as different as their neighborhoods. The staffs differed, too, in their provenance. "When you look at the family trees in Chicago," said Joly, "you have Bridget's protégés and Toby's protégés."

ONE OF MALONEY'S PROTÉGÉS was Kirk Estopinal, a New Orleanean in unexpected exile, thrown adrift by Hurricane Katrina. His wife worked for Saks. During the storm, the New Orleans store caught on fire, and she was transferred to Chicago. Kirk followed. A friend there got him a job at Terry Alexander's Del Toro. When the place closed and reopened as The Violet Hour, Estopinal and workmates Brad Bolt and Stephen Cole were offered jobs at the alien new bar. Estopinal had experienced nothing like it in New Orleans.

New Orleans, unlike Chicago, didn't need to be reminded what classic cocktails were. The city had never stopped drinking them. The Sazerac, Ramos Gin Fizz, and Vieux Carre, among other classic drinks, had been invented there, and the Pimm's Cup and Milk Punch were prized, drunk in bars as old as or older than the drinks themselves.

But by the twenty-first century, the drinking culture of New Orleans was passé. They were good at holding on to traditions, but they weren't creating any new ones. "We were still a little isolated down here," said bartender Chris Hannah, "and we were still making these old drinks."

Prior to Katrina, Chris McMillian was one of the few bartenders attempting anything adventurous. Big, shambling, with a face full of character and a mouth full of molasses and tall tales, he seemed like a lifelong barkeep, but was not. He had been in sales, but in 1994 he needed a job. His wife, who was pregnant with their sixth child, asked her boss to give Chris a job in catering. At the Clock Bar in the Royal Sonesta Hotel and at Arnaud's Richelieu bar and the Ritz-Carlton's Library Lounge, he began to piece together the history of his new profession.

"I was doing this path one drink at a time," he said.

At the old French Quarter eatery Tujague's, meanwhile, another crusty old man, Paul Gustings, was also working in isolation, conjuring up forty-three-item cocktail lists including the Aviation and others. Other than that, there wasn't much movement—until Katrina hit, and everyone was forced to move away. When they came back, they brought new ideas.

Estopinal went to Chicago. McMillian stayed with the DeGroffs on Long Island and went to Kentucky. Others, who had moved away from New Orleans before the storm hit, now knew it was time to go back. Neal Bodenheimer had been bartending in New York for Steve Hanson's BR Guest group, under the wing of Eben Klemm. In his off hours, he hung out at Milk & Honey, Employees Only, and his go-to bar, Grace, where he'd sample new bottles with owners Cory Hill and Fred McKibbin.

When Katrina hit, "I felt like I should be back in New Orleans," said Bodenheimer. "A lot of people who were from New Orleans, who didn't live in New Orleans, felt that if you didn't go home, there was a good chance the city wouldn't exist. So I came home, coupled with the idea that maybe it would be a good idea to be one of the first to have a stand-alone cocktail bar down there."

By the time he got back, a small group of bartenders who cared had created a makeshift community, partly brought together through the efforts of Chris Patino, a former New Orleans bartender who was now the area's brand ambassador for Plymouth gin. There was McMillian at the Library Bar, Hannah at the French 75 Bar, Danny Valdez at Commander's Palace, and Ricky Gomez at a dive bar called Harry's.

Bodenheimer found and bought a building in the lonely Freret neighborhood, far from the French Quarter. No one thought opening a bar there was a good idea.

"I had at least ten to twenty people come up to me and try to have interventions with me," he recalled. "'You really shouldn't do this. This will be a terrible idea.'"

Estopinal had moved back to the city, also with the idea of opening a cocktail bar. Bodenheimer pitched him on Cure, but he wasn't impressed. Instead, he tried to continue the consulting work he had begun in Chicago, hitting up local restaurant kings Donald Link and John Besh, with no success. "They were like, 'I got a guy who makes Sazeracs,'" said Estopinal. "Literally, that's what one of them said."

Bodenheimer had the pick of the litter in terms of staffing. Valdez and Gomez both signed on; Rhiannon Enlil, who had ridden out Katrina in Seattle, where she was inspired by Murray Stenson at the Zig Zag Club, and worked at Erin Rose in New Orleans; and Maksym Pazuniak, who was an apprentice. Estopinal became the final piece of the puzzle, joining shortly after Cure opened in 2009.

Like Death & Co, Cure was a bartender-led bar. In terms of drinks, Bodenheimer ceded control to his employees. But he did give the bar a dress code—no shorts, no flip-flops, no baseball caps—something Cure would never quite live down. "We spent the first nine months to a year trying to convince people they should drink cocktails and we weren't just pretentious assholes," he said. But the place was successful from the get-go anyway.

(That was a good thing, because, "We needed to be, or we would have gone under." So strapped for cash was Bodenheimer that, for the first two weeks, the bartenders used his stock of home booze.)

Like The Varnish in L.A. and The Violet Hour in Chicago, Cure wasn't at heart a local bar. "Neal brought it down from New York and Kirk brought it down from Chicago," pointed out local journalist Wayne Curtis. "It's a New York and Chicago bar." Some people thought that was a reason to knock it. Hannah's customers griped about the new kids in town, about how long it took to get a drink there. But Hannah refused to feed the fire. He liked Cure. "I knew we had a lot of bars that were resting on their laurels," he said.

Lu Brow said, "I thought it was very cool that the city was going to have a freestanding cocktail bar." Brow, who hailed from Shreveport and had befriended McMillian and Hannah before Katrina, renovated the cocktail program at the Brennan family's Café Adelaide and Swizzle Stick Bar, instituting fresh juices and classic cocktails. "It revitalized the neighborhood. The more competition we got, the better it was for the city."

It didn't take long, however, for Cure to develop its own personality independent of its New York and Chicago influences. Shortly after it opened, Pazuniak and Estopinal self-published *Rogue Cocktails*, a slim volume of radical recipes that became one of the most influential cocktail books of the decade.

"*Rogue Cocktails* was a reaction to how boring a lot of cocktail guys were," Pazuniak told *Wine Enthusiast*. "We were going through these old cocktail books, and they were cool. Then you'd read new books and couldn't make anything, because they involved crazy syrups and things you couldn't find."

One day, Estopinal made Pazuniak an Angostura Sour, a drink that turns the typical cocktail model on its head by using the bitters as its base. "My brain exploded," said Pazuniak. "I thought, *This is awesome. Why don't people know about this?*"

Pazuniak shifted the spotlight from gin, whiskey, and other traditional cocktail building blocks to unsung bitter and herbal liqueurs like Campari, Cynar, and Chartreuse.

The book "was a collection of our bitch sessions," said Estopinal. "Basically what we were into: amaro and bitters. Most recipes used just a bit of these. But bartenders were drinking the fuck out of them." Toby Maloney, Tonia Guffey, and other bartenders all made contributions.

It was a zeitgeist moment. Though only 277 copies of *Rogue Cocktails* were printed, the book had an impact. It was picked up by bartenders from around the country. A few drinks, like the Bitter Giuseppe and Gunshop Fizz (which called for two ounces of Peychaud's bitters), became cult classics.

Cure spread roots. Bodenheimer and his partners went on to open Bellocq, which had a quixotic focus on the ice-laden, nineteenth-century class of drink called cobblers; and Cane & Table, a quasi-tiki French Quarter bar. New Orleans continued to drink deeply as it always had done. But it drank differently.

"In a way, it was a decaying city," said Bodeheimer. "There were a lot of things that ended up being washed way. People started over."

Paper Plane

SAM ROSS, 2008, The Violet Hour, Chicago

¾ ounce bourbon

¾ ounce Nonino
Quintessentia amaro

¾ ounce Aperol

¾ ounce fresh
lemon juice

Sam Ross, the longtime bartender at Milk & Honey (now Attaboy), created this simple, equal-parts drink for the opening menu at The Violet Hour in Chicago, a bar where he never worked. "It's my second most well-traveled drink," after the Penicillin, said Ross. It is particularly popular in Toronto, for reasons that remain mysterious to Ross. "It is essentially the official drink of Toronto," he said. "It is on every cocktail menu in Toronto." It is made with the Italian bitter Aperol and the Italian amaro Nonino Quintessentia, two ingredients whose stars rose with the cocktail movement. (The original recipe contained Campari, but that was quickly supplanted with Aperol, which became the norm.) The drink was named after a song by the British rapper M.I.A. that Ross was listening to while he tried to come up with the recipe.

Combine all the ingredients in a cocktail shaker three-quarters filled with ice. Shake until chilled. Strain into a coupe glass.

Gunshop Fizz

KIRK ESTOPINAL and **MAKSYM PAZUNIAK**, 2009, Cure, New Orleans

2 ounces Peychaud's bitters

1 ounce fresh lemon juice

1 ounce simple syrup

2 strawberries

3 cucumber slices, plus one for garnish

3 swaths grapefruit peel

3 swaths orange peel

Sanbitter

This drink turned typical mixology rules on their head, using Peychaud's bitters not for an accent, but as the bulk of the drink. It first appeared in *Rogue Cocktails*, which challenged cocktail orthodoxy, putting bitter ingredients typically used as modifiers to significant use.

"Kirk had introduced me to the Angostura Sour, which he had adapted from the Angostura Fizz in Charles H. Baker's *Gentleman's Companion*," said Pazuniak. "This is around the time he and I were experimenting with these bitter- and amaro-heavy cocktails that ultimately led to *Rogue Cocktails*. We wanted to try doing something similar with Peychaud's, and Kirk had the genius idea to start with The Violet Hour Pimm's Cup template, which called for muddled strawberries and cucumbers, subbing out the Pimm's for Peychaud's. From there, it was just a matter of workshopping the drink to get the exact specs and ingredients down to make it delicious."

"I think the thing that we really liked is that it tastes like a fruit punch," said Estopinal, "so it's one of those cocktails that looks bad on paper, but tastes surprisingly good."

Add all the ingredients except the Sanbitter and garnish to a cocktail shaker. Muddle and set aside for two minutes to allow the flavors to blend. Add ice. Shake until chilled. Strain into a Collins glass filled with ice. Top with Sanbitter. Garnish with the cucumber slice.

XXXIII. A COCKTAIL CONVENTION

ANN ROGERS HAD TO START OVER, certainly. Her pet project, a tiny gathering of like-minded cocktail geeks called Tales of the Cocktail, was only a few years old when Katrina hit. Its major sponsor, Southern Comfort, had bailed after the storm. But Rogers was a tenacious sort. "I'm hardheaded," she admitted.

Rogers was born and raised in New Orleans, but she doesn't seem like it. High-strung and hard-nosed, she's more New Yorker than Southerner. That has a lot to do with her take-no-prisoners profession: marketing. When, while working for a television station, she realized the ban on liquor advertising was more a gentlemen's agreement than binding law, she signed on Seagram's. Soon she was meeting with people in the spirits business.

Always proud of the city's heritage, she began a walking tour of historical bars in 2002, inspired by *Obituary Cocktail*, a lavish photo book of old New Orleans taverns by photographer Kerri McCaffety. She convinced Southern Comfort, which has purported origins in the French Quarter, to sponsor it. A year later, she wanted to expand the event into a wider drinks-related affair and coined the name "Tales of the Cocktail."

In 2003, there were hardly enough cocktail personalities to fill a hotel room, let alone a hotel. But Rogers found them. She learned of Dale DeGroff from *Bon Appétit*. At the bookstore, she found other names: Ted Haigh, Barnaby Conrad III, Anistatia Miller, and Jared Brown. Then there were fringe characters like Stephen Visakay, an obsessive collector of antique cocktail shakers. Using Southern Comfort money, she flew them down and put them all up in the Hotel Monteleone. Entrance was free to the public. There were three events total: a ceremony in front of Brennan's restaurant; a cocktail hour at the Monteleone's Carousel Bar, where the authors sold their books; and ten "spirited dinners," where meals at restaurants were paired with cocktails instead of wine. A college kid with a pickup truck drove Rogers around to all ten.

The event grew slightly from year to year. But, ironically, it wasn't until after Katrina that it ballooned into the epicenter of cocktail-world networking and industry excess. Following the hurricane, Rogers took a temporary job marketing Illy coffee in New York and returned to New Orleans on January 1, 2006, with no money, no home (it had been flooded), and no husband, her ten-year marriage having fallen apart. Those circumstances didn't last long. She moved in with her mother, cashed in her 401(k) and life savings, took out a $100,000 loan from Chase, and borrowed a further $15,000 from the man who would become her second husband, Paul Tuennerman. "I think I caught him off guard," she said.

Savvy Simon Ford sniffed out the event and made Plymouth gin one of Tales's first new sponsors. Rogers determined that the fun could no longer be free. She started paperwork for a 501(c)(3), became a nonprofit, and began to charge for tickets. She also moved the event up from September to July and, at the suggestion of the Monteleone, lengthened it to a long weekend in order to attract more people. Aided by only a single intern, she began inviting people down. They came, four thousand strong.

The next year, more came. And by 2008, it was a near-mandatory obligation: If you were a cocktail bartender, author, or journalist, you set aside a week in July to head down to swelteringly hot New Orleans to hobnob and feed your mind and thirst in the educational bacchanalia that everyone simple calls "Tales." It was the perfect party for a growing national cocktailian community that was hungry for education and interaction. And there was simply nothing else like it.

New Orleans benefitted little from the first few Tales meetings. But the city would change its tune once Tales began pouring gobs of tourist dollars into the city coffers during the traditionally dead month of July. And for young bartenders not entirely sold on their choice of trade, it was a life-affirming fantasia.

"Tales 100-percent launched my career and drove my career, mainly because I met all the amazing bartenders from around the country," said Brooke Arthur, then of San Francisco, soon to become a sought-after consultant and brand ambassador.

"For those of us who were in undeveloped markets, there was no one I could ever talk to about drinks. Nobody at all," said Bobby Heugel, now owner of many cocktail bars in Houston. His initial Tales was the first time he could talk to people about cocktails outside of online forums. "It was exciting because I got to listen to people pronounce things. Is it Lillet? No? It's Lil-LAY."

It was a different experience for New Orleans barkeepers. Chris Hannah's pals in New York took advantage of his local position, asking for pre-Tales favors. "My favorite text is, 'Chris Hannah, you live in New Orleans, can you get me this?' One day a friend of mine at Whole Foods called me and said, 'I hate your bartender friends. I hate Tales. Why are you guys calling me and asking for star anise?'"

As it increased in power, Tales took on a Janus-like role in the cocktail world. On the plus side, its seminars spread cocktail information and appreciation like wildfire among consumers and professionals. It also provided a mecca where bartenders from London to Los Angeles could meet and confer. On the flip side, it was where money met mixology. Tales ran on sponsorship from big liquor conglomerates, who—while furnishing untold cash for parties, tasting rooms, and the Spirited Awards ceremony—were also able to get their hooks into the movement wherever they found purchase. By 2010, there was much talk that the tail was wagging the dog at Tales.

"I love going to New Orleans and seeing all my friends," said Phil Ward. "But Tales kind of pisses me off, because, let's see: let's have all the best bartenders, all the great bar owners, all these great spirit companies come down to Tales, and we'll have all these educational seminars. Only, the only people who can sponsor these seminars are the people who have enough money because they sell swill. I think it's grown into a big, giant monster."

Some prominent mixologists, like Toby Cecchini and Brian Miller, boycotted the event for years. "I hate the huge gatherings of cocktail people," explained Miller, "because it feels like I'm going to get whacked. It's like a meeting of the mob." But most came. Moreover, the next generation of mixologists, who grew up knowing only a calendar that orbited around Tales, flocked to it without professional reservations of any kind.

Whatever its pros and cons, the Rogers's idea was contagious. By 2015, nearly every American city of size had its own cocktail week, cocktail conference, or cocktail classic. The Arizona Cocktail Week, the San Francisco Cocktail Week, the San Antonio Cocktail Conference (set up by Sasha Petraske, it was unique in giving away all of its proceeds to charity), New York's Manhattan Cocktail Classic (which, less soulful and more greedy than Tales, imploded in 2015 when it changed hands), Portland Cocktail Week (more industry oriented), Kansas City's Paris of the Plains Cocktail Festival, and countless more.

Rogers, who became Ann Tuennerman in 2007, remains unimpressed.

"I'm thrilled that there are all those events," she said. "The difference is that they're not 'little Tales.' They try to say that. When people say we're going to have Pittsburgh Cocktail Week, and it's the next Tales of the Cocktail, it's really not. It needs to have its own identity. Tales is a global event. It's not a New Orleans event. It is the premier global cocktail event."

She enjoys watching as the new festivals learn to crawl. "Everyone thinks I'm a bitch, until they do one," she said. "It's not easy."

Though cocktail people still attend Tales by the droves, the regular litany is that the event has metastasized beyond recognition. From the Montelone, Tales went on to take over the nearby Royal Sonesta. Annual parties thrown by Pernod Ricard, Barcari, and William Grant & Sons have grown more lavish with each year, consuming local landmarks like the World War II Museum, Lakefront Airport, and Aquarium of the Americas in an unending quest to outdo one another. And seminar sponsoring fees have quadrupled.

Some have intimated that Tuennerman will divest herself of Tales one day, perhaps selling it to one of the big brands. Her response is, "I think you'd have to pry this event away from me. Paul and I have talked about it. If we both go down in a plane crash, we don't really have a plan."

XXXIV. A MAN IN A ROOM

ON MARCH 3, 2003, an "antiquarian lark" (as the *New York Times* put it) took place at the Oak Room in New York's Plaza Hotel. A group of mixologists and laypeople with a mixology bent gathered to each recreate one recipe from Jerry Thomas's 1862 book *How to Mix Drinks, or the Bon Vivant's Companion*. In attendance, and dressed in their best facsimiles of old-fashioned finery, were Dale DeGroff, Sasha Petraske, Ted Haigh, Robert Hess, Audrey Saunders, and Gary Regan. The man who organized the affair was probably the least famous of the bunch. Though that would change.

"I think it was a watershed moment," said Martin Doudoroff. "This is one of the things that brought Wondrich out into the light."

Beyond Dale DeGroff, there is no name in the cocktail industry more inescapable than that of David Wondrich. Wondrich is so well known that when he is referred to in cocktail circles by just his commonplace first name of Dave, everyone instantly knows who's being discussed. Through his books, he has arguably taught more mixologists how to build classic cocktails than DeGroff, Dick Bradsell, and all their disciples put together. First, and most important, was *Imbibe!*, which resurrected the name of Jerry Thomas and his school of nineteenth-century drink making. He followed it up with *Punch* (actually largely carved out of leftover sections of *Imbibe!*), which brought back the lost world of punch, cocktail's big-bowl predecessor, and resulted in

punch programs springing up at bars all across the world. If there's a hitherto unknown history to any famous drink, bar, or bartender, nine times out
of ten he's the guy who uncovered it. From his perch at *Esquire*, he decides
which are the best bars in the nation through an annual tally. Nearly alone
among liquor journalists, he has crossed the line between reporter and sub-
ject to become an industry player, leaving his mark on new brands of curaçao,
Cognac, gin, and other liquors that he has collaborated on.

In short, if something significant happened in the last decade that
pushed cocktail knowledge along in any way, he was probably involved. The
food and wine worlds have no parallel figure in terms of influence.

Not bad for a parvenu.

"Dave Wondrich is almost late to the game in this whole thing," observed
Simon Ford. "He was a hobbyist. He's one of the most important people in the
movement, but not at the beginning. The timing of his entry onto the scene
was perfect."

The timing was good for Wondrich, too. In the 1990s, he was a former
rocker going slowly mad with boredom in Staten Island's shabby groves of
academe, teaching Introductory English as St. John's University. Having
no fun and not liking the people around him, he took a year of unpaid
leave and began writing, first about music, then about drinks for *Esquire*, as
the magazine needed someone to edit an online version of a 1949 *Esquire*
cocktail book. Wondrich arranged the drinks in various families, and added
small essays for the cocktails that didn't have any. His editor liked the essays
and asked for more. He was given a couple hundred dollars, a booze budget,
and a stipend for old cocktail books, which he began to collect. The *Esquire*
database launched at the beginning of 2000. His cocktail entries were eventually compiled in a book that came out in 2002.

Esquire had picked the right man for the job. Wondrich, catholic in his
curiosity, had always been interested in cocktails. Born in Pittsburgh, he
attended high school in Port Washington (Audrey Saunders was a classmate,

though they didn't know each other at the time). The town had a WASPy culture: Martinis with dinner, Gin & Tonics, Gimlets. As a bass player pursuing the young dream of rock stardom, he drank Sidecars, Rob Roys, and Old-Fashioneds in the only bars that knew how to make them. "I was really poor and could only afford to drink in old man bars," he said. "Before I went on stage, I would have a couple gin Martinis." Like fellow musician Brother Cleve of Boston, Wondrich partly discovered cocktails in time-warp taverns while on the road.

He and his wife, Karen Rush, went to the Rainbow Room during DeGroff's reign, where the drinks were a "revelation." Karen, an aspiring actress who worked as a manager at chef Larry Forgione's trailblazing Manhattan restaurant An American Place, liked cocktails, too. She and the coat-checker—future *New York Times* food writer Melissa Clark—would sit at the bar, flip through the Mr. Boston manual, and have the bartender make up Fluffy Ruffles and French 75s. (Karen's post came in handy for the Sazerac-obsessed Wondriches when Emeril LaGasse did a guest gig at An American Place. Two days later, a Fed Ex package containing two bottles of Peychaud's bitters arrived from New Orleans.)

While studying at NYU, Wondrich bought William Grimes's cocktail history and Barnaby Conrad III's absinthe book when they came out. This led to a series of absinthe parties in which David served his own homemade hooch, basically Everclear infused with various botanicals.

Wondrich's counterpart at London *Esquire* was Jonathan Downey, who invited him to London, where Dale DeGroff was consulting for Downey. "That meant I got to spend a week with Dale," said Wondrich. "He totally changed my life in every way." Schooled on New York classicism, Wondrich found London to be unfamiliar country, and he didn't like everything he saw. "I had one of the worst drinks I ever had in my life at LAB. I asked for an Old-Fashioned. They said, 'We'll give you our version.' It was half passion fruit syrup, half Bacardi, in a short glass. It was revolting."

"Dave was a real fascist about the classics," remembered Downey, "but in a good way."

Wondrich spent much of his time digging for answers and fighting righteous battles online with Robert Hess, Gary Regan, Ted Haigh, and others on Drinkboy and eGullet. Sometimes it was the same fight over and over. The blind-alley repetitiveness of it all gave him an idea.

"There was no settled authority on cocktails, and there was no place to look it up," he said. "If you had old books, you had ammunition in these arguments. But people were very wary about letting the old books speak for themselves. When I sat down to write *Imbibe!,* that's what I wanted to do, put the old books on the page. Here is the actual recipe, verbatim."

Wondrich decided to structure the book around Jerry Thomas's seminal 1862 tome. A brief history of the man (whatever could be found, which wasn't much) was followed by a historical and analytical breakdown of every nonpunch drink in the book, explaining the arcane ingredients, the unfamiliar measurements. He was unlocking the puzzle of each formula, finding the simple, pleasing drink inside. "That's my Comp Lit background. Put a structure on it and analyze it.

"I've been very frustrated over the years," he explained, "because I'd find a historical recipe, and then I'd find the original recipe and it would be different, because the author had adapted the recipe rather than giving it to us straight. That was one of the original goals of the book. I'm going to give you the original recipe and put any adaptations in the comments. That way, if I'm wrong, you've got the original recipe. And you can see how I engage with these recipes."

At first, no one was interested. There was no modern precedent for a book that so completely immersed itself in cocktail history and habits. "Everybody still wanted *Cocktail Book 1.0: Your First Cocktail Book,*" he said. "I wanted to do *My Second Cocktail Book.* That was a hard sell."

Eventually, Perigee took the book on. While the cocktail movement blossomed in fits and starts, Wondrich spent four years working on it, begging colleagues for copies of old books, reading diaries, trolling the New York Public Library and newspaper databases. *Imbibe!* was published in 2007 as perhaps the weightiest, most comprehensive cocktail treatise of all time. The book didn't fly off the shelves, but it was almost instantly treated as a textbook for bartenders, a treasure map leading deep into America's drinking past.

"What's amazing about Dave is he's taken the rigor of the academy and applied it to spirits writing," observed Melissa Clark, a longtime friend. "Nobody had done that before. People had done that in food writing. But nobody had done it in spirit writing."

Imbibe! won a James Beard Award, which lent it additional currency. Wondrich was subsequently invited on talk shows as a sort of novelty guest, grilled amusingly about cocktails by the likes of Rachel Maddow, Stephen Colbert, and Conan O'Brien, who called him a "crazed Civil War general."

O'Brien's characterization wasn't far off. Wondrich's visibility was doubtless boosted by his singular appearance, the most recognizable profile in the business. Stout, bespectacled, with lank, shaggy hair and a long, scraggly goatee, you wouldn't mistake him for anyone else. On occasion, he would augment this by donning a velveteen top hat or a Soviet army marching hat. In an industry filled with tattooed, bearded, pierced, seersucker-wearing, bow-tied, hat-wearing dandies, he out-eccentric-ed everyone, all while somehow retaining the air of a kind of John Houseman-like professor of cocktails.

In 2006, Wondrich formed the Beverage Alcohol Resource (BAR) educational program with DeGroff, F. Paul Pacult, Steve Olson, and Doug Frost, a sort of intensive, one-week immersion course on cocktail scholarship, with attendees paying thousands to take part. That, in turn, evolved into the more streamlined BarSmarts, fueled by money from Pernod Ricard, a traveling road show that went from city to city training and certifying bartenders. Wondrich gave seminars and speeches, judged cock-tail competitions, and functioned as an all-around authority in myriad ways throughout the cocktail world. Distillers sought out his help in creating historically accurate recreations of spirits and lost liqueurs. (Many of the products whose absence he bemoaned in the pages of *Imbibe!* were back on the market by the time he updated the book in 2015.)

But it was through his continued scholarship that he retained a prom-inent perch in the renaissance. Though others, like Ted Haigh, Wayne Curtis, Jeff Berry, and Eric Felten, had done their own digging into the cocktail's past alongside him, and many more have done so since, Wondrich remained mixology's answer desk, an industry unto himself. At one semi-nar at Tales of the Cocktail, a brand ambassador suggested, not without a little sarcasm, that Wondrich be kept in a room where all would have access to him. There, he could be asked any cocktail question that might come up.

XXXV. THE BIGGER TIME

SIMON FORD'S STATURE ONLY GREW. He had a sixth sense about where to sink his boss's money. After Hurricane Katrina nearly ended Tales of the Cocktail, Plymouth and then Beefeater swooped in as sponsor saviors. He financed cocktail history tours led by David Wondrich in San Francisco, New Orleans, Los Angeles, and London. The tours were "insanely funded," recalled Wondrich. "We'd meet at a bar, everybody got a flask of punch. Sometimes it was a bus, sometimes just walking. We'd stop a place and have a drink. If the place was no longer there, we'd have a drink on the sidewalk. It was a slam dance toward the night."

If bartenders were worried about the conflicts intrinsic in climbing aboard the Ford bandwagon—and those of the ambassadors of other brands who came after them—they were learning too much, having too much fun, and feeling too good about their profession's new prospects to give it much thought.

Other liquor companies, both big and small, took note of Ford's success. By 2010, brand ambassadors, once a novelty, were thick on the ground.

"Everybody and their uncle became a brand ambassador the way that ten years before in the UK everybody had become consultants," recalled Angus Winchester. "They were suddenly bartenders with business cards."

Liquor companies had no problem finding more ambassadors, because young cocktail bucks desperately wanted the jobs. They were lucrative exits from backbreaking bar work that could pay from $60,000 to $100,000 a year, not to mention the travel and entertainment perks.

Ford, who graduated to the position of director of trade outreach and brand education at Pernod Ricard USA—basically, Lord High Master of all ambassadors—was approached constantly by bartenders who wanted to join his army. Most applicants, he felt, were not suited to the work and also didn't know what they were getting into.

"Being a brand ambassador, here's the trick," explained Ford. "It's not that difficult, but it's extremely time-consuming. It wears on you, your physical well-being and health and sleep. It takes you eighty hours to do forty hours of work because of all the travel."

Erick Castro, a popular bartender at Rickhouse in San Francisco, was tapped by Ford to be an ambassador for Plymouth and Beefeater gins in 2010 and did the job for two years, before leaving to open his own bar. He didn't regret the detour, but departed understanding the negatives.

"Part of the reason it's a difficult job is because, in all honesty, the brands don't care about you," said Castro. "They hire a bartender who has a lot of contacts in the industry, and they hire them with a two-year mindset. We're going to put this guy through the wringer for two years and get all his contacts, and then [they'll] hire another guy and do the same thing to him for two years. I didn't realize this at the time, but that's kind of what they do. A lot of the job isn't built with longevity. They're kind of, like, 'This guy is exhausted, he looks like hell, but whatever. We'll just hire another bartender.'"

Some began to think that the rise of the ambassador, while seemingly giving striving bartenders a leg up, was strip-mining the new cocktail bars of their best talent—what Ford himself termed "a loss of personalities."

Not everyone saw ambassador gigs as a golden ticket. "You have to kiss ass," said Sam Ross. "And I don't like kissing ass. Never have. Not for one second did I consider that. And never would."

AS THE COCKTAIL RENAISSANCE ENTERED its second decade in earnest (if we date it back to the Atlantic in England and Milk & Honey in the United States), the stakes grew for both bars and bartenders. Some were happy to simply open respectable cocktail bars that become popular local haunts. Others wanted a bit more. The Spirited Awards at Tales of the Cocktail had grown with the convention to become the Oscars of the drinks industry. In 2012, the James Beard Foundation added an award category for Outstanding Bar Program. In addition, in 2011 a magazine called *Drinks International* invented something called the World's 50 Best Bars, an annually announced list of top dogs in cocktaildom. The new breed of uber-cocktail bar that chased after these prizes had goals that went far beyond serving a good drink—goals that were often backed by the big liquor corporations.

In the past, "You're a bartender because you either really loved it or you're not the 9-to-5 type," theorized Tom Chadwick, a Brooklyn bar owner. "Now, I think we're getting a personality type that's really kind of going into it to be famous. There's a social media presence, there's cocktail competitions; you have a drink in *New York* magazine, and you start to feel famous. And the brands are there and you do another charity event. 'Hey, you want to guest bartend?' Or, 'Hey, Bulldog gin is doing a rooftop thing; you want to work for us?' You just feel like a celebrity for it. And you're being flown around to places, to a seminar, to guest bartend, all sponsored by the brands."

By 2015, the top celebrity bartenders were commanding five-figure "day rates" and had business relationships with clothing lines. Chadwick thinks that in such a heady atmosphere the guest, the neighborhood in which the bar is located, and the actual drinks have become "secondary."

Sean Muldoon is as ambitious a person as the cocktail resurgence has produced. As the Belfast man put together what would become the Dead

Rabbit Grocery and Grog in New York City, he was pretty up front that he wanted to create a "hundred-year bar," the best bar in the world.

Situated in a narrow, four-story building on a historic block in lower Manhattan (the Fraunces Tavern, where Washington bid good-bye to his troops, is around the corner), Dead Rabbit was the mixology microculture's most ambitious attempt yet to capture the tippling past in a bottle. Its vision of New York history had a Dickensian scope, showing both the low and the high end of social drinking. On the first floor was a sawdust-strewn beer and whiskey pub, as might have been patronized by the Irish-American roughnecks who thronged the waterfront in the mid-1800s (including, perhaps, members of the notorious street gang that gave the saloon its name). The second floor was a cocktail bar fit for the bon vivants of the same period who favored elegant watering holes around lower Broadway.

Muldoon's partner was young Jack McGarry, another Irishman. McGarry holed himself up with fifty books and read for a year and a half in preparation for creating the drinks for Dead Rabbit's opening menu. He tested thousands of ancient drinks, including various bishops, cobblers, fixes, and slings, of which more than seventy found their way onto the expansive cocktail menu. It was all a bit cocktail Disneyland, but it slayed the media and public. Dead Rabbit was a destination for the drinking world from the moment it opened.

Muldoon knew how to court the cocktail elite. He had been through the process before. He won an international reputation as a barman while working at the Merchant Hotel bar in Belfast, Northern Ireland, which opened in 2006 in a historic building that formerly housed the Ulster Bank. Muldoon saw it as a potential Belfast version of Lanesborough, the London hotel that had made Salvatore Calabrese a celebrity.

"What we tried to do was make a cocktail bar in a hotel as opposed to a hotel cocktail bar," said Muldoon. He labored over the menus. The first was leather-bound and broken into categories: gin, whiskey, and so on.

The second divided the drinks by the time of day you might imbibe them. Another menu had pictures of cocktails and a glossary. Within two to three years of opening, the Merchant was winning awards.

But for all his efforts, in 2008, the Merchant was beat out by Milk & Honey as World's Best Cocktail Bar at the Spirited Awards. Muldoon didn't like that. He asked *Class* publisher Simon Difford how to win. "He said, 'Nobody knows about your bar, nobody knows where the Merchant is, nobody knows where Belfast is. You've got to bring your bar to these people.'"

Muldoon approached the big liquor companies for money, and he used it to fly the cocktail movement's reigning grandees from New York and London to Belfast. "We spent a lot of money getting the right people over."

In 2009, the Merchant won three Spirited Awards. In 2010, it won the World's Best Cocktail Bar prize Muldoon so desired. "It seems to have worked," he said, in retrospect, of his efforts.

The Dead Rabbit, too, would become a big award magnet. "At Dead Rabbit, they're on a mission," said Elayne Duff, a cocktails consultant who worked for Diageo and who did some shifts at the bar. "Sean and Jack are so hardcore. It's very serious."

Beginning in 2014, Dead Rabbit entered a sort of winner-takes-all grudge match with Artesian in London, another bar that would routinely shoot the moon in its pursuit of accolades. The World's Best or top Spirited Awards would routinely go to one or the other. Artesian had an edge, arguably because British bars are allowed to accept money from brands—something that is, at least on paper, illegal in the United States, though observers think the law is often skirted. (Alex Kratena and Simone Caporale, the leaders of Artesian, surprised the industry when they left the bar in late 2015.)

"That's a fantastic bar," said Naren Young about Artesian. "But their budget is so big, they have the money to buy these really expensive, unique vessels. It's all paid for by brands." The Aqui Estoy drink, for instance, which was served in a skull wearing a sombrero, was paid for by Don Julio tequila. Not coincidentally, the drink contained Don Julio tequila.

Which leads to questions: Are the award-winning headline-grabbers really the world's best bars, or merely the world's best-funded bars? And who's winning here? The bar owners, or the brands? Is there a difference? And where does the customer benefit in all this?

No other food or drink revolution has as tangled a relationship between the corporate and the craft as the cocktail movement does. As American cuisine pulled itself out of the bland, convenience-fueled torpor of post-WWII home cooking, no chef felt the need to deal with, or even think about, food giants like Kraft, General Mills, and Nabisco. Any self-respecting, creative kitchen can easily do without their products. Craft brewers didn't have to navigate around Bud and Miller as they went about forging their finer, tastier brews. And young ambitious vintners on either coast didn't give Gallo a thought, except as a standard they wanted to soar far above.

But bartending is different. Bartenders don't work from scratch the way a chef or brewer does. They are creative plagiarists, piecing together exciting new liquid short stories with pages ripped from the existing canon. Even the bravest, most idealistic mixologist must turn to established brands with familiar labels that have held sway in liquor stores and backbars for generations. (London's White Lyan, which uses its own house spirits wherever possible, is a rare exception.) Liquor conglomerates play a complicated but undeniably large role in the cocktail revival. The Acme Liquor Corporation may be an evil empire adept at churning out Pandering Potion Nos. 1, 2, 3, 4, and 5. But it may also make that venerable gin that works just perfectly in your nifty Negroni variation. And it probably holds the rights to a whiskey, rum, tequila, and brandy equally as good. In this respect, every great new cocktail to come out of the cocktail renaissance has been an ambiguous deal with the devil.

The same symbiotic situation, however, can be viewed from the opposite angle. Once the cocktail movement gathered serious steam in the mid-'00s, it became popular among some bartenders and journalists to cynically view representatives of Big Liquor—the ever-morphing, ever-expanding monoliths that are Diageo, Pernod Ricard, William Grant & Sons, Beam Suntory, and others—as rampaging carpetbaggers, throwing their tentacles around every creative corner, slapping their sponsorship on each major cocktail conclave and convention, and luring away the best and brightest of the bartending community with promises of business-class travel, fame, exposure, and brand ambassador jobs with bottomless expense accounts—all in hopes of wringing further profit out of a revolution that had largely rebuked their products. But that view is somewhat naive, for the corporations were there at the very beginning and in many ways got the ball rolling and kept it rolling at critical junctures during the renaissance. An argument can be made that the cocktail revival could not have happened—or happened as quickly—without the help of Big Liquor.

Still, it's a worrisome relationship. Today, no cocktail event of any significance happens without the backing of the major brands. The principled days of chasing brand reps out of your cocktail bar because they dared to hawk bad booze to you are gone; today, those same reps are embraced because they come bearing ready funding. Bartenders' careers are made at World Class, a global cocktail competition funded by Diageo. Young bartenders are granted legitimacy through certification by the BarSmarts program, which is backed by Pernod Ricard. Certainly, it can be argued that these companies are furthering education, but it can't be denied that the schooling comes with strings attached.

Independent mixologists and brand ambassadors, who are often former bartenders, are often pals and socialize. The most prominent of the ambassadors have deftly fashioned themselves as industry leaders, primarily because they are often everywhere at once, from Melbourne to Moscow, and have the wherewithal to make things happen; and no one seems overly concerned that, however well-meaning, the ambassadors are walking, talking conflicts of interest who must at the end of the day sell a case of dragonberry vodka.

Cocktail and spirits writers, meanwhile, are routinely tapped by brands for speeches, cocktail competitions, and seminars, lending their tacit imprimatur to the products that back their appearances. As the revolution was co-opted, this situation changed how the cocktail business is covered for a scrupulous few.

"I feel my job has changed from being more of a crusader to being more of a cop," said Wayne Curtis, the cocktail journalist and author. He sees some of the newer players as "all mustache, no merit. I think a lot of younger bartenders just like the limelight. They see it as more of a career option."

Bobby Heugel, who owns a slew of cocktail bars in Houston, is one of the few prominent bar owners to speak out against the cozy relationship between the profession and liquor brands. He is particularly concerned about the effect large companies are having on the future of tequila and mezcal as they plunder Mexico in pursuit of an agave payday.

"We see chefs who are so proud about where they source produce and the ingredients they use in their kitchen," said Heugel. "That same agricultural consciousness is never applied to spirits. I just think it's inconsistent. I rub people the wrong way when talking about these issues. People say, 'You really shouldn't do that. This is a relationship business. There's no room for that perspective.' People tell me that all the time. So why don't we have relationships with the people who make these spirits then?"

"If it is a relationship business," he continued, "I think a lot of those relationships are the ones we would prefer to have, the recreational relationships, or the relationships that benefit our publicity, or that net financial benefits or trips around the world. All of those things are great, but I feel there's a lot more to the industry that we don't talk about."

Asked if he thought being hired by brands sometimes prevented bartenders from speaking their minds, he didn't pause. "Yes. Absolutely."

XXXVI. OPEN 24 HOURS

NEW YORK TIMES REPORTER WILLIAM GRIMES'S long-ago worry, in the early 1990s—that haute cocktails would just be a fad—lingered in minds of skeptical journalists, critics, chefs, and prognosticators for another fifteen years or so. Today, it has vanished. Even with a concerted effort, it would take a quarter century to erase the progress that has been made behind the bar. New York, San Francisco, and London no longer see only a few important new cocktail bars every year; there are dozens. Chicago, Los Angeles, Portland, and Texas give them runs for their money. Paris and Moscow and Mexico City are cocktail destinations. Nearly every secondary and tertiary market in the United States and UK has at least two or three decent cocktail bars. Those bars offer much in variety. Some of the children of the cocktail renaissance have strived to open bars that are more welcoming and casual, while never stinting on quality. Others have veered into the even more ornate and high end, embracing elitism. When there are so many choices, there's room for all tastes.

Chefs and bar directors no longer war with one another. No respectable restaurant today opens up without a well-considered cocktail program, preferably designed by a noted mixologist. Restaurant critics have been forced to assess the cocktail list in their reviews. (And "forced" is the apt word, as few restaurant critics yet understand the bartender's art as well as they do the chef's, and their reviews often betray a lingering condescension toward, ignorance of, and impatience with the field.)

Bartenders' expectations have changed a hundredfold. The young ones enter the trade not as time-wasters, but as careerists. They leap from bar to bar, carve out their media profile, hopscotch around the planet attending conventions, enter competitions, and visit distilleries, where they are courted and pampered. They travel as much as they bartend, and they pitch book deals and accept speaking engagements. They are businesspeople. Some dream of attaining the status of household name, the way some celebrity chefs do. And once they achieve that level, it's hard to find them behind the bar that gave them a platform in the first pace. "Everyone wants to be startenders now," complained Todd Thrasher, who has trouble retaining bar staff. "Everyone wants to be Jim Meehan."

Dale DeGroff probably remains the most famous bartender in the world. He's done well enough. He's a roving celebrity, an ambassador of the drinking life done well, and a sought-after speaker and judge. Tony Abou-Ganim, long gone from the Bellagio, is the same, the star of a never-ending mixology road show. Dick Bradsell, in contrast, never wished for fame, and retreated into near-invisibility, spending the 2010s bartending only at a basement bar below a Mexican restaurant in SoHo, before exiting even that. After a long battle with brain cancer, he died on February 27, 2016, at the age of fifty-six. He left no single bar behind to carry on his legacy, but his protégés' bars crowd the London streets from SoHo to Shoreditch, and his Vodka Espresso and Bramble are still downed from Dublin to Dubai.

His one-time business partner, Jonathan Downey, is still in the game, but, save the lasting Milk & Honey, no longer owns any of the bars that once made him a titan of the industry. Oliver Peyton was awarded an honorary Order of the British Empire for services to catering in 2013.

Paul Harrington willingly left the industry years ago, but keeps the smallest of toeholds, running a small bar in Spokane, Washington, a city on the circuit of no cocktail maven. Robert Hess married Audrey Saunders after a long courtship, creating the most prominent power couple in cocktails. Saunders never opened another sustained bar after Pegu Club, instead throwing her energies into a projected bartender academy built on Hess's estate in Washington. But nearly every bartender who worked for Saunders at Pegu now has a saloon of their own, including Phil Ward, owner of the well-respected Mayahuel, though he seems to enjoy bartending at others' bars more.

Julie Reiner did the opposite of Saunders, opening several other bars after Pegu, finding the most success in Brooklyn with the accessible Clover Club and Leyenda. David Kaplan built on the popularity of Death & Co to become a multicity cocktail bar mogul in partnership with his former bartender Alex Day. (The Death & Co cocktail book, *Death & Co: Modern Classic Cocktails*, published in 2014, netted a quarter-million-dollar advance.) Ford left the corporate grind to become his own brand ambassador, crisscrossing the world to promote the 86 Co. line of spirits he formed with Dushan Zaric and Jason Kosmas of Employees Only. In 2016, the latter bar announced plans to go global with their brand, opening locations in Austin, Miami Beach, and Singapore.

Jeff Berry, after decades of talking and writing about tiki and inspiring countless tiki bars, finally opened his own bar, Latitude 29, in New Orleans. Toby Cecchini wandered barless for years after losing his bar Passerby before finally opening a new bar, Long Island Bar, inside a 1930s diner near the Brooklyn waterfront. It quickly became as beloved as Passerby had been. In Melbourne, Vernon Chalker and Matt Bax are still doing pretty much what they always did, Chalker still reigning over his Gin Palace, and Bax opening bars just as eccentric as Der Raum. Around them, in both Melbourne and Sydney, a thriving cocktail scene has grown and grown.

Sam Ross and Michael McIlroy, after years of service to Milk & Honey, were bequeathed the Lower East Side space, and reopened it as Attaboy.

Their former boss, Sasha Petraske, moved his brainchild uptown to 23rd Street. But when the building was suddenly sold, he had to vacate a little over a year later. For the first time in fourteen years, New York did not have a bar called Milk & Honey.

Petraske vowed to reopen in another location. But it was not to be. He died on August 21, 2015, in Hudson, New York, where he was doing some consulting work for a local hotel. He was found by his wife, journalist Georgette Moger, whom he had married in May. Petraske died of a heart attack. He was forty-two and in debt, as he had been for most of his career.

Matt Piacentini, the owner of a couple of Manhattan cocktail bars, tweeted that day, "If not for Sasha Petraske, we'd all be shaking Manhattans. Except many of us wouldn't be bartenders, and most of our bars wouldn't exist."

The cocktail world shuddered, as a house can only when one of its support beams is knocked out. But by that time, the foundations Petraske had laid were so sturdy and embedded that there was no danger of the cocktail movement collapsing. On August 31, between 9 and 10 p.m., at bars in each time zone, bartenders and patrons hoisted a Daiquiri in Petraske's honor. Each one of those bartenders knew how to make a proper Daiquiri.

Trinidad Sour

GIUSEPPE GONZALEZ, 2008, Clover Club, Brooklyn

1½ ounces Angostura bitters

1 ounce orgeat

¾ ounce fresh lemon juice

½ ounce rye

The origin story of this drink is disputed, and the disagreement has to do with that ounce-plus of Angostura bitters required in the recipe.

"I invented it for Star Chefs," recalled Gonzalez, then head bartender at Clover Club in Brooklyn, which was run by Julie Reiner. "I didn't win. I presented it to Julie Reiner at Clover Club. Julie said 'Nobody's going to drink it.' I said, 'I'm the head bartender; I want to put it on the menu.' She said it was too expensive. It was one of those ideas she shot down. She took one of these consulting trips, and I put it on the menu. I reprinted the menu without her knowing. Nobody knew it. One of the bartenders who came in and tried it was Johnny Gertsen. He said, 'An ounce and a half of Angostura? An ounce of orgeat? Are you kidding?' I said, 'Just try it.' The reason that drink became so popular had nothing to do with me. He started making this drink at Drink, and it took off. And when I was at Dutch Kills I made it all the time."

Reiner doesn't remember this story, or recall the drink ever being on the menu at Clover Club. However it came to first be noticed, the Trinidad Sour is now served from England to the Far East.

Combine all the ingredients in a cocktail shaker three-quarters filled with ice. Shake until chilled. Strain into a coupe glass.

EPILOGUE

IN SPRING OF 2015, I sat down with Dave Wondrich to interview him about the newly expanded edition of his book *Imbibe!*, which had just been released. Wondrich had never stopped researching the history of cocktails, and the fresh volume was considerably fatter than the first.

I had first met Wondrich in 2007, when I interviewed him about the original *Imbibe!* I asked him some novice questions at the time, like why he didn't think the Sazerac was the first cocktail. ("Because it isn't," he said.) I also asked him how he dealt with working in a field where even the most central questions are essentially unknowable. Who created the Martini? Why is it called the Martini? Who invented the Manhattan? For God's sake, we didn't even know where did the word "cocktail" came from. He told me it was the nature of the beast; he had long since made his peace with it.

Eight years later, there weren't quite as many unsolved mysteries. He even thought he had cracked the "cocktail" case. It was an appropriately off-color explanation. "Ginger was used in the horse trade to make a horse stick its tail up," he said. "They'd put it in its ass. If you had an old horse you were trying to sell, you would put some ginger up its butt, and it would cock its tail up and be frisky. That was known as 'cock-tail.' It comes from that. It became this morning thing. Something to cock your tail up, like an eye-opener. I'm almost positive that's where it's from."

And that's why they're called cocktails. Maybe. How far we had come.

After the interview, we went out for a drink at the nearest bar, Lavender Lake, just steps from Brooklyn's fetid, eternal-punch-line waterway, the Gowanus Canal. Owned by artists, the bar had an artsy rep, but it was not known as a cocktail bar. Still, Dave said they made a passable Manhattan.

Manhattans were what we ordered.

From the end of the bar, I watched the bartender make our drinks. It was a habit I'd gotten into, part writerly curiosity, part quality control. He used rye whiskey. The sweet vermouth was fetched from the fridge, where it was kept fresh. He dashed in the bitters, and stirred the drinks patiently until they were chilled. All told, it wasn't much of a show. But it was a ballet and fireworks next to what we would have gotten a mere fifteen years before.

"See that," said Dave. "There's the cocktail revival in action."

The Manhattans were delicious. We ordered two more.

SHOULD-BE CLASSICS

Brancolada

JEREMY OERTEL, 2012, Donna, Brooklyn

1 ounce Appleton
V/X rum

1 ounce Branca
Menta

1½ ounces pineapple
juice

¼ ounce fresh
orange juice

¾ ounce coconut
cream (recipe
follows)

Mint sprig and
orange wedge, for
garnish

A highly unusual tiki drink that uses the difficult-to-mix
Branca Menta to spectacular ends. A rare modern tiki
classic.

Combine all the ingredients except the mint sprig and
orange wedge in cocktail shaker with a few ice cubes.
Shake until chilled. Strain over crushed ice in a hurricane
glass. Garnish with the mint sprig and orange wedge.

To make the coconut cream, combine 3 parts Coco
Lopez with 1 part coconut milk.

Siesta

KATIE STIPE, 2006, Flatiron Lounge, New York

1½ ounces tequila

¾ ounce fresh
lime juice

¾ ounce simple syrup

½ ounce fresh
grapefruit juice

¼ ounce Campari

Lime wheel, for
garnish

A tequila-Campari spin on a Hemingway Daiquiri.

Combine all the ingredients except the lime wheel in a cocktail shaker three-quarters filled with ice. Shake until chilled. Strain into a chilled coupe. Garnish with thelime wheel.

Moon Cocktail

THOMAS WAUGH, 2008, Death & Co, New York

**2 ounces
Plymouth gin**

**¾ ounce Lustau
Amontillado sherry**

**1 barspoon Massenez
Crème de Pêche
peach liqueur**

**¼ ounce acacia
honey syrup (recipe
follows)**

**Lemon peel, for
garnish**

A drink of impeccable balance and elegance. Created as
Waugh's idea of a Martini varation on La Perla, a popular
drink by San Francisco bartender Jacques Bezuidenhaut.

Combine all the ingredients except the lemon peel in
a mixing glass three-quarters filled with ice. Stir until
chilled. Strain into an coupe glass. Squeeze the lemon
peel over the top and discard.

To make the acacia honey syrup, combine equal parts
water and acacia honey in a saucepan. Heat until the
honey dissolves, then allow to cool.

Laphroaig Project

OWEN WESTMAN, 2009, Bourbon & Branch, San Francisco

1 ounce Green Chartreuse

1 ounce fresh lemon juice

½ ounce Laphroaig Quarter Cask Scotch

½ ounce maraschino liqueur

½ ounce Yellow Chartreuse

2 dashes Fee Brothers Peach Bitters

Lemon peel, for garnish

The ingredients are high end in the extreme, making this an expensive drink to make, but the results are worth it. Westman is an Australian bartender who journeyed to San Francisco to learn at Bourbon & Branch. He invented the drink while in San Francisco.

Combine all the ingredients except the lemon peel in a cocktail shaker three-quarters filled with ice. Shake until chilled. Strain into an ice-filled Old-Fashioned glass. Garnish with the lemon peel.

Bitter Giuseppe

STEPHEN COLE, 2006, The Violet Hour, Chicago

2 ounces Cynar

¾ ounce Carpano Antica

2 dashes Regan's orange bitters

Lemon peel with a little meat on it, for garnish

Lemon slice, for garnish

Created in Chicago, it gained a wider audience when included in *Beta Cocktails*, the second edition of the cocktail booklet put out by Cure in New Orleans. It often makes an appearance when a customer orders "bartender's choice."

Combine all ingredients except the lemon peel and slice in an Old-Fashioned glass filled with ice. Twist the lemon peel over the glass, spraying oils over the surface, with about 11 to 15 drops of juice going into the glass. Stir in the glass until chilled. Garnish with the lemon slice.

Division Bell

PHIL WARD, 2009, Mayahuel, New York

---

1 ounce Del Maguey
Vida

¾ ounce Aperol

½ ounce maraschino
liqueur

¾ ounce fresh
lime juice

Grapefruit peel, for
garnish

A mezcal-fueled twist on the Last Word.

Combine all the ingredients except the grapefruit
peel in a cocktail shaker three-quarters filled with ice.
Shake until chilled. Strain into a coupe glass. Twist the
grapefruit peel over the glass, rub along the rim of glass,
and discard.

ACKNOWLEDGMENTS

I WOULD FIRST LIKE TO THANK Emily Timberlake and Aaron Wehner at Ten Speed Press for having the faith that the story of the cocktail revival deserved to be told and would have an audience. Thanks for David Black and everyone at the David Black Agency for all their help and guidance throughout the long process of this book's creation, particularly for their assistance in getting me to Paris and Australia. Thanks for everyone I interviewed for their time, perspective, and memories. Special thanks for the creators of the cocktails found in these pages. Gratitude to every venue I used for the interviews for letting me temporarily use their bars, cafés, and restaurants as my office. Most of all, thanks to my son, Asher, for whom I do everything I do.

PEOPLE AND DATES

In chronological order.

Dale DeGroff (1/21/14, Tazza, Brooklyn)

Julie Reiner (1/22/14, Clover Club, Brooklyn; 4/7/14, Clover Club)

Jonathan Downey (1/24/14, Char No. 4, Brooklyn; 4/17/15, Luke's, London)

Jeff Berry (1/26/14, Katz's Deli, NYC)

Audrey Saunders (1/27/14, Pegu Club, NYC; 9/15/14, Pegu Club, NYC)

Eben Freeman (1/29/14, Lupe's, NYC; 2/27/14, The Butterfly, NYC)

Sasha Petraske (1/29/14, Milk & Honey, NYC; 6/25/14, Milk & Honey, NYC)

Del Pedro (1/31/14, Tooker Alley, Brooklyn; 2/20/14, Tooker Alley)

Martin Doudoroff (1/31/14, Tooker Alley, Brooklyn; 2/20/14, Tooker Alley)

Eben Klemm (2/4/14, Bien Cuit, Brooklyn)

William Grimes (2/5/14, *New York Times* building, NYC)

Gerry Holland (2/11/14, Mike's Diner, Astoria, Queens)

Toby Maloney (2/11/14, Mother's Ruin, NYC)

Gary Regan (2/12/14, Fraunces Tavern, NYC)

Jim Meehan (2/18/14, McSorley's Old Ale House, NYC)

Vincenzo Errico (2/20/14, email interview)

Albert Trummer (2/25/14, Soho Grand Hotel, NYC)

Ben Pundole (2/25/14, offices of Morgans Hotel Group, NYC)

T. J. Siegal (2/26/14, Professor Thom's, NYC)

Jerri Banks (2/28/14, McSorley's Old Ale House, NYC)

Ravi DeRossi (3/4/14, Maybelle's Cafe, Brooklyn)

Greg Boehm (3/6/14, Cocktail Kingdom, NYC)

Don Lee (3/6/14, Cocktail Kingdom, NYC)

David Kaplan (3/6/14, Schiller's Liquor Bar, NYC)

Cory Hill (3/10/14, Fifth Avenue Diner, Brooklyn)

Chad Solomon (3/10/14, Pegu Club, NYC)

Jay Savulich (3/11/14, Joe, Greenwich Village, NYC)

Robert Haynes (3/13/14, Analogue, Chicago)

Charles Joly (3/13/14, Longman & Eagle, Chicago)

Paul McGee (3/14/14, Three Dots & A Dash, Chicago)

Bridget Albert (3/14/14, Berghoff Cafe, Chicago)

Mike Ryan (3/15/14, Joe's Seafood, Chicago)

Lynnette Marrero (3/17/14, NoMad Library Bar, NYC)

Jim Kearns (3/18/14, NoMad Library Bar, NYC)

Lynn House (3/20/14, NoMad Restaurant, NYC)

Francis Schott (3/22/14, Stage Left, New Brunswick, NJ)

Phil Ward (3/26/14, Long Island Bar, Brooklyn)

Toby Cecchini (3/28/14, Long Island Bar, Brooklyn)

Colin Appiah (3/31/14, Soho House, NYC)

Gillian Duffy (4/1/14, Cafe Duke, NYC)

Wylie Dufresne (4/1/14, WD-50, NYC)

Brian Miller (4/7/14, Bien Cuit, Brooklyn)

Martin Cate (4/10/14, Original Joe's, San Francisco)

Scott Beattie (4/10/14, Comstock Saloon, San Francisco)

Brian Sheehy (4/10/14, Bourbon & Branch, San Francisco)

Thad Vogler (4/11/14, Vesuvio Cafe, San Francisco)

Julio Bermejo (4/11/14, Tommy's Mexican Restaurant, San Francisco)

Marco Dionysus (4/12/14, 15 Romolo, San Francisco)

Neyah White (4/12/14, Comstock Saloon, San Francisco)

Jacques Bezuidenhaut (4/13/14, Vesuvio Cafe, San Francisco)

Jonny Raglin (4/14/14, Comstock Saloon, San Francisco)

Todd Smith (4/14/14, Vesuvio Cafe, San Francisco)

Eric Adkins (4/14/14, Comstock Saloon, San Francisco)

Duggan McDonnell (4/15/14, Kin Khao, San Francisco)

Scott Baird (4/15/14, Vesuvio Cafe, San Francisco)

Jeff Hollinger (4/15/14, Comstock Saloon, San Francisco)

H. Joseph Ehrmann (4/15/14, Elixir, San Francisco)

Jon Santer (4/15/14, The Prizefighter, Emeryville, CA)

Liza Weisstuch (4/22/14, Molly's Shebeen, NYC)

Sean Muldoon (4/22/14, Dead Rabbit, NYC)

Sam Kinsey (4/22/14, Pegu Club, NYC)

Ted Haigh (4/27/14, Clover Club, Brooklyn)

Joseph Schwartz (4/30/14, Black Forest, Brooklyn)

Thomas Waugh (5/7/14, Pegu Club, NYC)

Simon Difford (5/8/14, The Roger Hotel, NYC)

Simon Ford (5/10/14, Fraunces Tavern, NYC)

Eric Seed (5/13/14, Aloft Hotel, Brooklyn)

Ted Breaux (5/14/14, Le Veau d'Or, NYC)

Dominic Venegas (5/15/14, Kellogg's Diner, Brooklyn)

Kirk Estopinal (5/20/14, Bellocq, New Orleans)

Wayne Curtis (5/20/14, Contemporary Arts Center Café, New Orleans)

Chris Hannah (5/21/14, Arnaud's, New Orleans)

Ann Teunnerman (5/21/14, Booty's Street Food, New Orleans)

Lu Brow (5/22/14, Café Adelaide, New Orleans)

Chris McMillian (5/22/14, Kingfish, New Orleans)

Neal Bodenheimer (5/22/14, Bellocq, New Orleans)

Juliette Pope (5/28/14, Gramercy Tavern, NYC)

Charles Shumann (6/2/14, PDT, NYC)

Dushan Zaric (6/2/14, Macao Trading Company, NYC)

Mark Brown (6/5/15, NoMad Library Bar, NYC)

Joaquín Simó (6/5/14, Ganso Ramen, Brooklyn)

Will Guidara (6/5/14, NoMad Library Bar)

Todd Thrasher (6/10/14, Starbucks, Arlington, VA)

Derek Brown (6/10/14, Mockingbird Hill, Washington, DC)

Brother Cleve (6/13/14, Eastern Standard, Boston; 12/11/14, phone)

John Gertsen (6/13/14, Barrington Coffee Roasting Company, Boston)

John Myers (6/14/14, Eastern Standard, Boston)

Jackson Cannon (6/14/14, The Hawthorne, Boston)

Misty Kalkofen (6/15/14, Eastern Standard, Boston)

Wayne Collins (6/17/14, Joe's Southern Kitchen, London)

Tony Conigliaro (6/17/14, offices of Drink Factory, London)

Dick Bradsell (6/18/14, La Bodega Tapas Bar, London)

Ben Reed (6/18/14, Salusbury pub, London)

Nick Strangeway (6/19/14, offices of Strange Hill, London)

Peter Dorelli (6/19/14, Duke's Bar, London)

Douglas Ankrah (6/20/14, Foxcroft and Ginger, London)

Oliver Peyton (6/20/14, Inn the Park, London)

Nick Blacknell (6/20/14, Reform Club, London)

Ryan Chetiyawardana (6/21/14, White Lyan, London)

Romee de Goriainoff (7/2/14, La Compagnies des Vins Surnaturels, NYC)

Tony Abou-Ganim (7/16/14, Café Fleur-de-lis, New Orleans)

Paul Gustings (7/17/14, Cafe Beignet, New Orleans)

Paul Harrington (7/18/14, Marti's Restaurant, New Orleans)

Darcy O'Neill (7/20/14, Hotel Monteleone, New Orleans)

Jamie Boudreau (7/20/14, Ritz-Carlton, New Orleans)

Melissa Clark (7/30/14, *New York Times* building, NYC)

St. John Frizell (7/31/14, Fort Defiance, Brooklyn)

Katie Stipe (8/2/14, Long Island Bar, Brooklyn)

Peggy Boston (8/4/14, phone)

David O'Malley (8/4/14, phone)

Nick Mautone (8/5/14, Heartwood, NYC)

Richie Boccato (8/6/14, Park Plaza Restaurant, Brooklyn)

Dave Arnold (8/7/14, Booker & Dax, NYC)

David Wondrich (8/11/14, his office, Brooklyn; 9/15/14, his office)

Sam Ross (8/13/14, Fort Defiance, Brooklyn)

Dre Masso (8/14/14, email interview)

Alex Day (8/20/14, 151 Bar, NYC)

Mickey McIlroy (8/22/14, De Robertis Pasticceria, NYC)

Angus Winchester (9/8/14, NoMad Library Bar, NYC)

Chris Patino (9/19/14, Norwood Club, NYC)

Jacob Briars (9/22/14, Diageo offices, NYC)

Tom Chadwick (9/24/14, Törst, Brooklyn)

Damon Boelte (9/25/14, Wilma Jean, Brooklyn)

Sam Mason (9/27/14, OddFellows Ice Cream Co., NYC)

Leo Robitchek (9/27/14, NoMad Library Bar, Brooklyn)

John Deragon (9/29/14, Pershing Square, NYC)

Bobby Heugel (9/30/14, Bien Cuit, Brooklyn)

Murray Stenson (9/30/14, phone)

Robert Hess (9/30/14, phone)

Jason Kosmas (10/6/14, phone)

Erick Castro (10/7/14, McSorley's Old Ale House, NYC)

Chuck Taggart (10/7/14, phone)

LeNell Smothers (10/9/14–10/14/14, email interview)

Colin Peter Field (10/10/14, Mark Hotel, NYC)

Philip Duff (10/14/14, Tooker Alley, Brooklyn)

Shingo Gokan (10/17/14, White Horse Tavern, NYC)

Ryan Maybee (10/19/14, Ace Hotel, Portland, OR)

Lucy Brennan (10/20/14, Ace Hotel, Portland, OR)

Jeffrey Morganthaler (10/20/14, Pepe Lo Moko, Portland, OR)

Daniel Shoemaker (10/21/14, Ace Hotel, Portland, OR)

Ryan Magarian (10/21/14, Heart Coffee Roasters, Portland, OR)

Karen Casey (10/23/14, Portland, OR)

Alex and Kristina Kossi (11/11/14, Zinc Bar, NYC)

Giuseppe Gonzalez (11/11/14, Remedy Diner, NYC)

Barnaby Conrad III (11/12/14, Bemelmans Bar, NYC)

Camper English (11/13/14, Katz's Deli, NYC)

Naren Young (11/18/14, Swift Hibernian Lounge, NYC)

Andy Ricker (11/18/14, phone)

Ed Hamilton (11/20/14, phone)

Eric Alperin (11/20/14, phone)

Paul Clarke (12/4/14, phone)

Charles Hardwick (12/8/14, Cafe Orlin, NYC)

Cedd Moses (12/9/14, Ludlow Hotel, NYC)

Francesco Lafranconi (12/10/14, phone)

Nico de Soto (12/10/14, Miracle on 9th Street, NYC)

David Nepove (12/11/14, phone)

Steve Olson (12/16/14, Smyth Hotel, NYC)

Brian Shebairo (12/22/14, phone)

Doug Biederbeck (1/12/15, phone)

Elayne Duff (1/13/15, Diageo Bar, NYC)

Damon Dyer (1/14/15, Iris Cafe, Brooklyn)

Philip Kirschen-Clark (1/19/15, Ninth Street Espresso, NYC)

Patrick Sullivan (1/26/15, phone)

Linden Pride (2/2/15, Le Pain Quotidien, Soho, NYC)

Sean Kenyon (2/11/15, Peter McManus Cafe, NYC)

Andrew Knowlton (2/11/15, *Bon Appétit* offices, NYC)

Shinichi Ikeda (2/13/15, B-Flat, NYC)

Waldy Malouf (2/16/15, phone)

Mike Werner (2/17/15, phone)

Jeremiah Tower (2/24/15, Tavern on the Green, NYC)

Frank Caiafa (3/10/15, Peacock Alley, Waldorf-Astoria, NYC)

Hugh Garvey (3/11/15, phone)

Brooke Arthur (3/11/15, phone)

Jared Brown (3/12/15, Old John's Luncheonette, NYC)

Michael Bauer (3/13/15, Batard, NYC)

Jake Burger (3/18/15, Caffe Reggio, NYC)

Christy Pope (3/19/15, phone)

Michelle Connolly (3/19/15, phone)

Mark Fleckenstein (3/23/15, Union Square Park, NYC)

Amy Sacco (3/24/15, Barchetta, NYC)

Grant Achatz (3/30/15, Bowery Hotel, NYC)

Danny Meyer (3/31/15, USHG offices, NYC)

Carina Tsou (4/10/15, Hero, Paris, France)

Tomas Estes (4/14/15, La Perla, London)

Alex Kratena (4/14/15 Artesian, London)

Erik Lorincz (4/15/15, American Bar, The Savoy Hotel, London)

Simone Caporale (4/15/15, Artesian, London)

Alex Turner (4/16/15, Termini Bar, London)

Danny Smith (4/16/15, Hawksmoor Spitalfields, London)

John Humphries (4/17/15, La Perla, London)

Salvatore Calabrese (4/17/15, Salvatore's, Playboy Club, London)

Jörg Meyer (4/23/15, NoMad Library Bar, NYC)

Greg Lindgren (5/4/15, phone, NYC)

Stanislav Vadrna (5/6/15, Ace Hotel, NYC; 5/11/15, Ace Hotel)

Jonathan Gold (5/22/15, Ledlow, Los Angeles)

Jamie Terrell (5/22/15, Barbershop, Sydney, Australia)

Jason Crawley (5/23/15, Grace Hotel, Sydney)

Matthew Bax (5/25/15, Traveler Coffee Shop, Melbourne, Australia)

Sebastian Reyburn (5/25/15, The European, Melbourne)

Vernon Chalker (5/25/15, Gin Palace, Melbourne)

Michael Madrusan (5/26/15, The European, Melbourne)

Eugene Masat (6/17/15, Sweetwater Grill, Brooklyn, NY)

Mike Enright (7/17/15, Kingfish, New Orleans)

Jonathan Pogash (9/9/15, Café Mogador, NYC)

Robert Cooper (9/9/15, phone)

Ago Perrone (9/15/15, email interview)

Maks Pazuniak (9/23/15, email interview)

ABOUT THE AUTHOR

ROBERT SIMONSON writes about cocktails, spirits, bars and bartenders for the *New York Times*, for which he has written since 2000. He is the author of *The Old-Fashioned: The Story of the World's First Classic Cocktail* and is a contributor to *The Essential New York Times Book of Cocktails* and *Savoring Gotham*. His writings have appeared in *Saveur, GQ, Lucky Peach, Whisky Advocate, Imbibe,* and many others. A native of Wisconsin, he has lived in Brooklyn since 1988.